Field Operations
Diller Scofidio + Renfro

Friends of the High Line
The City of New York

Designing the High Line
Gansevoort Street to 30th Street

First Edition ©2008 Friends of the High Line

ISBN: 978-0-615-21191-6

Friends of the High Line
529 West 20th Street, Suite 8W
New York, NY 10011
USA

www.thehighline.org

Printed and bound in the USA by Finlay
Printing, LLC

High Line design:
Field Operations and Diller Scofidio + Renfro

Book design:
Patrick Hazari, Friends of the High Line

Friends of the High Line is committed to
environmentally responsible practices,
including sustainable sourcing for our
printed material.

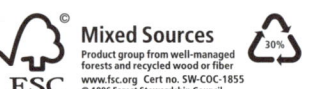

Mixed Sources
Product group from well-managed
forests and recycled wood or fiber
www.fsc.org Cert no. SW-COC-1855
© 1996 Forest Stewardship Council
FSC

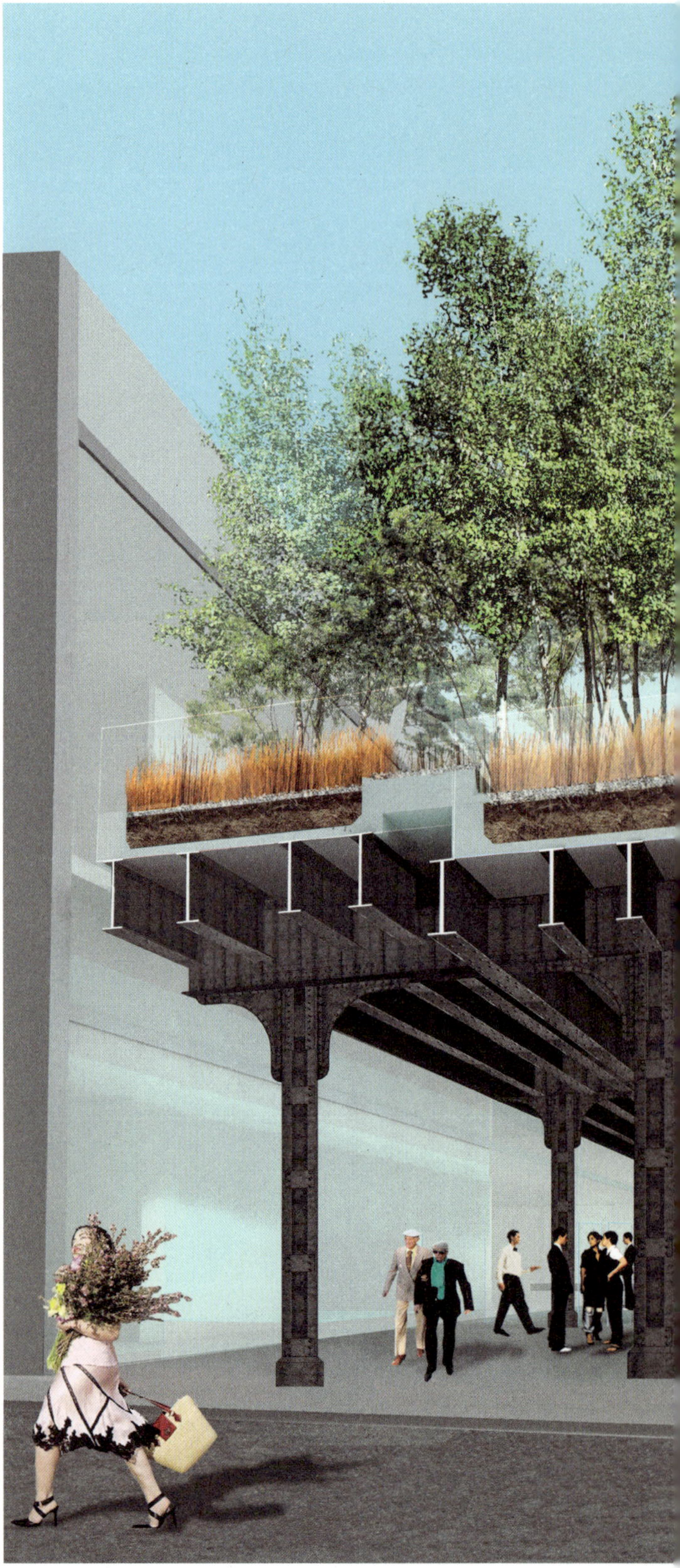

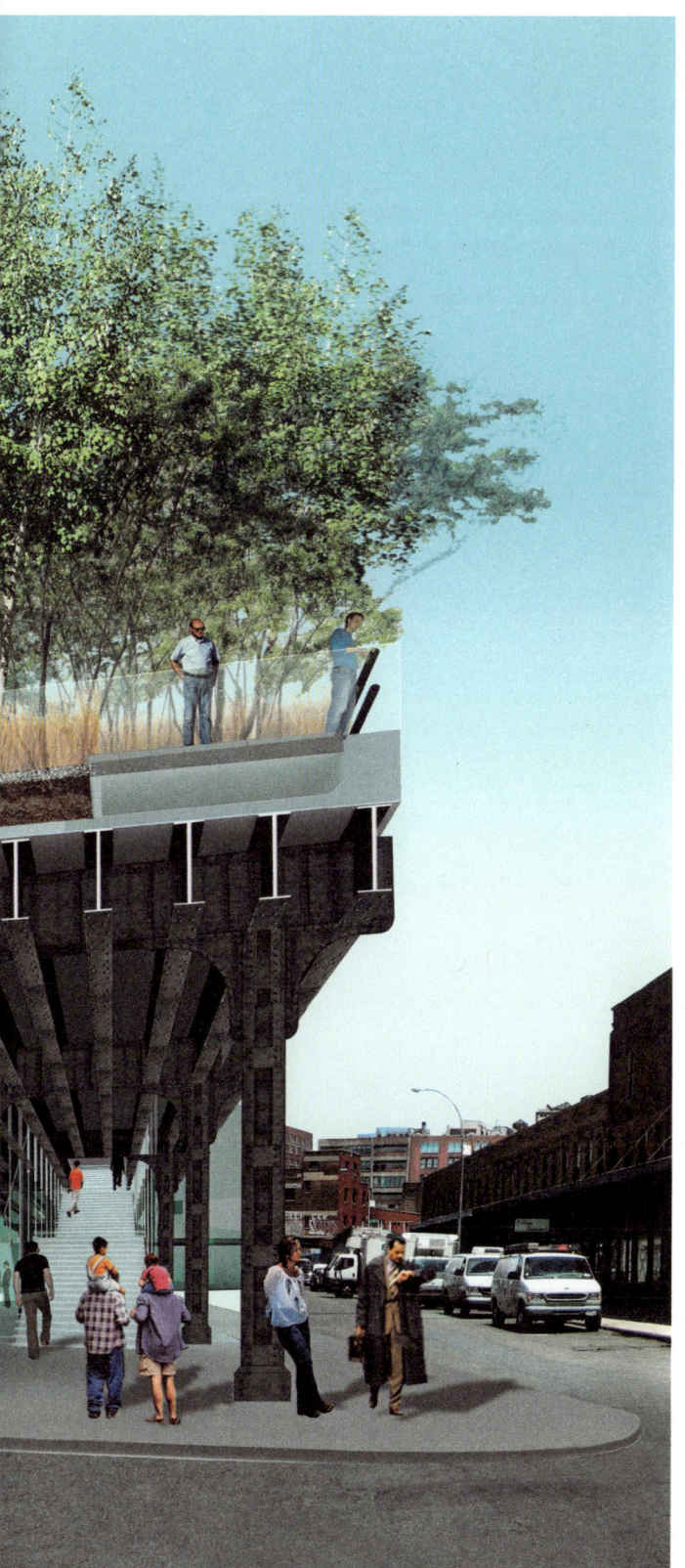

CONTENTS

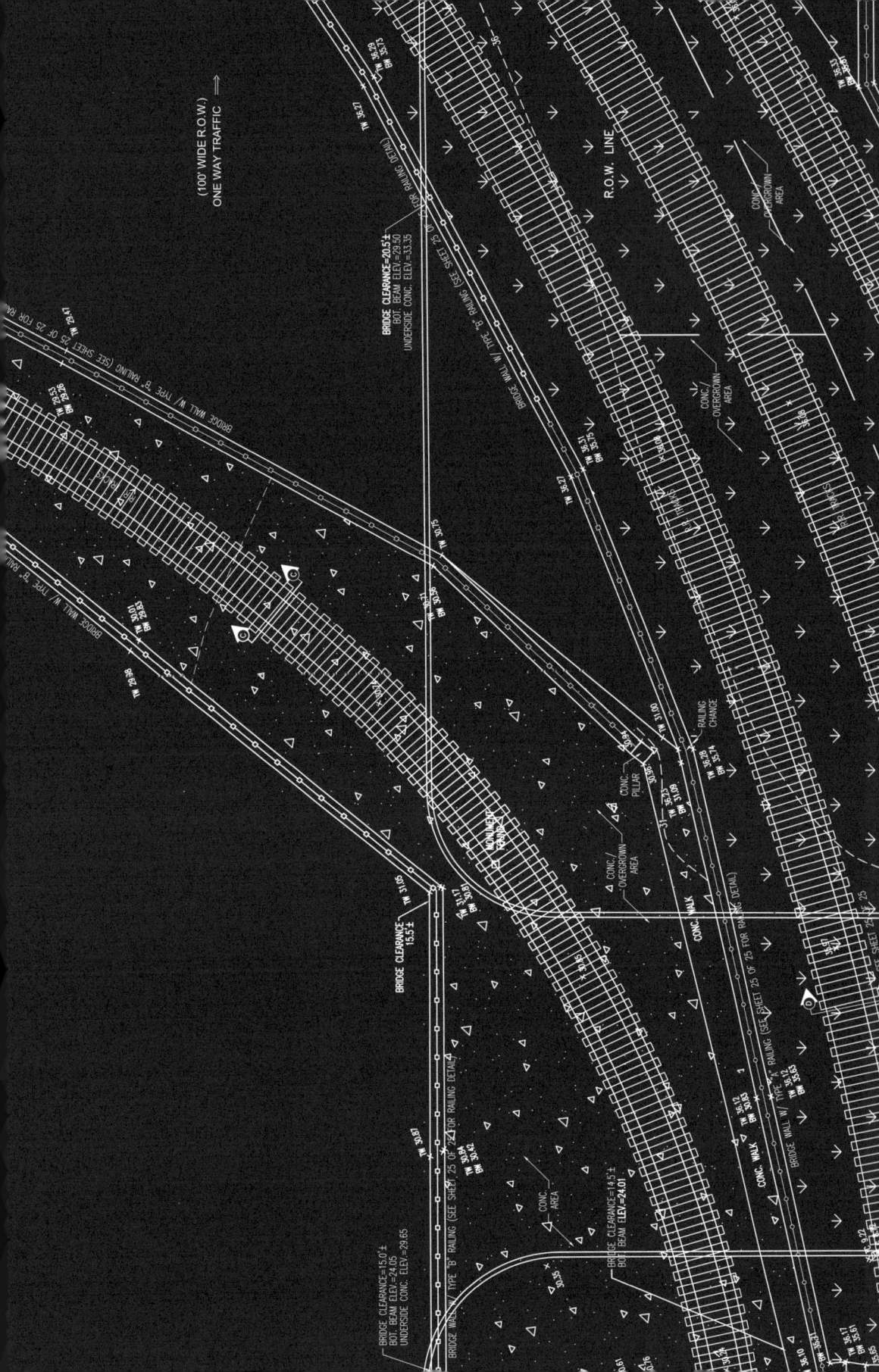

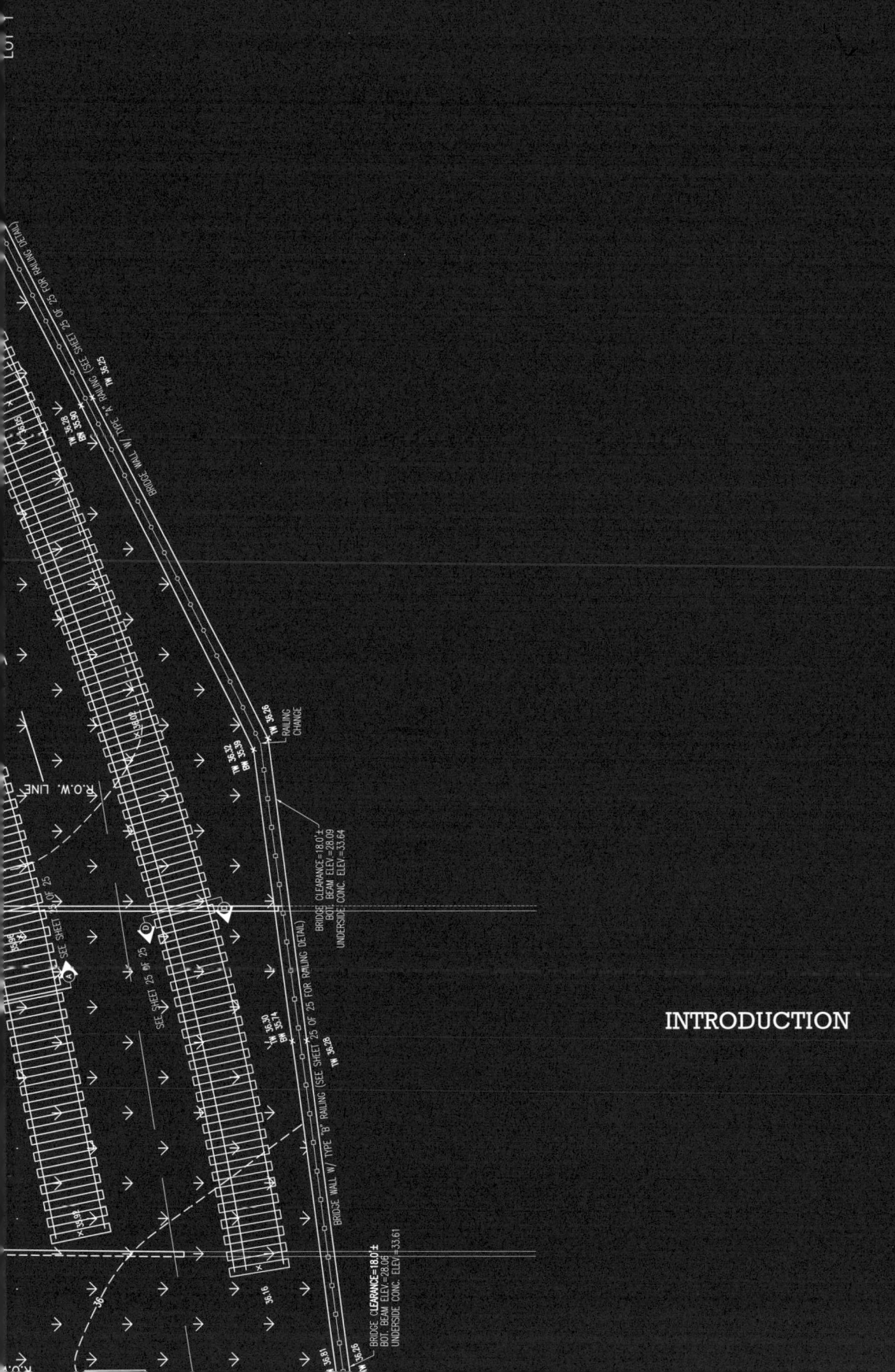

INTRODUCTION

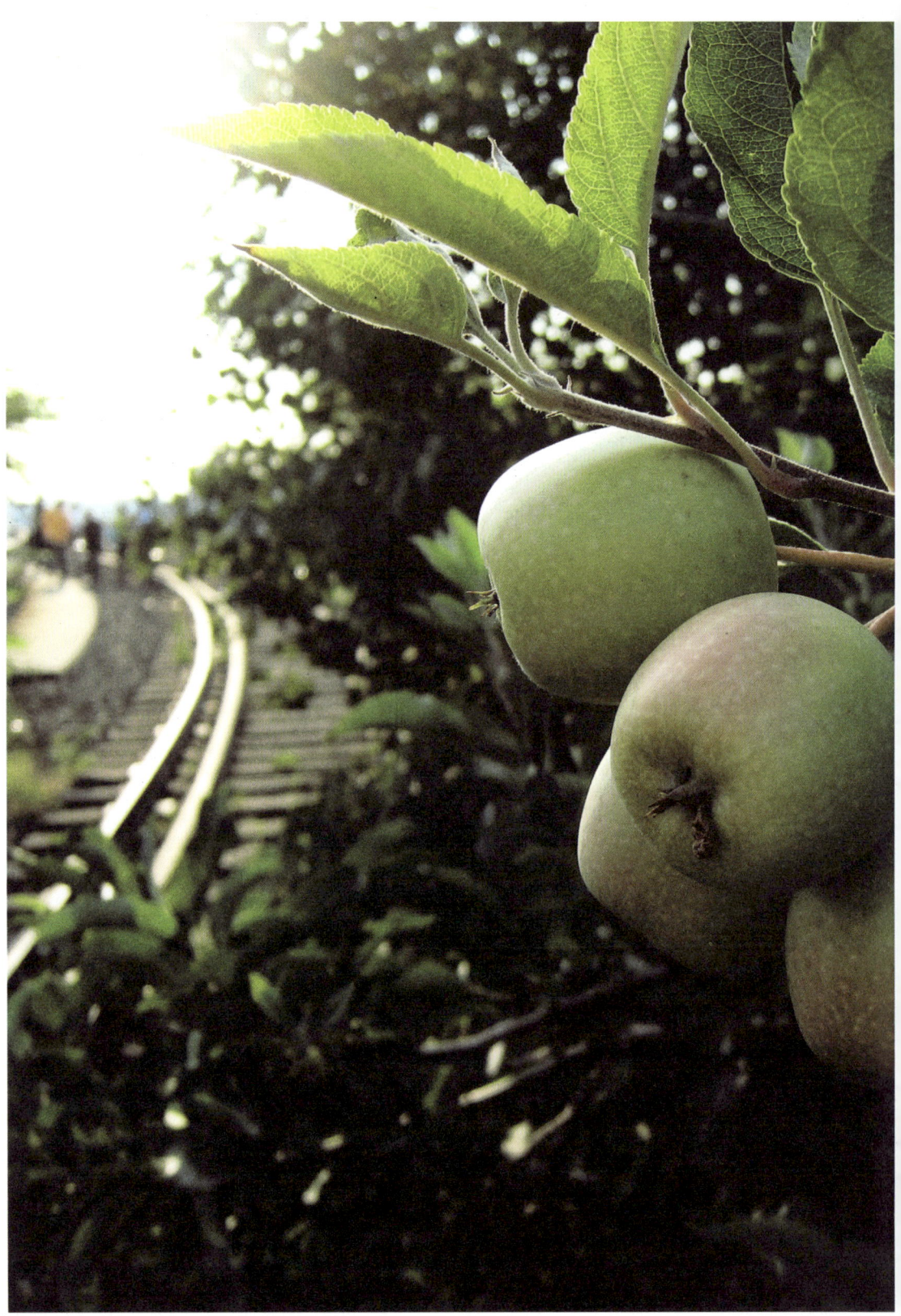

In the summer of 1999, we both read the same newspaper article, which said the High Line was going to be torn down. We didn't know each other then, but we had each become fascinated by the High Line and the opportunity it offered. Hoping to find a group working to save it, we went to a community board meeting, where we met and started Friends of the High Line.

We wanted to save the High Line to make something extraordinary for New York City. It wouldn't be enough to build stairs and add a few planters and benches. The design for the High Line had to be as interesting and unusual as the structure itself.

Like others, we had fallen in love with the landscape that had reclaimed the monumental structure. We hoped to save this self-sown wilderness, which, thanks to Joel Sternfeld's photography, had become the defining image of the High Line – but to repair the underlying structure and make the High Line sound for years to come, this landscape had to be removed.

In their 2004 competition entry, Field Operations and Diller Scofidio + Renfro showed us a proposal that retained the sense of wildness and mystery of the original High Line landscape. It celebrated all that was great about the High Line's past while making the High Line accessible and giving it a future.

When the preliminary design was displayed at the Museum of Modern Art, in 2005, it was enthusiastically received. But skeptics told us it could never be built – that it would prove impractical or too experimental for a city park. Which is why we are so pleased to share this final design with you today: a design that includes all the best ideas of the original vision – ideas that have been refined, improved upon, but never diluted; ideas that are becoming reality right now.

This publication is a kind of map – a literal map of the park we are building, and a guide to the transformation of the High Line that will allow it to be rediscovered. This project has always been driven by images, so we've chosen to let the visual material speak for itself, with minimal text.

We owe thanks to many. What began as an unlikely dream is becoming reality because of the help of our elected officials, board of directors, staff, donors, volunteers, and thousands of supporters, who all shared a vision of New York reinventing itself.

Many challenges remain. We need to complete a $50 million private capital campaign to ensure that Section 2 can be built to the design standards shown in these pages. And the High Line will need to be scrupulously maintained to be the place we've worked to build. It will require more annual operations support than the City can provide. So we have a new job. Once an advocacy group, we now become the conservancy that partners with the Parks Department and is charged with providing the resources and leadership to guarantee a long, healthy life for the High Line. At this transformative moment, we rededicate ourselves to the High Line and its place in the future of New York City. We hope you will join us.

Joshua David & Robert Hammond
Co-Founders, Friends of the High Line

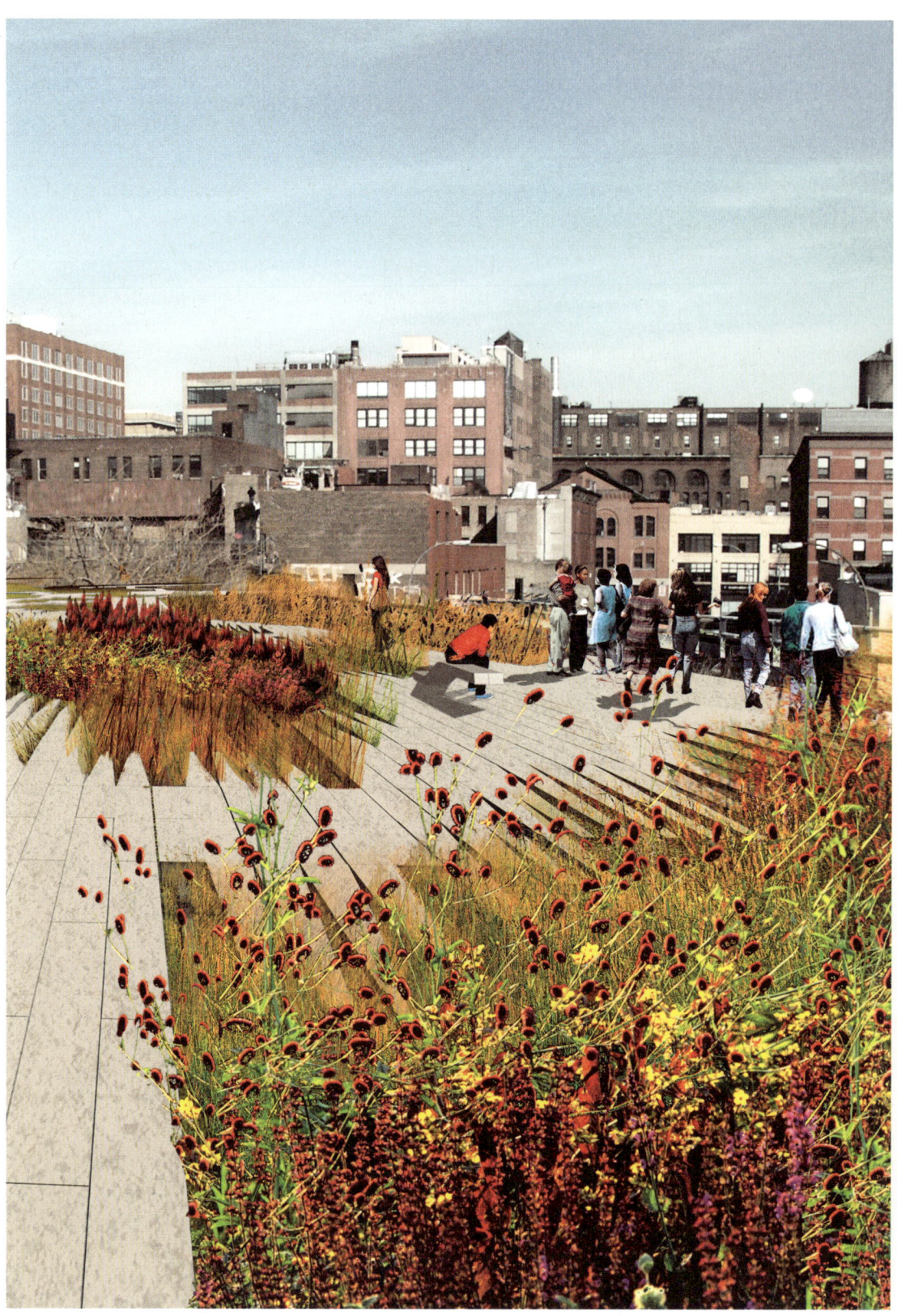

In 2002, when I first took office, the High Line was one court decision away from demolition. Unused by freight service for more than two decades, it was seen by many as an eyesore and a barrier to development; a vestige of a bygone era that had outlived its practical use. A small group of New Yorkers, though, realized that the High Line presented an opportunity: the chance to transform an abandoned remnant of our past into a vital part of our future.

Thanks to these visionaries' dedication, Section 1 of the High Line will open to the public at the end of this year. It represents everything we want New York City to be: bold, innovative, and environmentally sustainable. Standing 29 feet in the air and stretching 22 blocks, it will provide vital open space – one of the most important goals of PlaNYC, our vision of a greener, greater New York. It is also a testament to how much we can accomplish through public-private partnerships, which combine the best talents and resources of government, the business community, and nonprofit organizations. As you will see in the following pages, the High Line will be a one-of-a-kind park in our one-of-a-kind city; like so much of what we do here, it will be a model and an inspiration for others all around the world.

After so much hard work, we're finally beginning to see the High Line take shape. Soon, the first visitors will enjoy the greenery, tranquility, and history of this new park, along with its breathtaking views of our skyline. In the years to come, it is destined to become one of our city's most treasured and iconic public spaces.

Michael R. Bloomberg
Mayor, City of New York

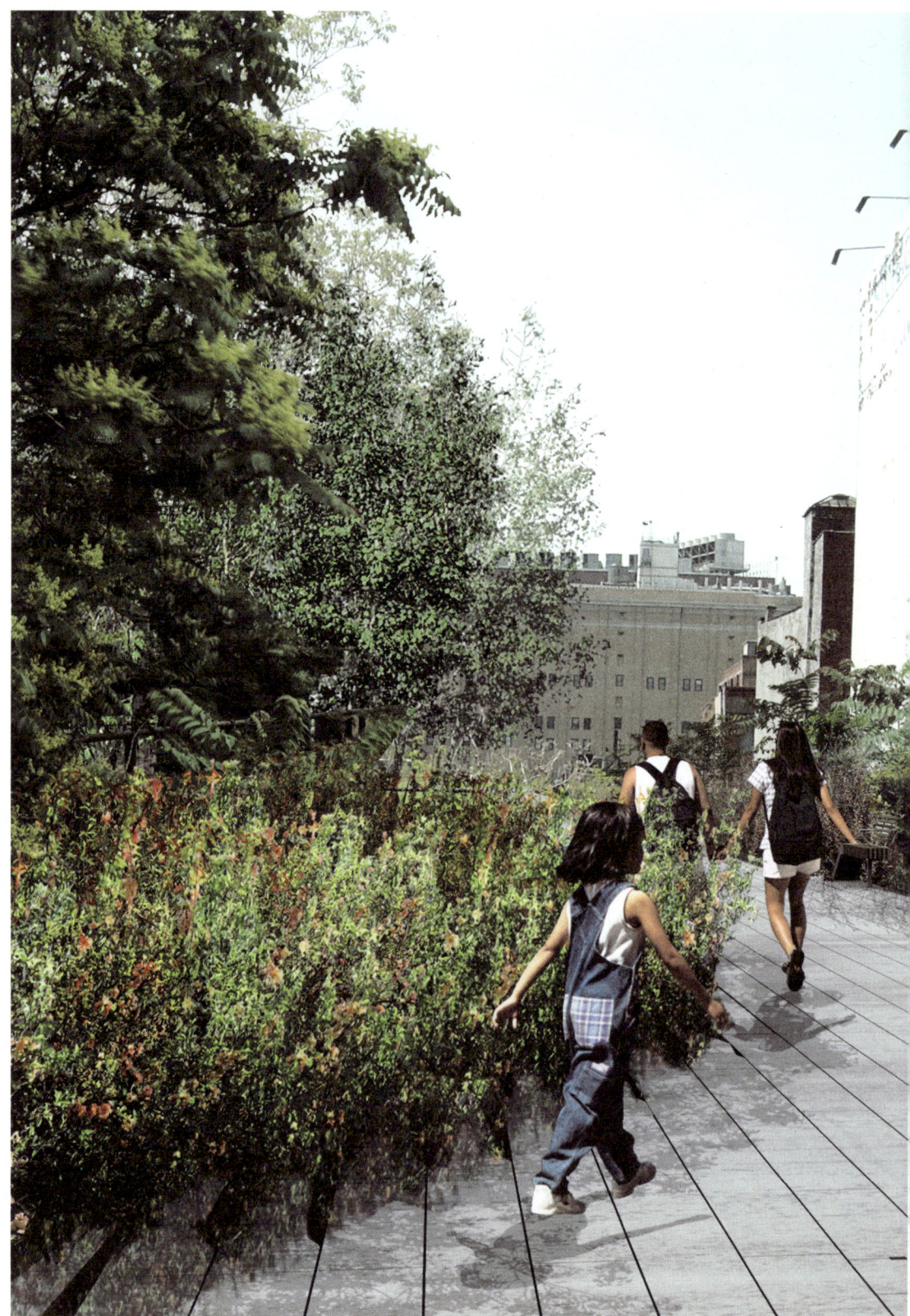

Since 1999, when the High Line project began, I have been deeply committed, personally and professionally, to advancing the creation of a park on this unique historic structure.

As a resident of the High Line neighborhood, I know how badly we need more parks. Creating much-needed green space on the High Line – a monument to the industrial and transportation history of the West Side – showcases the creativity and original thinking that makes New York great.

And as Speaker of the New York City Council, I'm proud of the Council's leadership in the creation of this unique park.

In 2001, when Mayor Giuliani's administration moved to tear the High Line down, the Council passed a resolution, which I co-sponsored, in favor of saving it. This was the first major governmental show of support for High Line preservation. Later that same year, the Council joined Friends of the High Line in a lawsuit that challenged the Giuliani administration and effectively halted the demolition efforts.

The Council also gave the project its first major capital funding allocation, in 2003. The Council is now the project's second largest public funder, after the Bloomberg administration, with over $33 million in capital allocations devoted to the project to date.

In 2005, the Council also helped establish the planning rationale for the High Line's future use with the passage of the West Chelsea rezoning. And, right now, in a related planning effort, we are hard at work to ensure that the entire historic High Line is preserved for park use at the West Side Rail Yards.

The High Line is a project of citywide importance, but it began as a community-driven initiative by residents in my Council district. I point that out because it demonstrates how ordinary New Yorkers can shape their neighborhoods, and the city as a whole. The New York City Council is proud to be part of this historic project, where government works in partnership with the citizens it represents to build something great for the future of the city.

Christine C. Quinn
Speaker, New York City Council

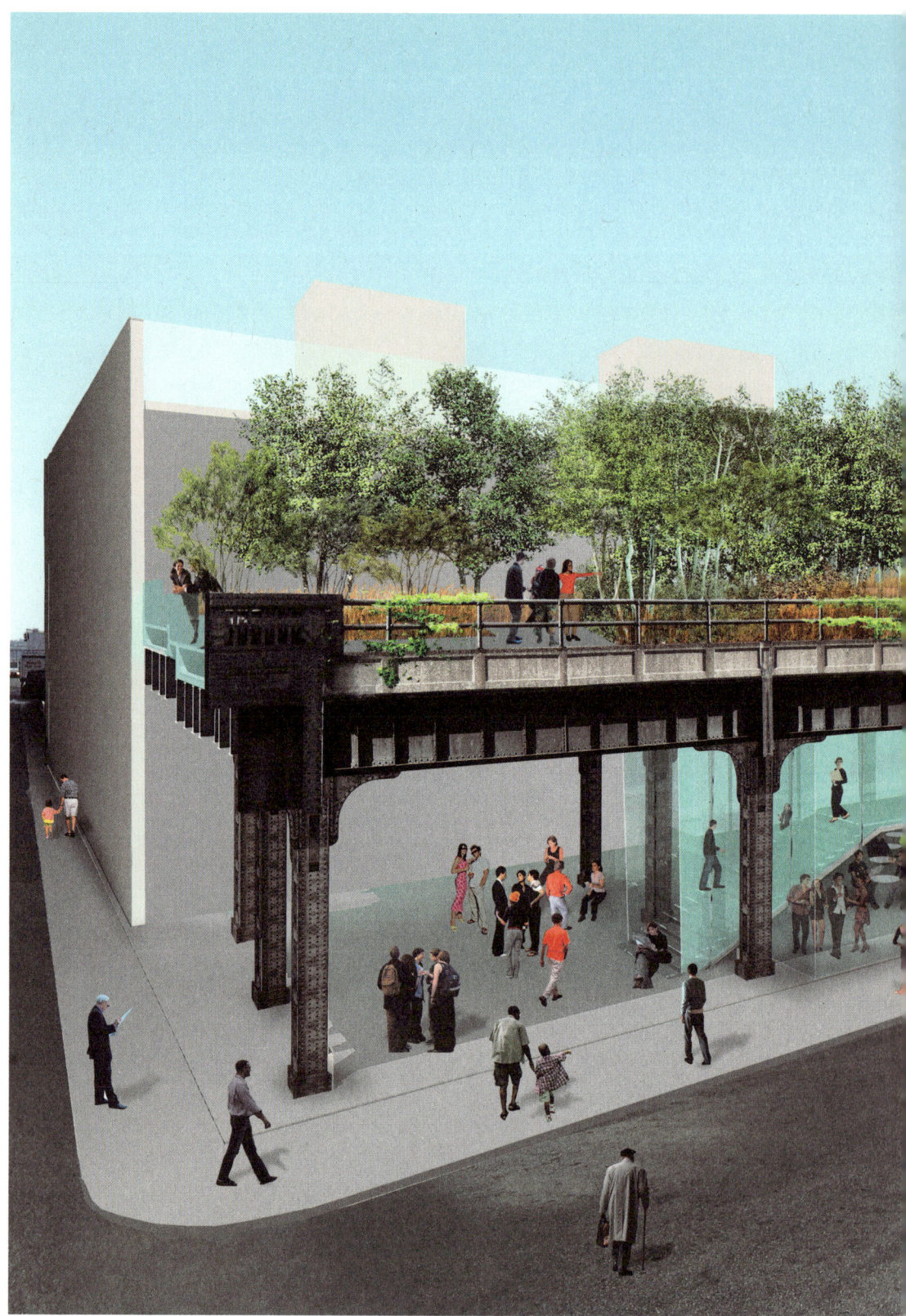

High Line construction broke ground shortly after I took office as Manhattan Borough President. At that historic moment, recognizing the positive impact the High Line would have on New York City's future, I decided that I had to make the High Line a funding priority. I am thrilled that I have been able to allocate $3 million in capital funds for the restoration of the ornamental steel railings. This year I plan to contribute additional funds for the construction of the 23rd Street Lawn, an oasis that is sure to become one of the High Line's best-loved gathering spots.

As we acknowledge the transformative effect this visionary project will have on three Manhattan neighborhoods, I also want to note that the idea first arose at a meeting of Manhattan's Community Board 4, when two residents came to a meeting hoping to save a unique structure – and ended up founding Friends of the High Line.

With the help of Community Boards 2 and 4, Friends of the High Line has built the broad base of governmental and community support that continues to be crucial to the project's success. Not only is the High Line going to be a wonderful park, loved by its neighbors and by people from all over the city; it will demonstrate the very real opportunity for any New Yorker to help shape their neighborhood and our city. Finally, the project shows how New York City's community boards are indispensable avenues for community-based planning. Congratulations to Friends of the High Line and all of the supporters and volunteers!

Scott M. Stringer
Manhattan Borough President

With the High Line, preservation and innovation come together in a forward-thinking project that shows how New York honors its history while building for the future. Inspired by nature, which overtook a forgotten railroad viaduct, the design for the High Line employs green-roof technologies in creative ways to turn an unused piece of infrastructure into a park that will provide needed open space for the rich diversity of urban life. I'm pleased to help build this future landmark for New York City.

Hillary Rodham Clinton
U.S. Senator

Once called the "Life Line of New York," for decades this historic railway played a vital role in the life of the West Side, bringing food, goods, and raw materials into the city. Its transformation into a public park means that the High Line will benefit generations of New Yorkers for decades to come. As a member of the New York Assembly, I fought for its preservation in the 20th century, and I am thrilled to have contributed to its rebirth in the 21st.

Jerrold L. Nadler
U.S. Representative

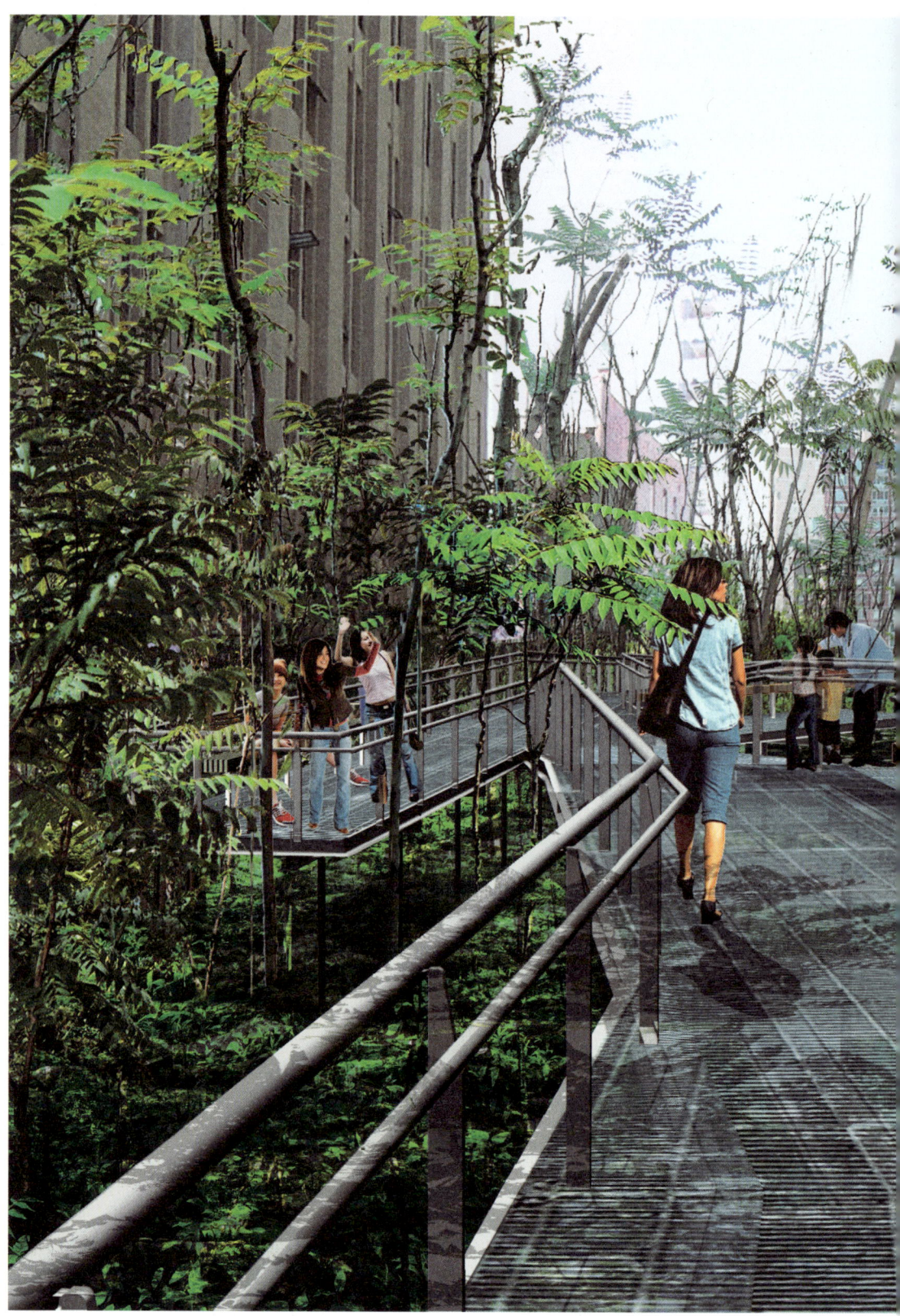

There are few occasions as exciting for a city as the creation of a new park. In New York City, our parks simultaneously allow us to escape the pressures of life on the streets and allow us to join with other New Yorkers in harmonious surroundings.

Possessing these qualities, the High Line will be like other parks in our city's system, but it will also be distinct. A park unlike any other, the High Line will be lifted 29 feet above the street, linking 22 blocks, connecting three neighborhoods, even passing through the interiors of buildings.

The High Line's unique qualities create unique challenges, which is why I'm glad that we have formed a strong partnership with Friends of the High Line. Private partners, such as the Friends of the High Line, are a fundamental reason for the incredible transformation of New York City's parks over the past decade. Each partner makes an invaluable contribution to our parks, many of them raising funds for capital projects, maintenance, and public programs.

In addition to committing to raise $50 million in capital funds for the High Line's construction and endowment, Friends of the High Line has committed to raise a major portion of the High Line's maintenance funds each year, for years to come. Thus, the future of the High Line is very much linked to the future of Friends of the High Line. I hope you will do all you can to support Friends of the High Line in its efforts, so that its partnership with the Parks Department continues successfully and the High Line is always maintained at a level of excellence commensurate with the innovative design shown in these pages.

Adrian Benepe
Commissioner, New York City Department of Parks & Recreation

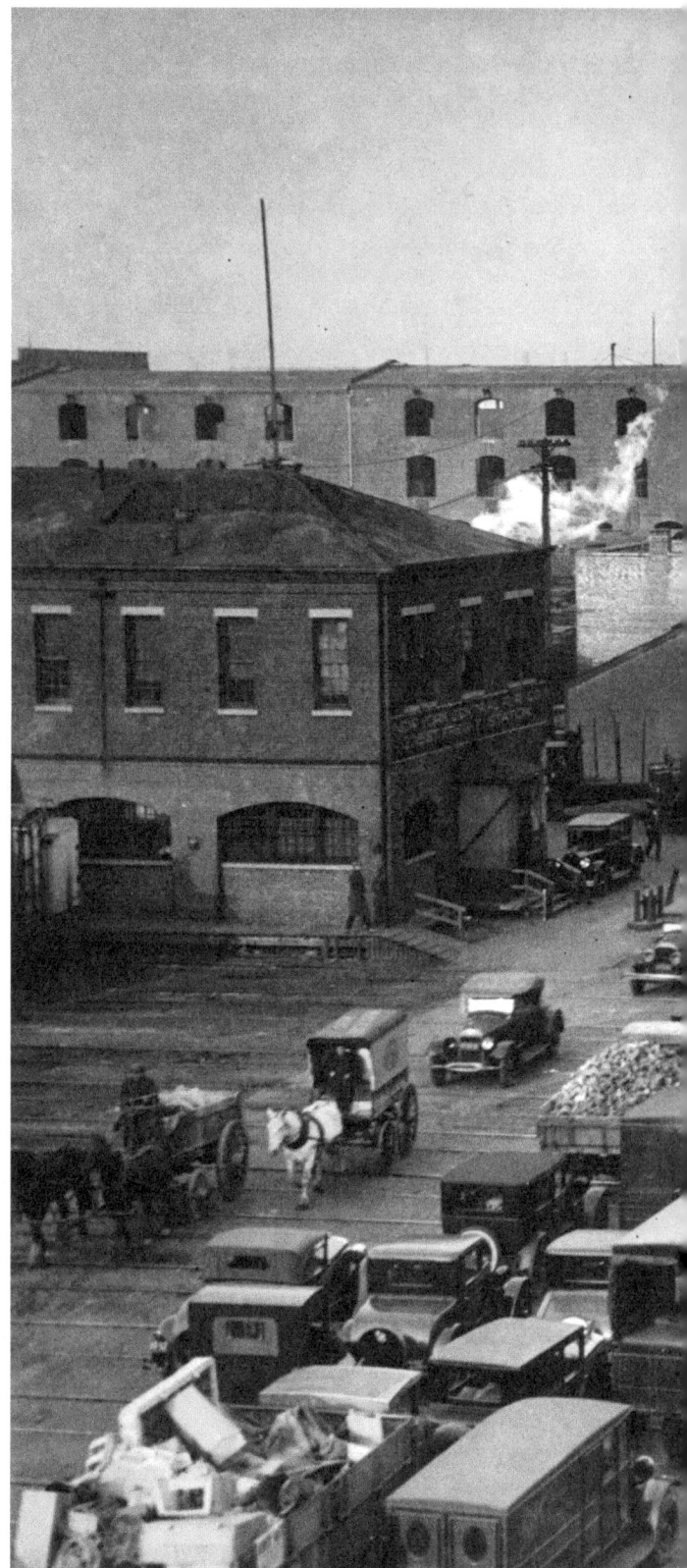

The City authorized freight train tracks to run down the West Side in 1847. Collisions between trains, pedestrians, and other traffic caused so many fatalities that the route was called "Death Avenue."

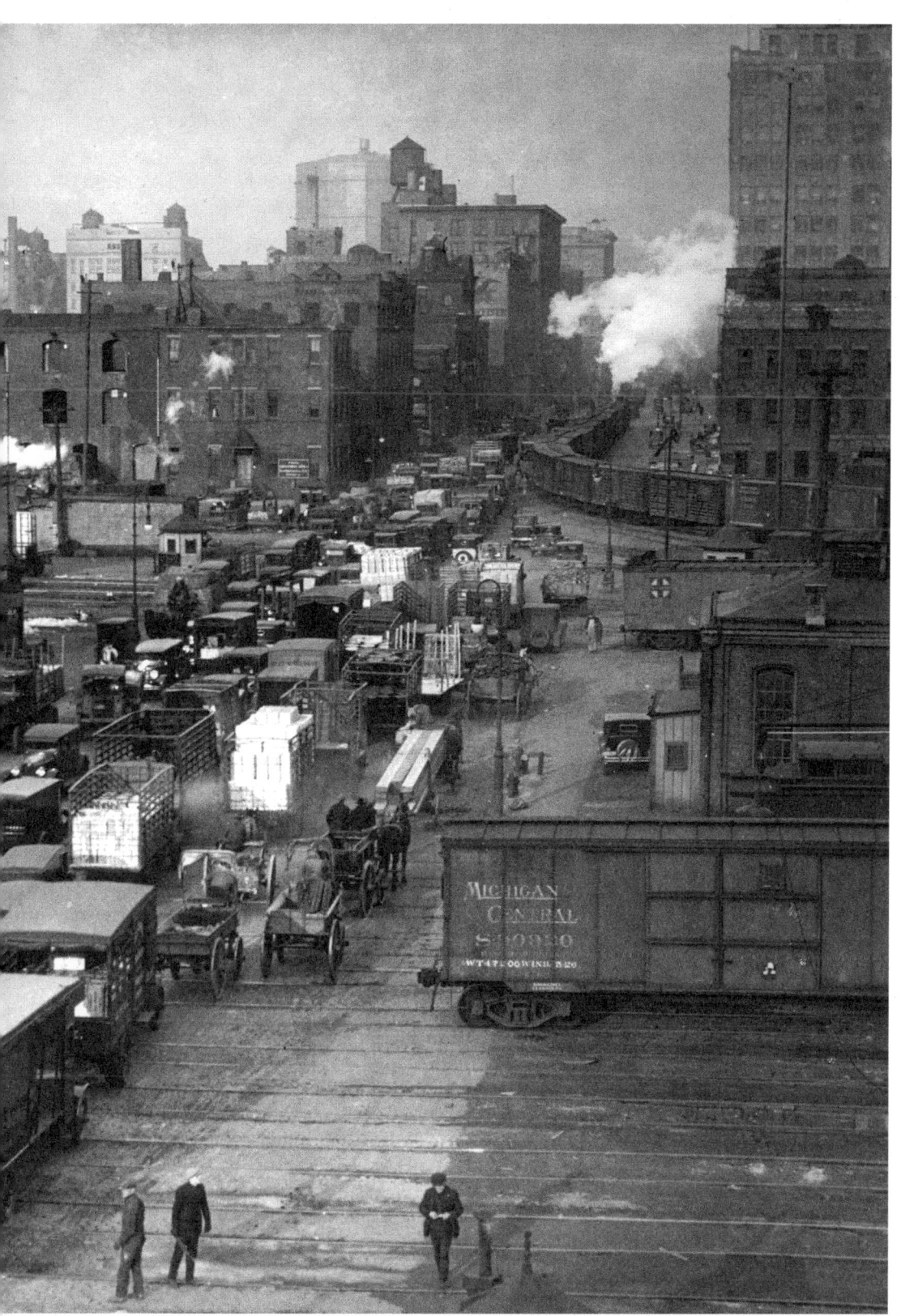

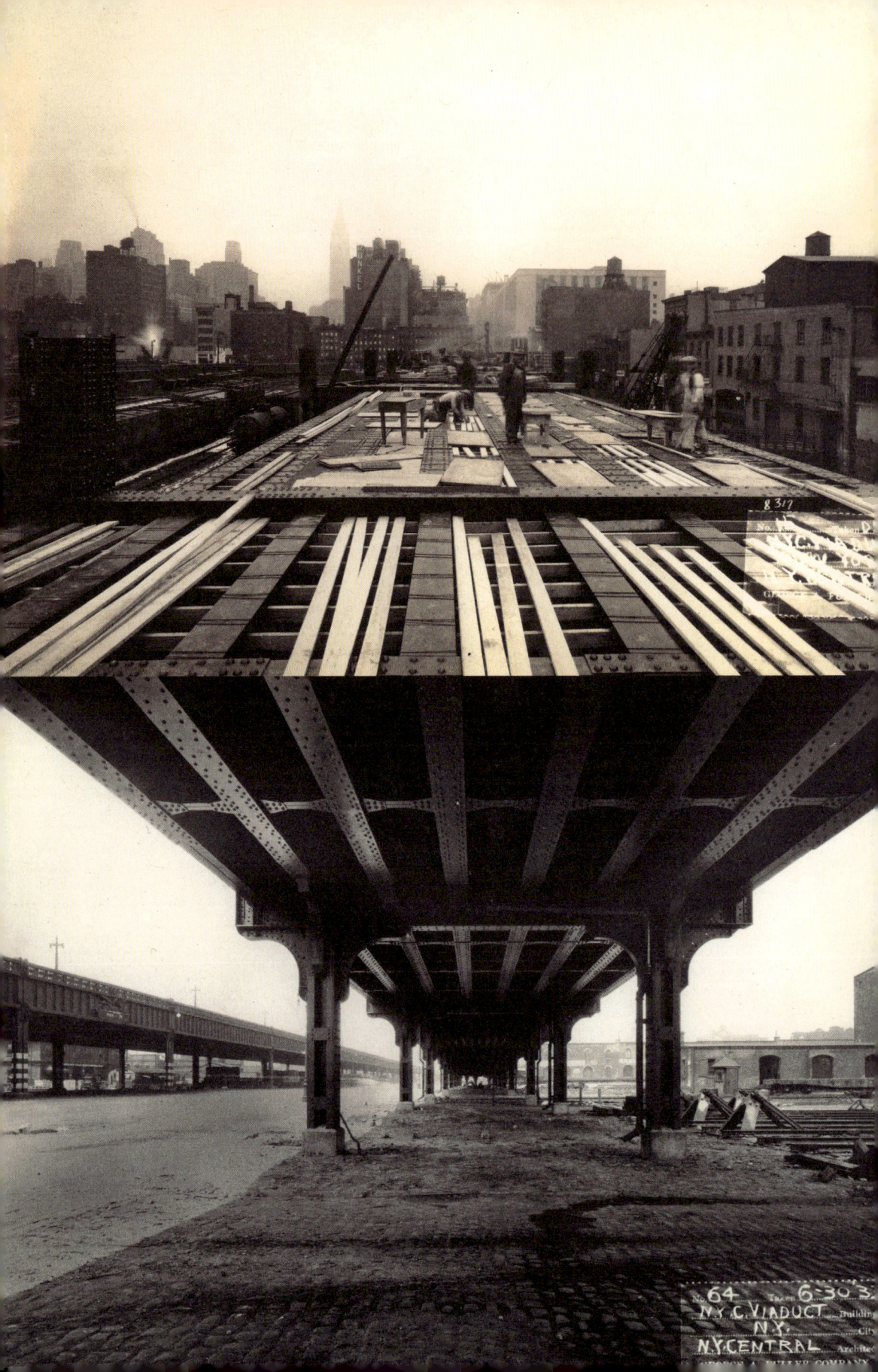

No. 64   6-30-3.
N.Y.C. VIADUCT
N.Y.
N.Y. CENTRAL

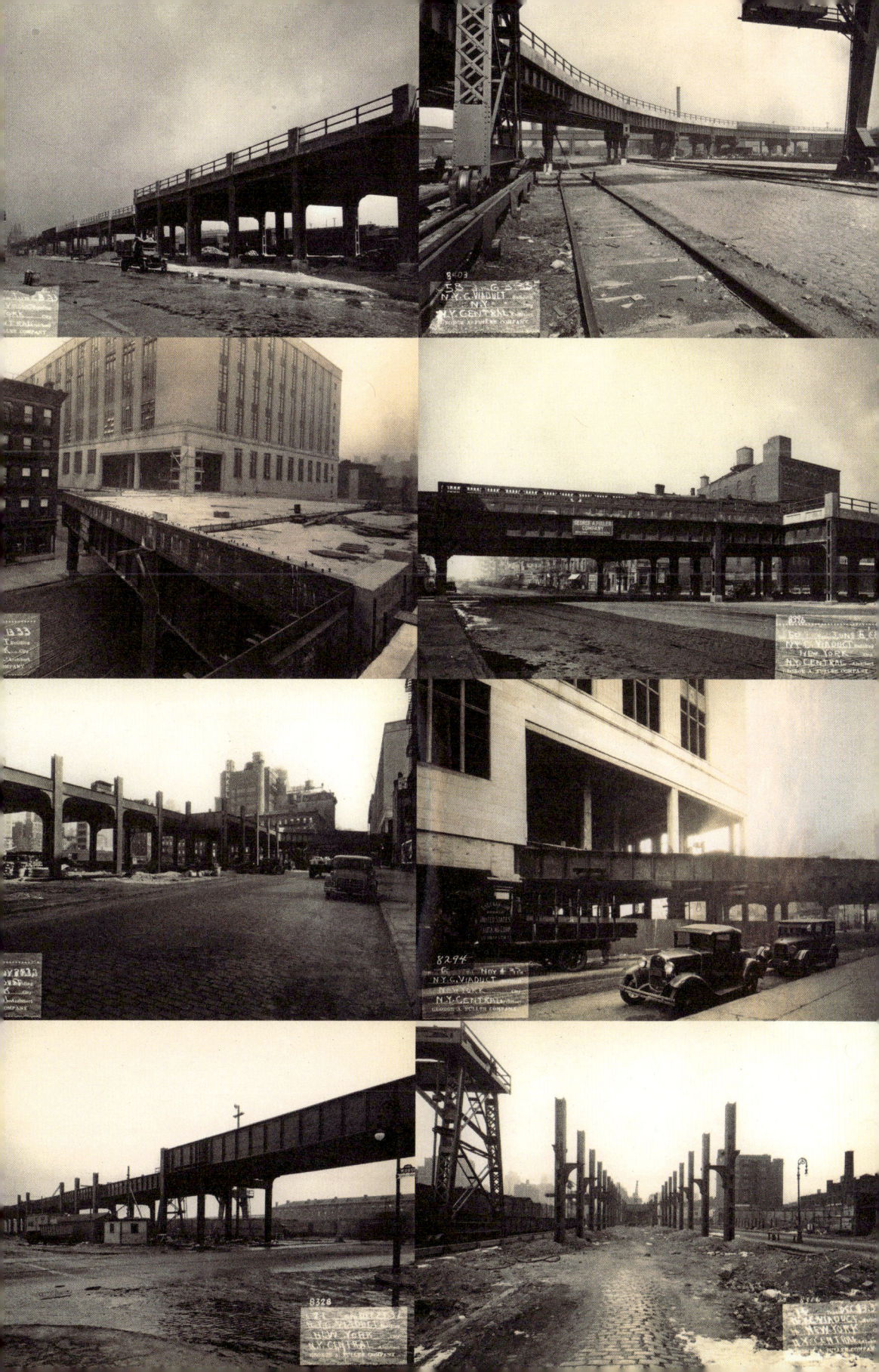

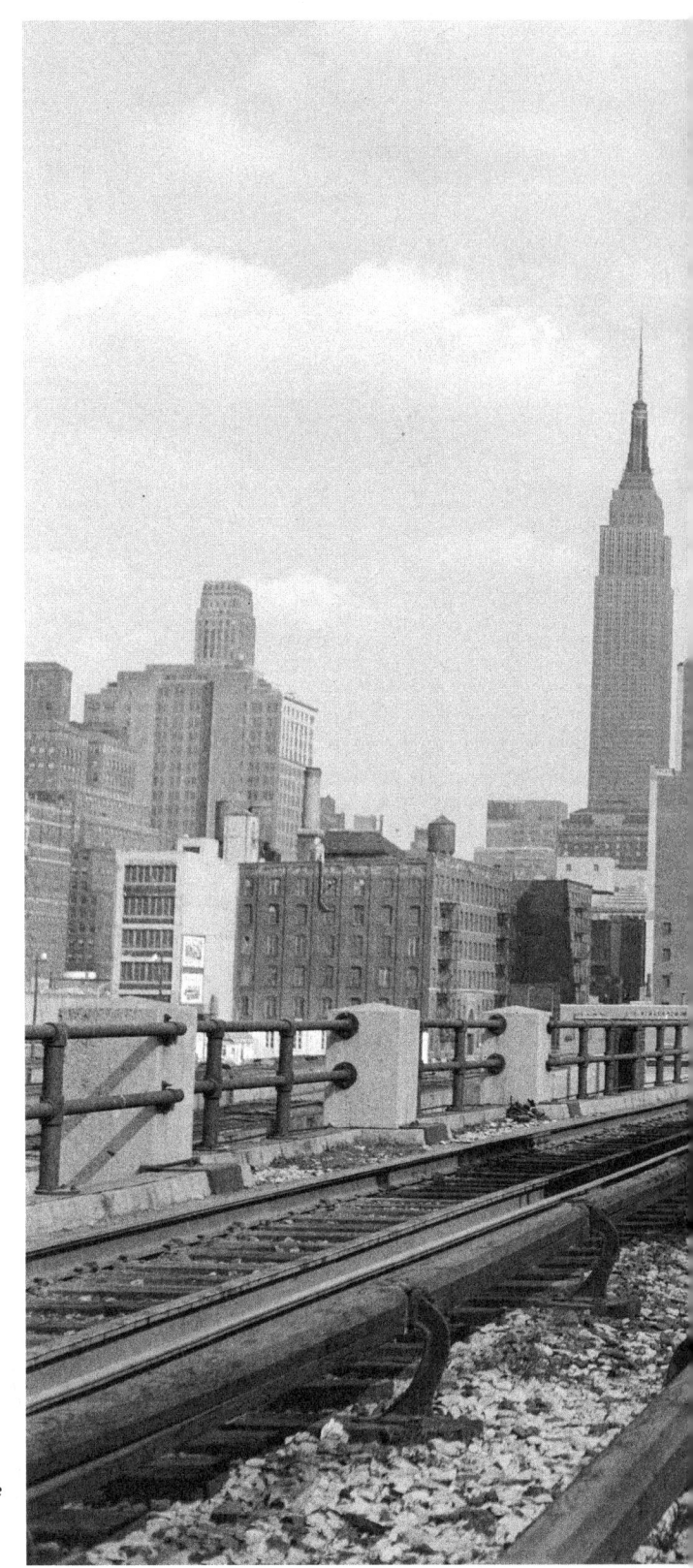

An agreement between the City of New York and New York Central Rail Road was finalized in 1929 for the West Side Improvement, an infrastructure project that eliminated street-level rail crossings in Manhattan. South of 35th Street, tracks were raised on the High Line, constructed 1929-1934. The High Line originally ended at the St. John's Park Terminal, at Spring Street.

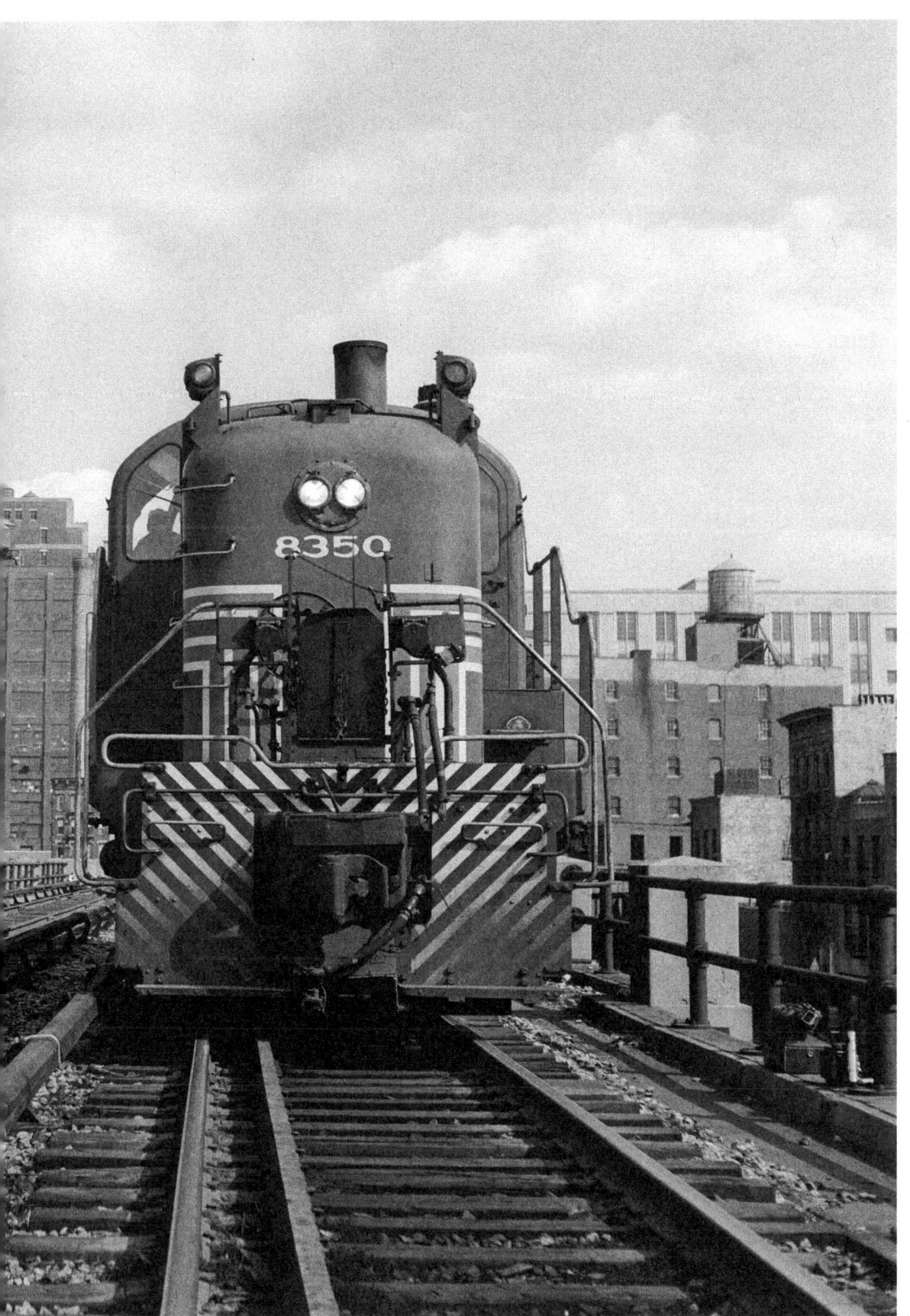

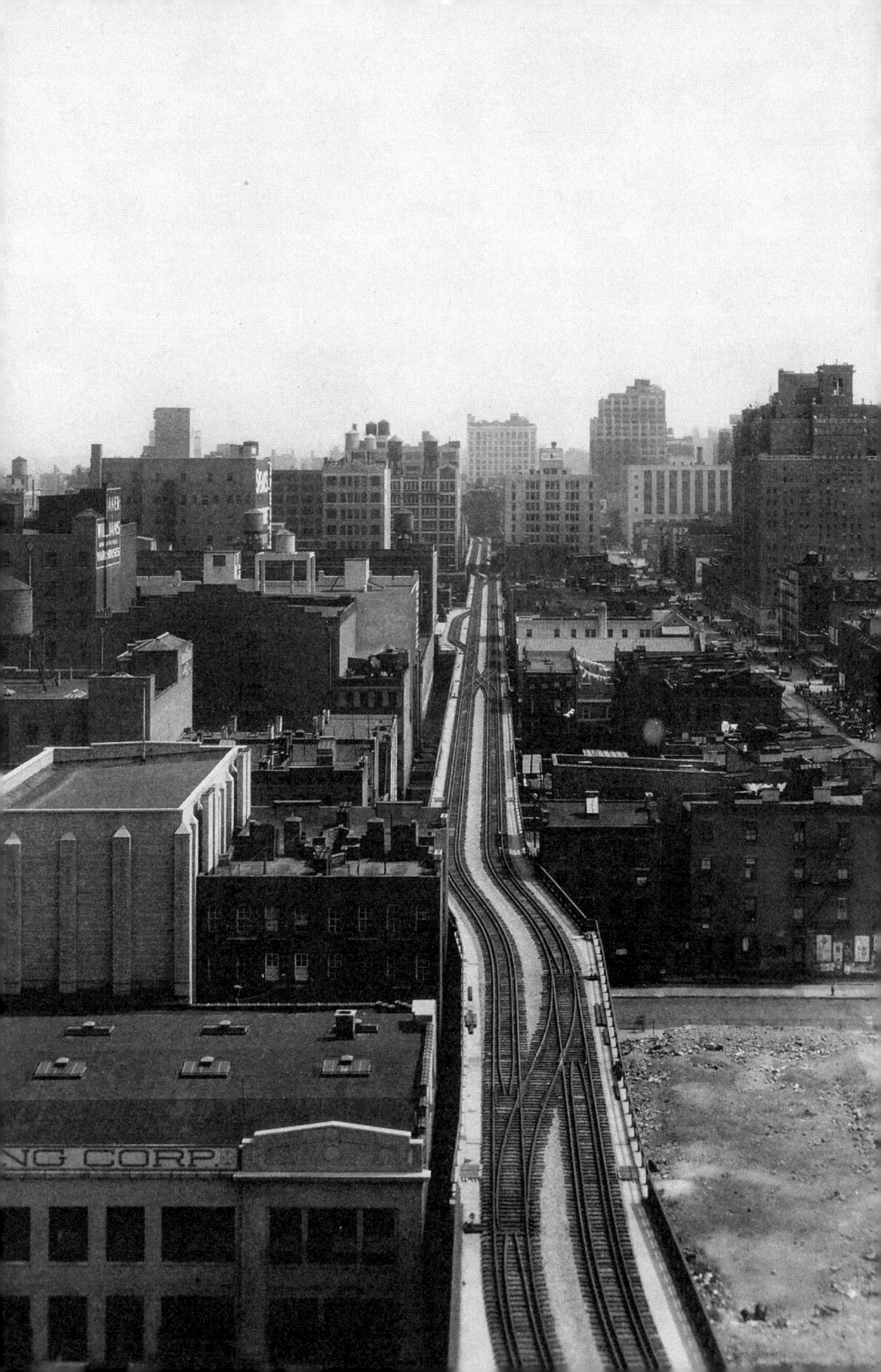

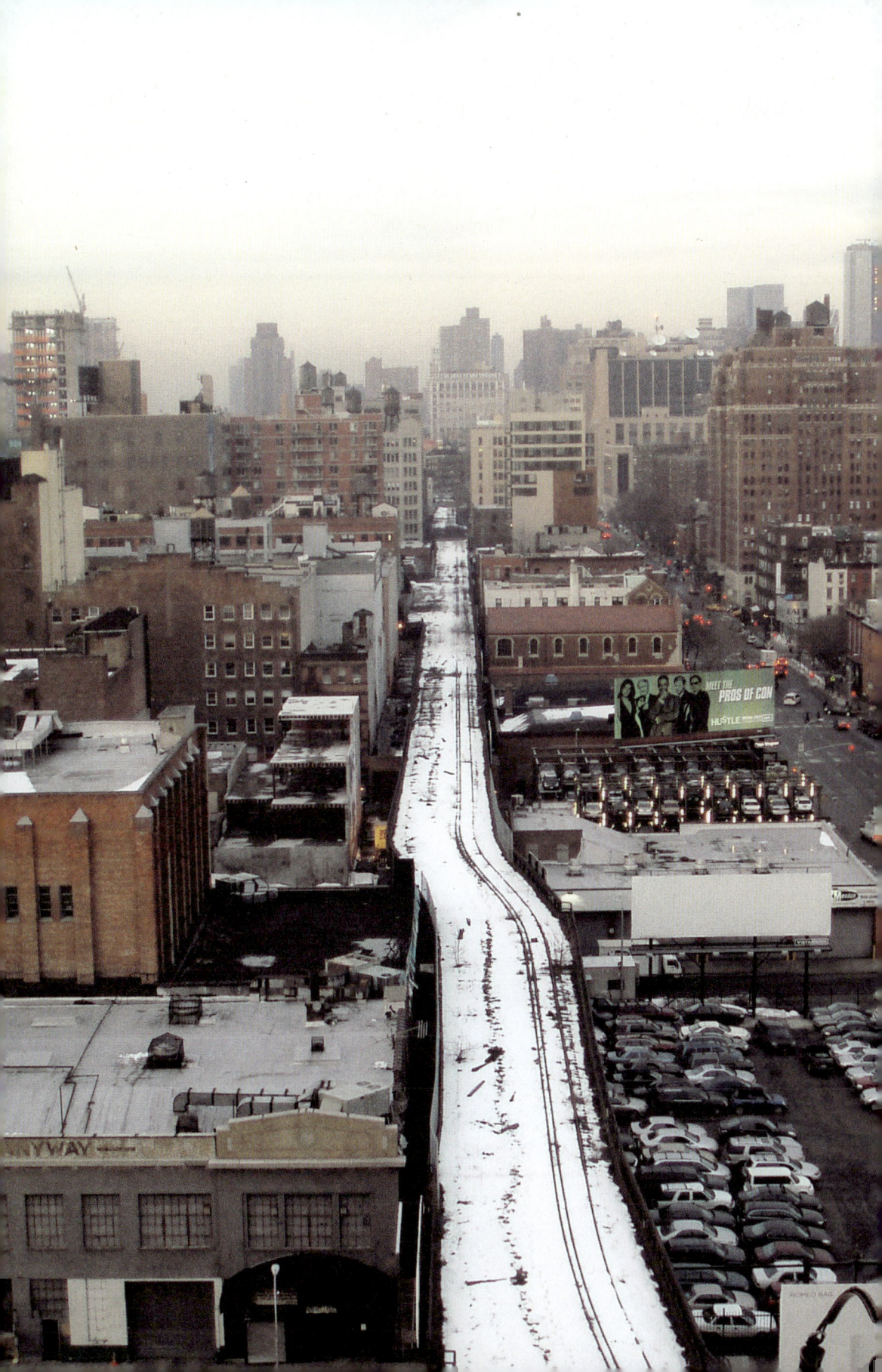

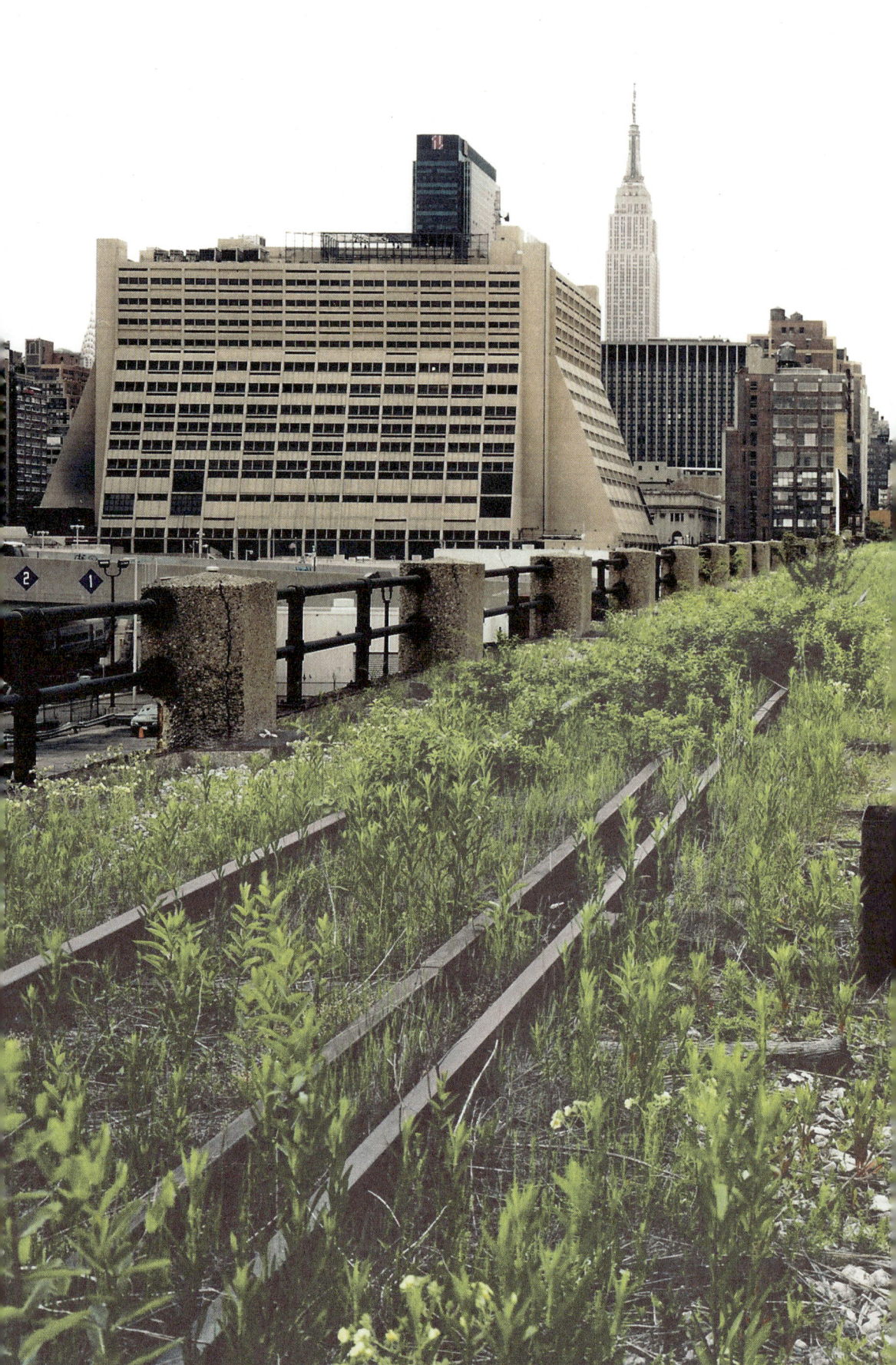

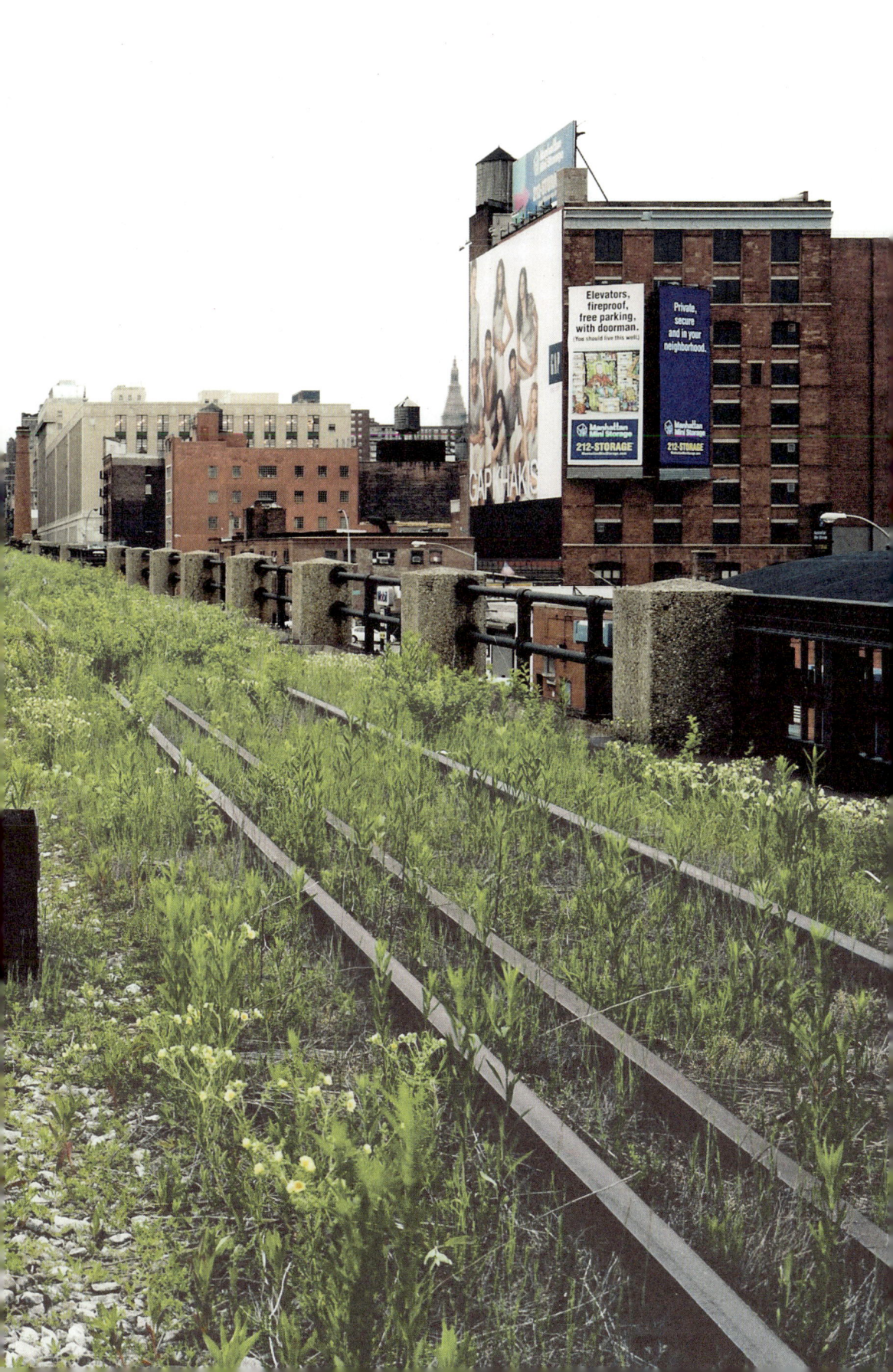

Self-Sown Landscape

Trains were active on the High Line from 1934 until the early 1960s, when rail traffic declined and a southern section was torn down. The last train ran in 1980, and the High Line, less than 50 years old, went silent. Seeds, dropped by trains, birds, and breezes, grew in the gravel ballast. Photographer Joel Sternfeld's images of the self-sown landscape, taken over the course of a year in 2000 and 2001, supported efforts to save the High Line when it was threatened with demolition.

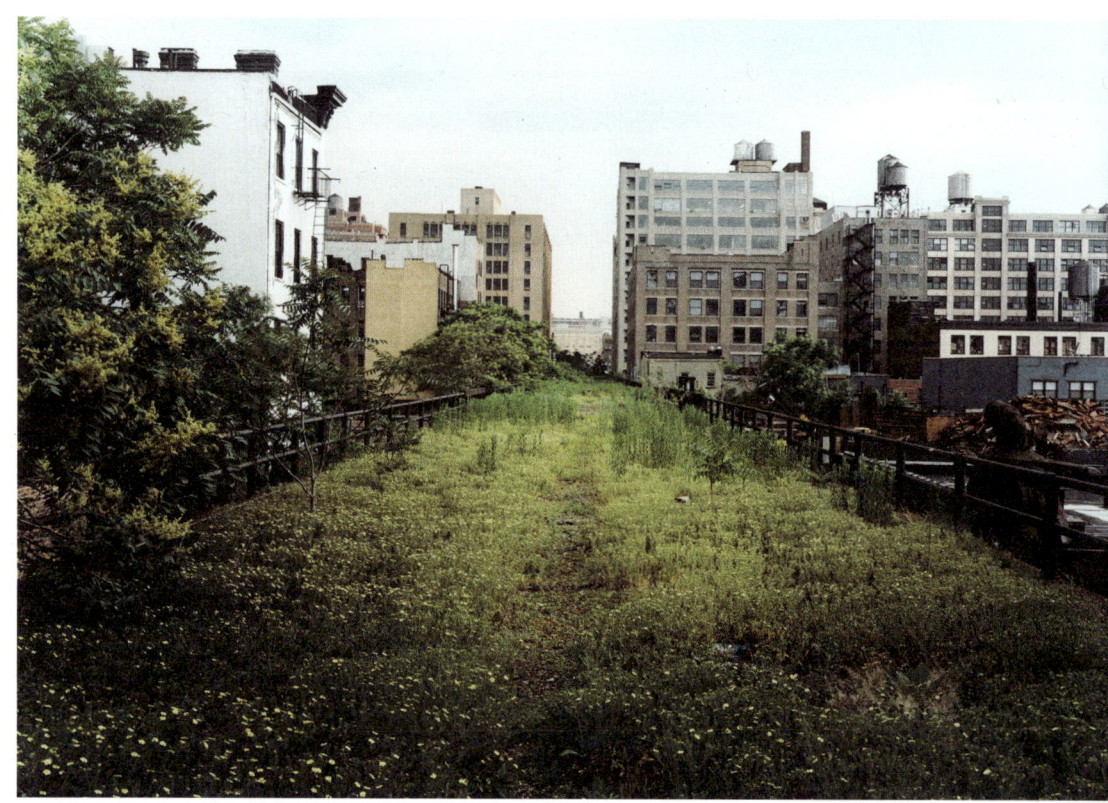

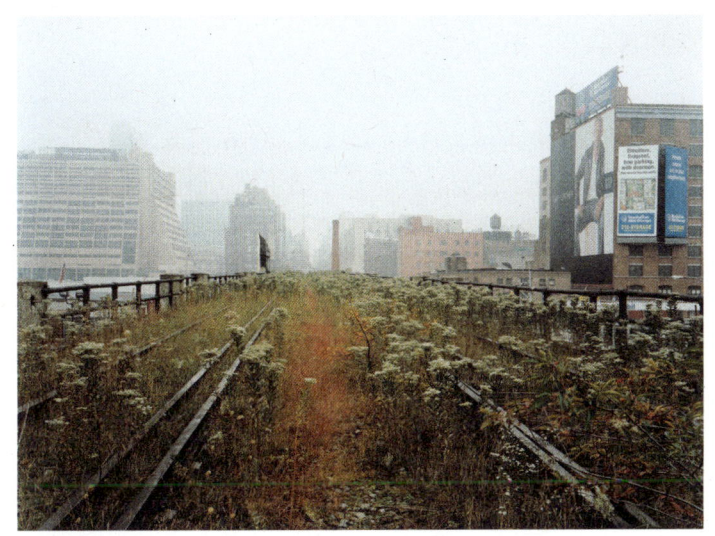

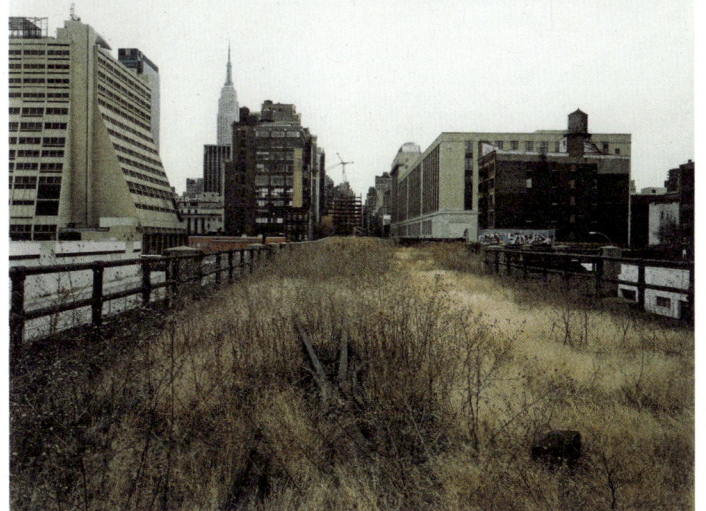

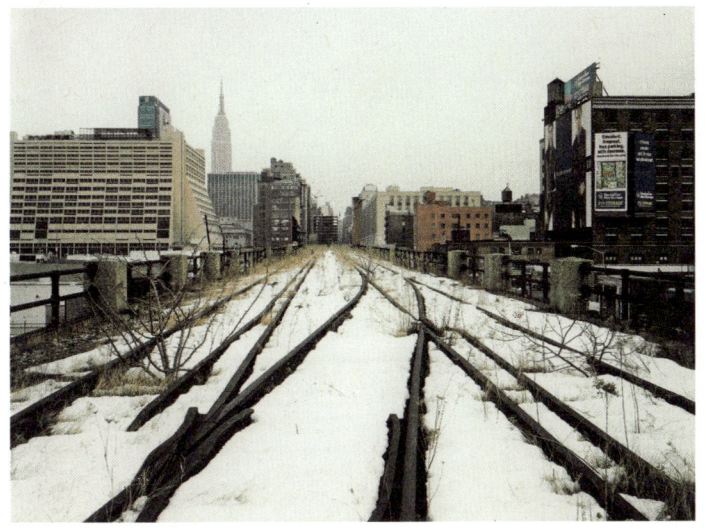

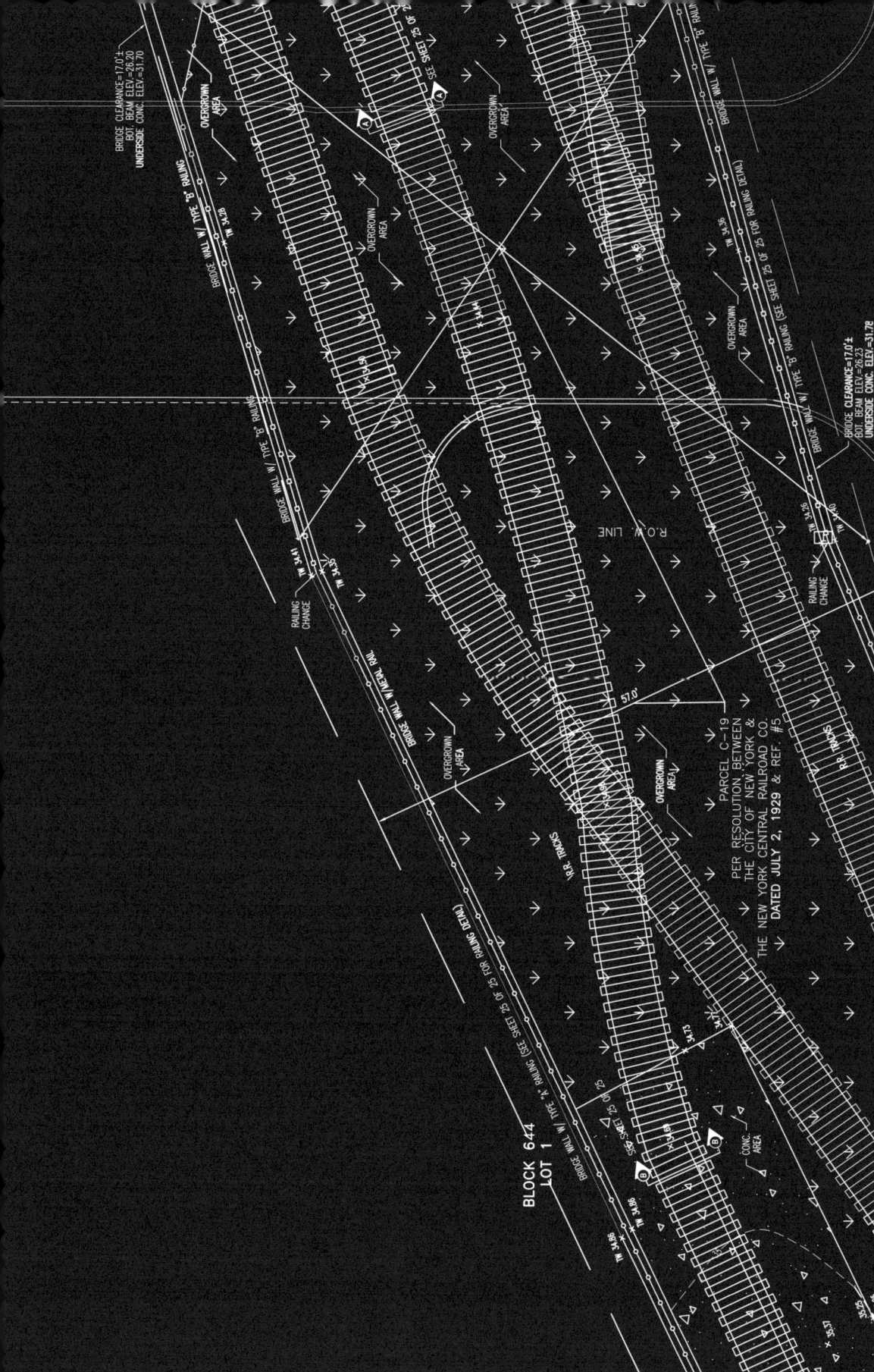

DESIGN: CONCEPT

From an aesthetic and design standpoint, it has always been our position to try to respect the innate character of the High Line itself: its singularity and linearity, its straight-forward pragmatism, its emergent properties with wild plant-life — meadows, thickets, vines, mosses, flowers, intermixed with ballast, steel tracks, railings, and concrete.

Our solution is primarily threefold: first the invention of a new paving system, built from linear concrete planks with open joints, specially tapered edges and seams that permit the free flow of water (collected for irrigation) and the intermingling of organic plant-life with harder materials. Less a pathway and more a combed or furrowed landscape surface, this intermixing of plants with paving creates a rambling, textural effect of immersion, strolling "within" and "amongst" rather than feeling distanced from. The selection and arrangement of grasses and plants further helps to define a wild, dynamic character, distinct from a typical manicured landscape, and representative of the harsh, arid conditions of the shallow rooting depth. The second strategy is to slow things down, to promote a sense of duration and of being in another place, where time seems less pressing. Long stairways, meandering pathways, and hidden niches with seating encourage taking one's time. The third approach involved a careful sense of dimension and scale, minimizing the current tendency to make things bigger and obvious and seeking instead a more subtle gauge of the High Line's measure.

The result is an episodic and varied sequence of public spaces and landscape biotopes set along a simple and consistent line — a line that cuts across some of the most remarkable elevated vistas of Manhattan and the Hudson River, each view unfolding through an otherworldly synaesthesia of motion.

James Corner, Principal
Field Operations

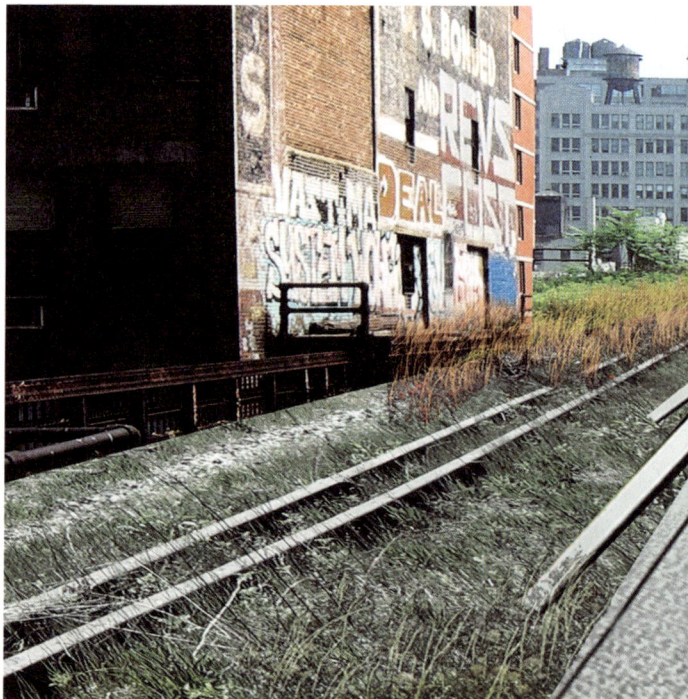

Inspired by the melancholic, unruly beauty of this postindustrial ruin where nature has reclaimed a once-vital piece of urban infrastructure, the new park will be an instrument of leisure, a place to reflect about the very categories of "nature" and "culture" in our time.

Through a strategy of agri-tecture that combines organic and building materials into a vegetal/mineral blend, the park accommodates the wild, the cultivated, the intimate, and the social. In stark contrast to the speed of Hudson River Park, this parallel linear experience is marked by slowness, distraction, and an otherworldliness that preserves the strange character of the High Line. New plantings build upon the existing landscape character, working with specific environmental urban conditions and microclimates associated with sun, shade, wet, dry, wind, noise, open and sheltered spaces. Access points are durational experiences designed to prolong the transition from the frenetic pace of the city streets to the slow, otherworldly landscape of the High Line. Wherever possible, access points cut through the massive steel structure with slow stairs, ramps, and elevators to strategically position the body at varying elevations under, within, and above the High Line.

Providing flexibility and responsiveness to the changing needs, opportunities, and desires of the dynamic context, the project will remain perpetually unfinished, sustaining emergent growth and change over time.

Ricardo Scofidio, Principal
Diller Scofidio + Renfro

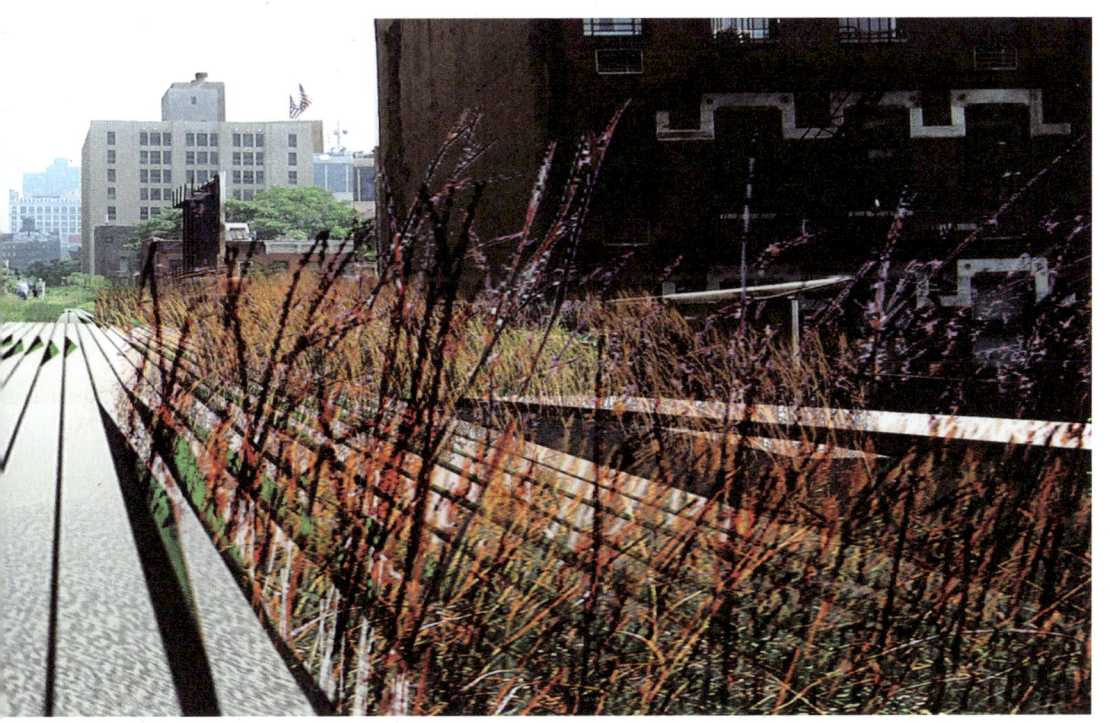

WHAT WILL GROW HERE ?

By changing the rules of engagement between plant life and pedestrians, our strategy of **AGRI-TECTURE** combines organic and building materials into gradients of changing proportions that accommodate a variety of natural and programmatic conditions. Part agriculture / part architecture the system digitizes the High Line surface into discrete units of paving and planting that could be organized in any combination from 100% hard paving to 100% soft richly vegetated biotopes, or any gradation in between. The surface is built from individual pre-cast concrete planks with open joints to encourage emergent growth like wild grass through cracks in the sidewalk. The long, gradually tapering units are designed to comb into planting beds creating a "pathless" landscape' where the public can meander in unscripted ways.

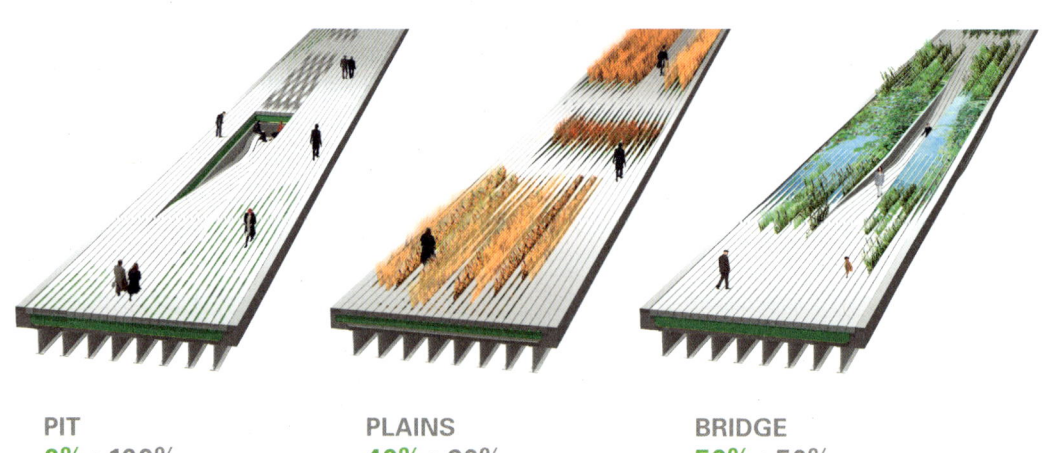

PIT
0% : 100%

PLAINS
40% : 60%

BRIDGE
50% : 50%

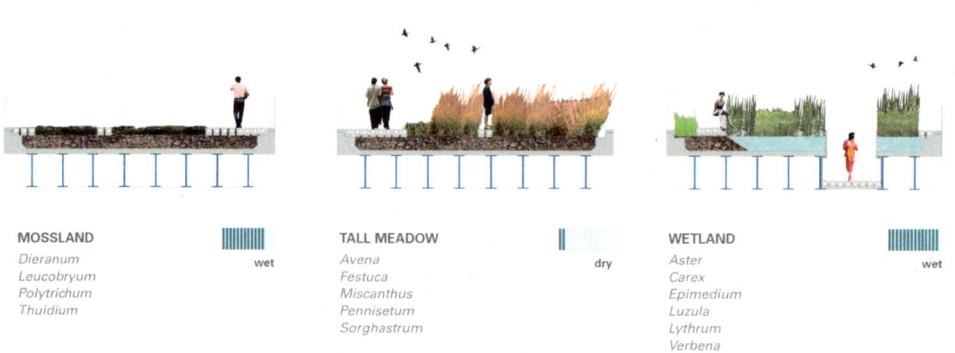

MOSSLAND	TALL MEADOW	WETLAND
Dieranum	*Avena*	*Aster*
Leucobryum	*Festuca*	*Carex*
Polytrichum	*Miscanthus*	*Epimedium*
Thuidium	*Pennisetum*	*Luzula*
	Sorghastrum	*Lythrum*
		Verbena

MOSSLAND — wet

TALL MEADOW — dry

WETLAND — wet

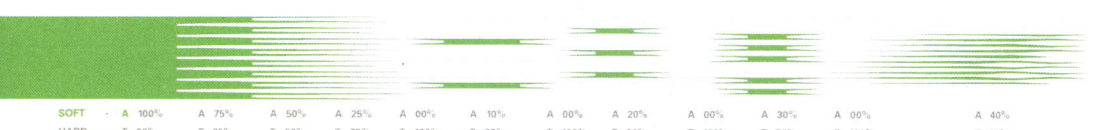

SOFT	· A 100%	A 75%	A 50%	A 25%	A 00%	A 10%	A 00%	A 20%	A 00%	A 30%	A 00%	A 40%
HARD	T 00%	T 25%	T 50%	T 75%	T 100%	T 90%	T 100%	T 80%	T 100%	T 70%	T 100%	T 60%

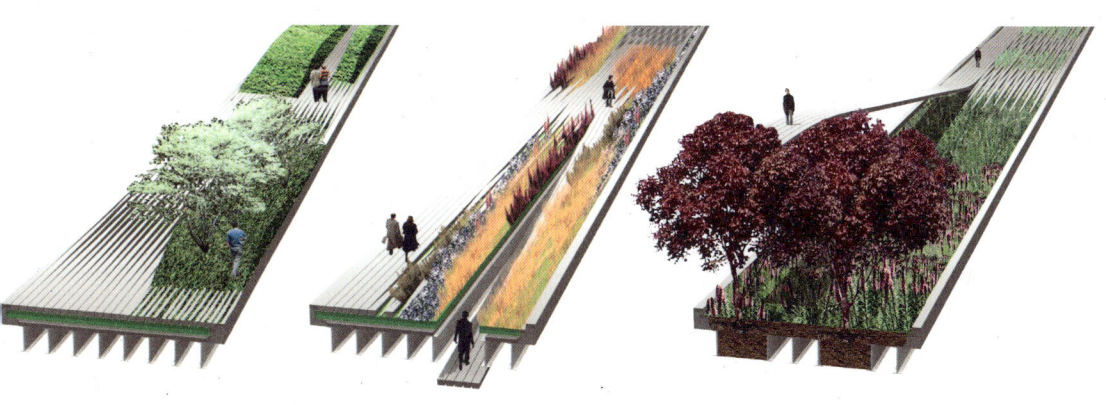

MOUND
55% : 45%

RAMP
60% : 40%

FLYOVER
100% : 10%

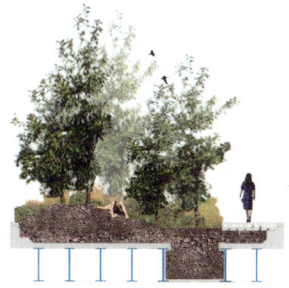

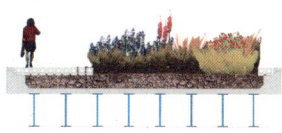

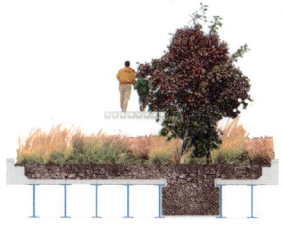

WOODLAND THICKET

wet/average

Adiantum spp.
Asarum
Betula nigra 'Heritage'
Clethra barbinervis
Sassafras albidum
Osmunda spp.
Viburnum dilitatum

MIXED PERENNIAL MEADOW
dry/average

Artemisia
Eryngium giganteum
Heuchera
Monarda
Persicaria
Sanguisorba officinalis
Salvia

YOUNG WOODLAND
average

Agastache
Buxus sempervirens
Cercis canadensis
Lavatera
Rhus chinensis
Salix eleagnos

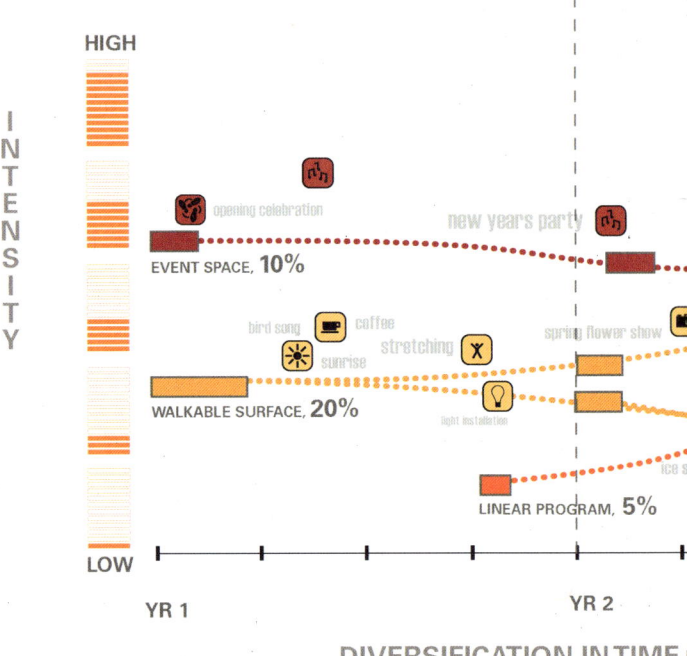

I
N
T
E
N
S
I
T
Y

HIGH

opening celebration

new years party

EVENT SPACE, **10%**

bird song   coffee

sunrise   stretching

spring flower show

WALKABLE SURFACE, **20%**

light installation

ice s...

LINEAR PROGRAM, **5%**

LOW

YR 1   YR 2

DIVERSIFICATION IN TIME

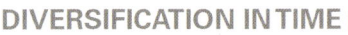

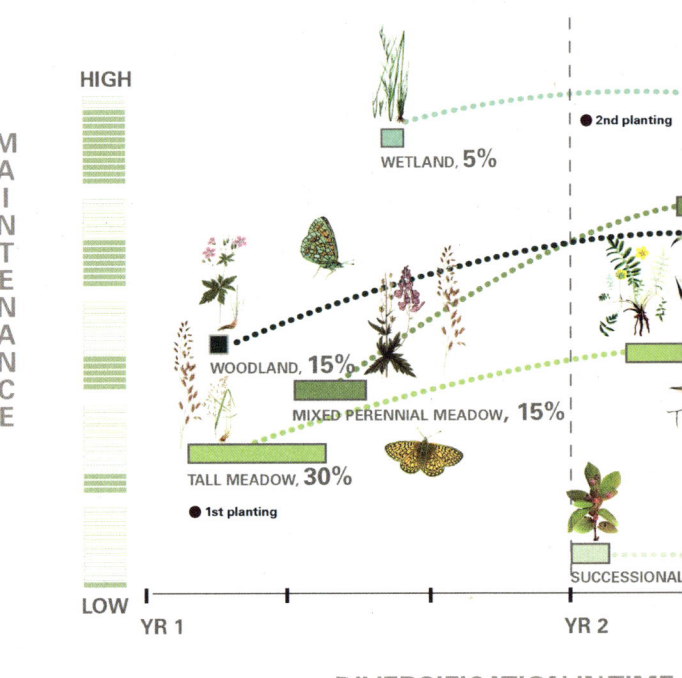

M
A
I
N
T
E
N
A
N
C
E

HIGH

● 2nd planting

WETLAND, **5%**

WOODLAND, **15%**

MIXED PERENNIAL MEADOW, **15%**

TALL MEADOW, **30%**

● 1st planting

SUCCESSIONAL

LOW

YR 1   YR 2

DIVERSIFICATION IN TIME

Field Operations and Diller Scofidio +
Renfro's 2004 design competition entry
proposed to blur boundaries between
walkways and plantings and suggested
evolutions of programs, plant life, and
bird life.

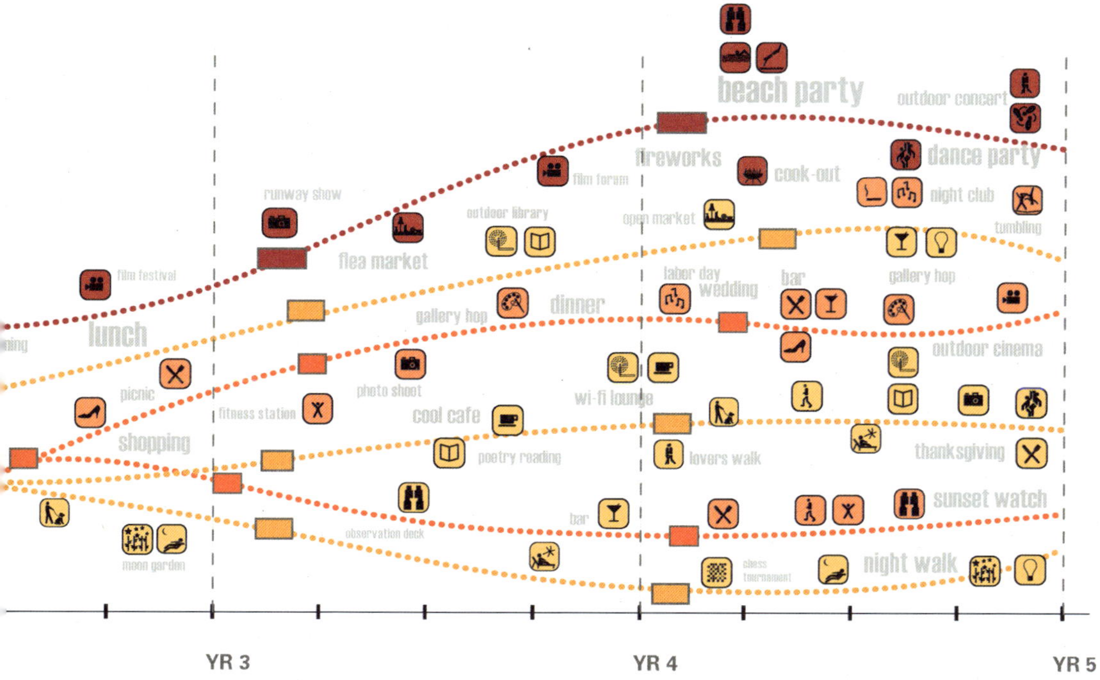

beach party

outdoor concert

runway show

fireworks   cook-out   dance party

film forum

outdoor library   night club

flea market   open market   tumbling

film festival

labor day   wedding   bar   gallery hop

lunch   gallery hop   dinner   outdoor cinema

dining

picnic   photo shoot   wi-fi lounge

fitness station   cool cafe   lovers walk   thanksgiving

shopping   poetry reading

bar   sunset watch

observation deck   bar   night walk

moon garden   chess tournament

YR 3   YR 4   YR 5

ED PERFORMANCE / INCREASED POTENTIAL]

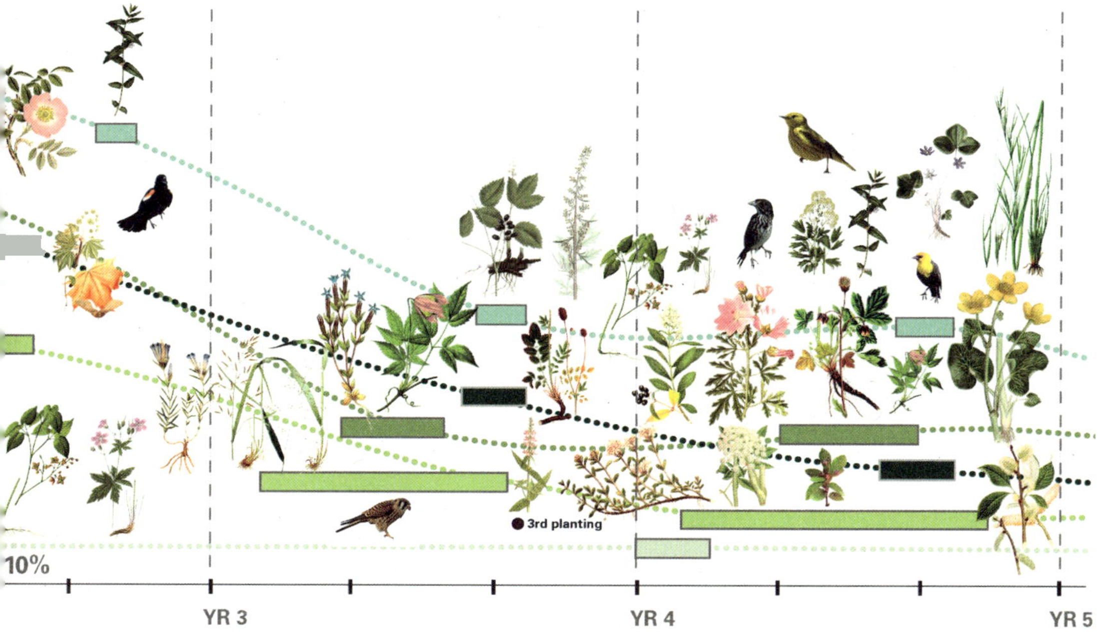

3rd planting

10%

YR 3   YR 4   YR 5

D MAINTENANCE / ENHANCED BIODIVERSITY]

35

Design Principles

Framework Plan, February 2005

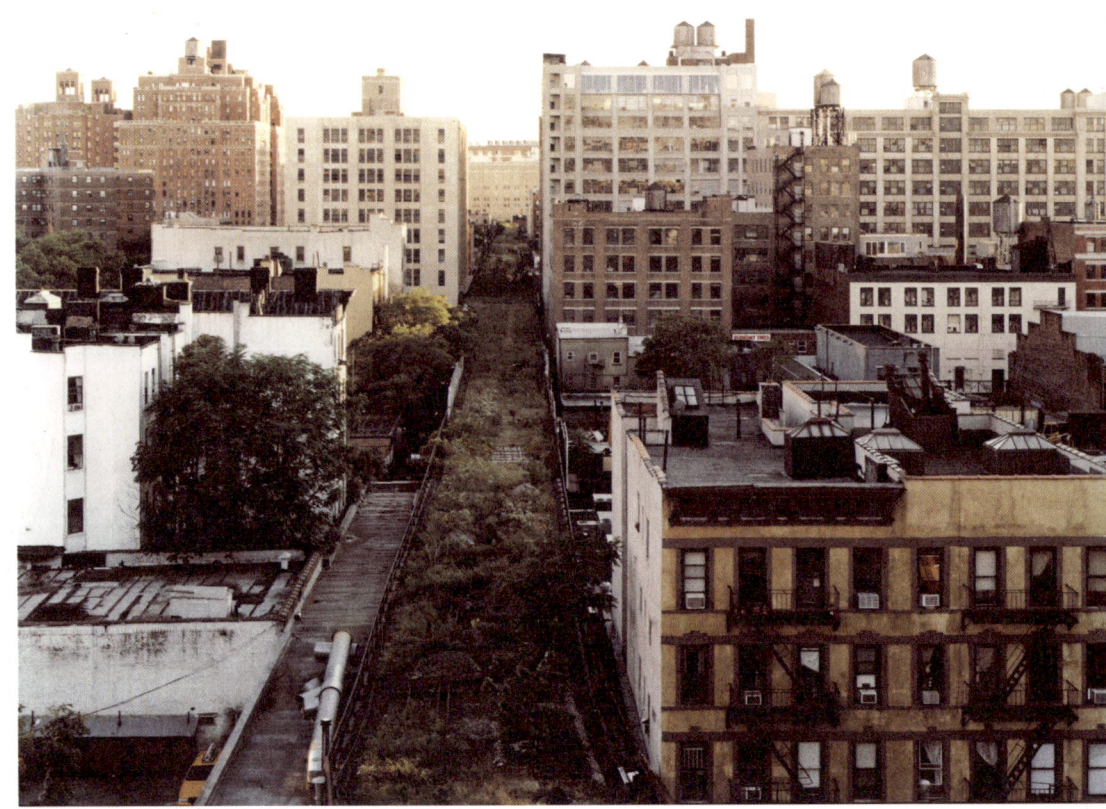

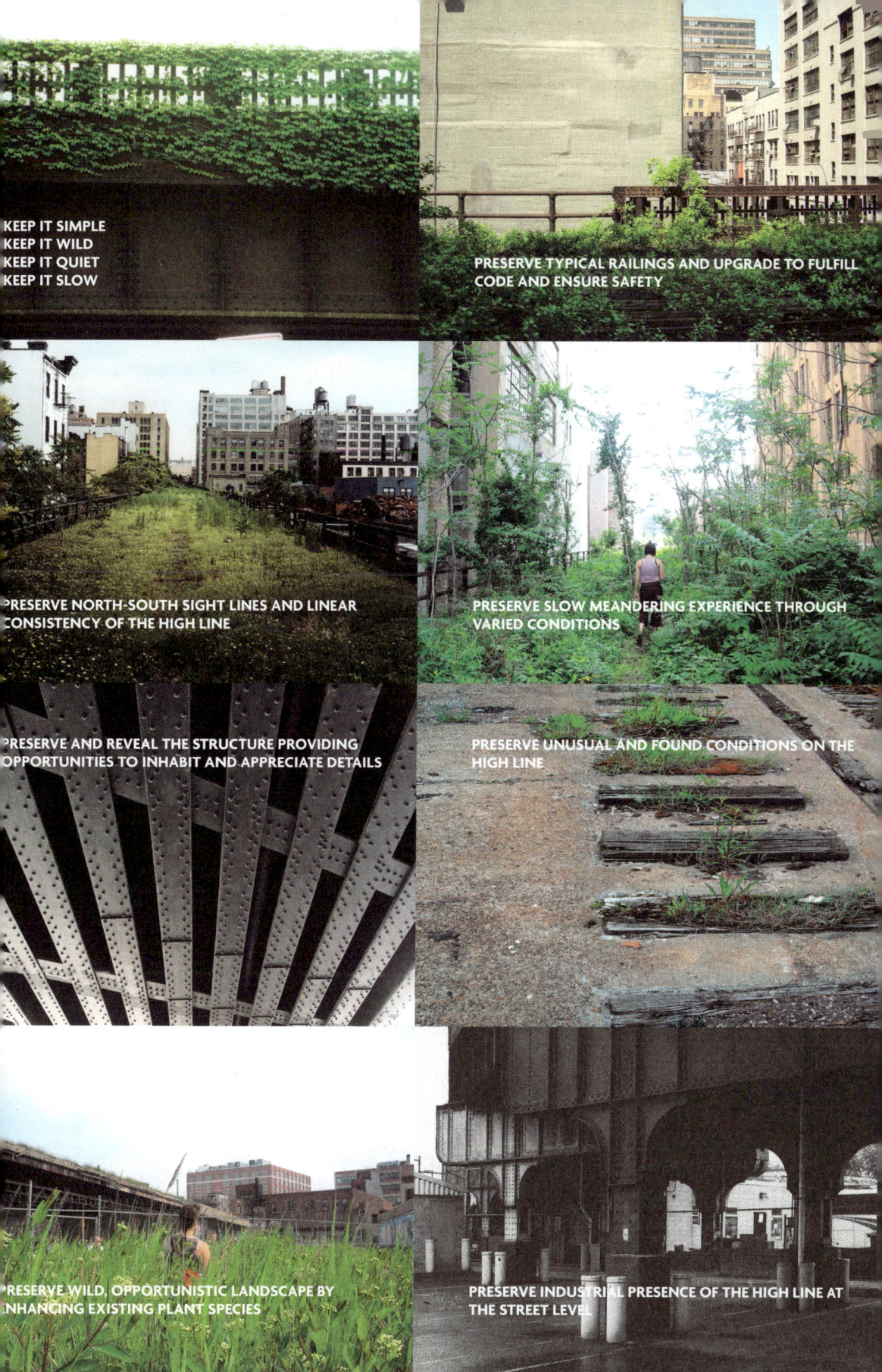

KEEP IT SIMPLE
KEEP IT WILD
KEEP IT QUIET
KEEP IT SLOW

PRESERVE TYPICAL RAILINGS AND UPGRADE TO FULFILL CODE AND ENSURE SAFETY

PRESERVE NORTH-SOUTH SIGHT LINES AND LINEAR CONSISTENCY OF THE HIGH LINE

PRESERVE SLOW MEANDERING EXPERIENCE THROUGH VARIED CONDITIONS

PRESERVE AND REVEAL THE STRUCTURE PROVIDING OPPORTUNITIES TO INHABIT AND APPRECIATE DETAILS

PRESERVE UNUSUAL AND FOUND CONDITIONS ON THE HIGH LINE

PRESERVE WILD, OPPORTUNISTIC LANDSCAPE BY ENHANCING EXISTING PLANT SPECIES

PRESERVE INDUSTRIAL PRESENCE OF THE HIGH LINE AT THE STREET LEVEL

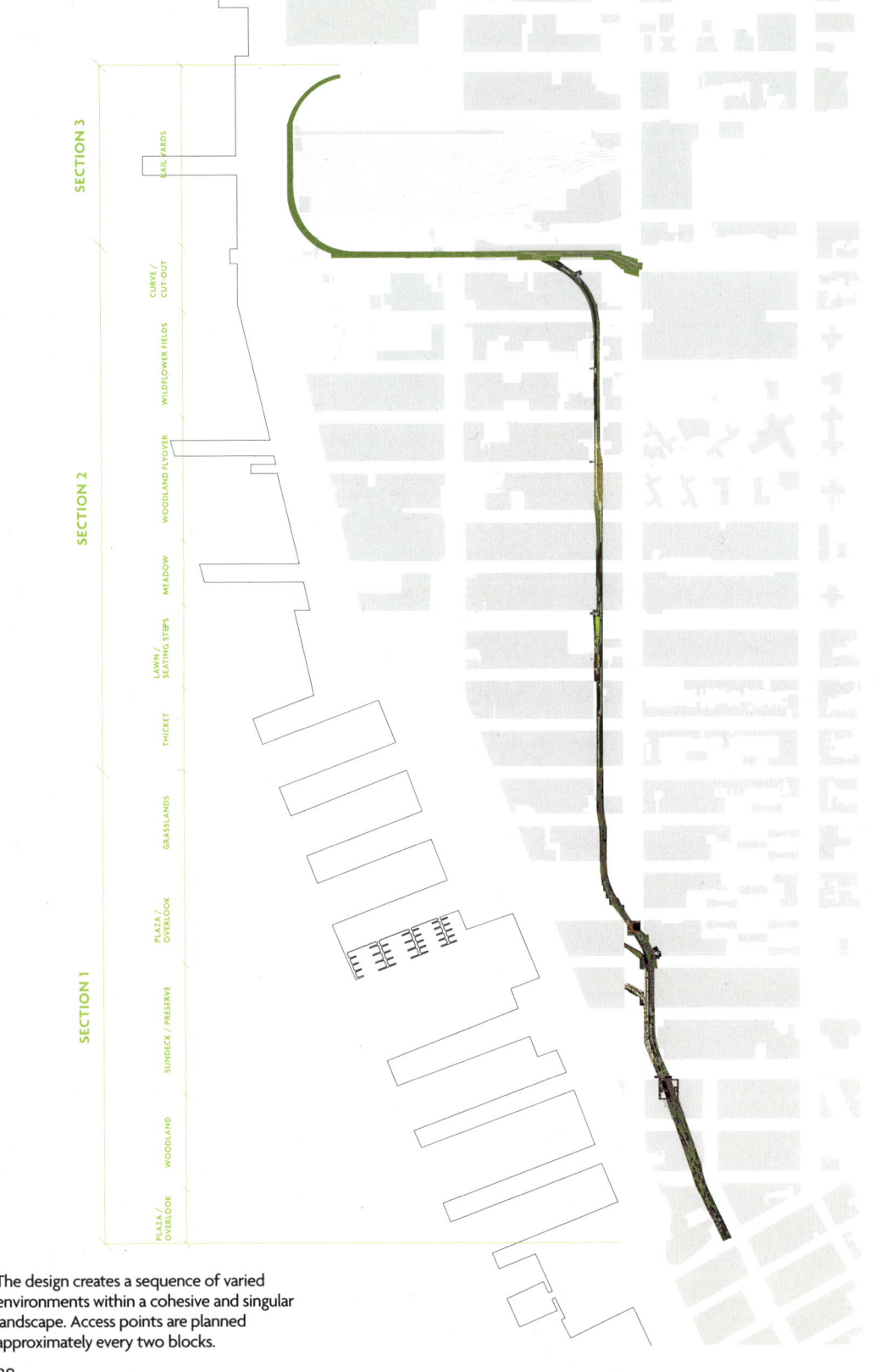

The design creates a sequence of varied
environments within a cohesive and singular
landscape. Access points are planned
approximately every two blocks.

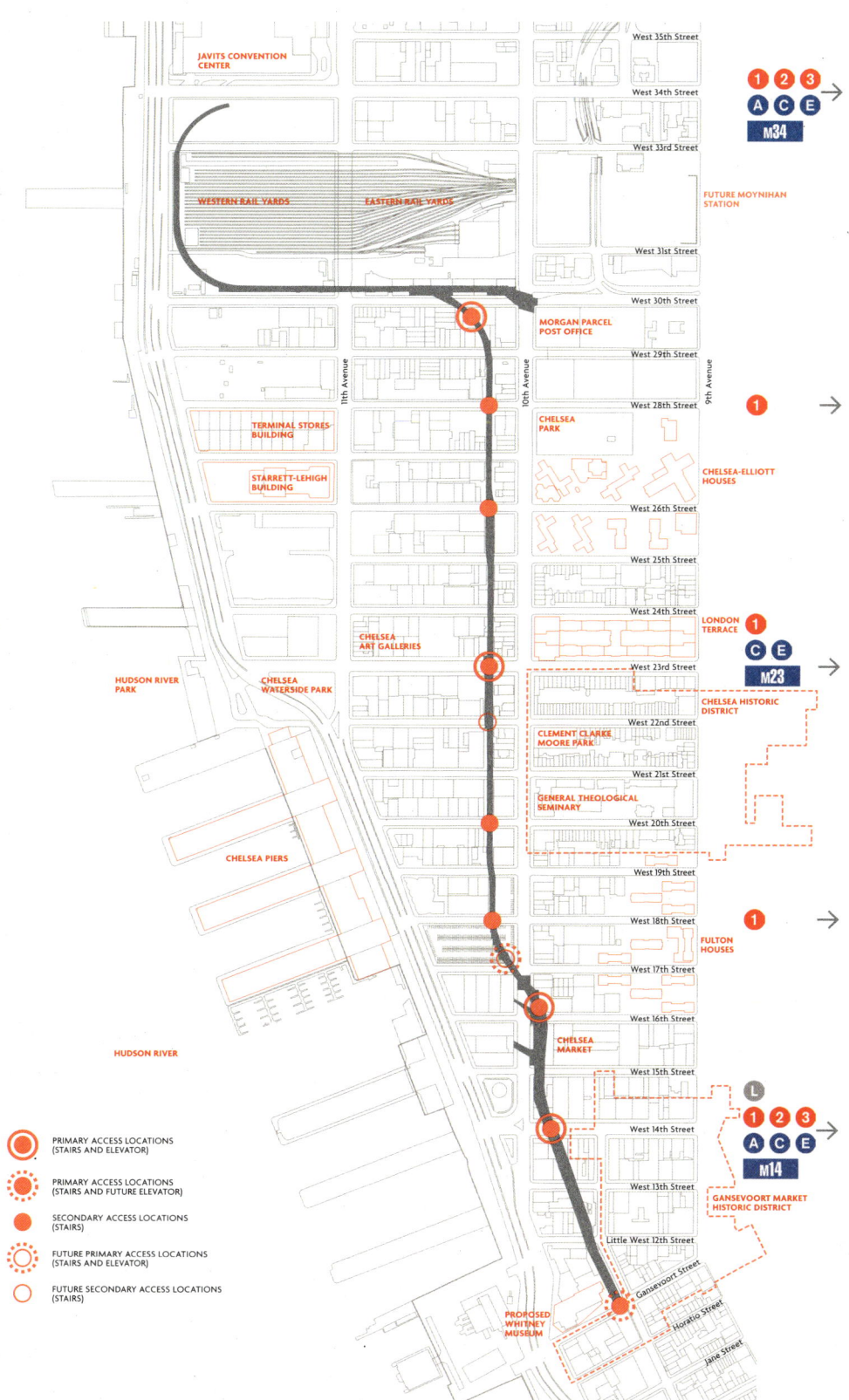

JAVITS CONVENTION CENTER

West 35th Street

West 34th Street

①②③
Ⓐ Ⓒ Ⓔ
M34

West 33rd Street

FUTURE MOYNIHAN STATION

WESTERN RAIL YARDS   EASTERN RAIL YARDS

West 31st Street

West 30th Street

MORGAN PARCEL POST OFFICE

West 29th Street

①

West 28th Street

TERMINAL STORES BUILDING

CHELSEA PARK

CHELSEA-ELLIOTT HOUSES

STARRETT-LEHIGH BUILDING

West 26th Street

West 25th Street

West 24th Street

LONDON TERRACE   ①

CHELSEA ART GALLERIES

West 23rd Street

Ⓒ Ⓔ
M23

CHELSEA HISTORIC DISTRICT

HUDSON RIVER PARK

CHELSEA WATERSIDE PARK

West 22nd Street

CLEMENT CLARKE MOORE PARK

West 21st Street

GENERAL THEOLOGICAL SEMINARY

West 20th Street

West 19th Street

CHELSEA PIERS

West 18th Street

FULTON HOUSES

①

West 17th Street

West 16th Street

CHELSEA MARKET

HUDSON RIVER

West 15th Street

Ⓛ

West 14th Street

①②③
Ⓐ Ⓒ Ⓔ
M14

West 13th Street

GANSEVOORT MARKET HISTORIC DISTRICT

Little West 12th Street

PROPOSED WHITNEY MUSEUM

Gansevoort Street

Horatio Street

Jane Street

⬤ PRIMARY ACCESS LOCATIONS (STAIRS AND ELEVATOR)

⬤ PRIMARY ACCESS LOCATIONS (STAIRS AND FUTURE ELEVATOR)

● SECONDARY ACCESS LOCATIONS (STAIRS)

○ FUTURE PRIMARY ACCESS LOCATIONS (STAIRS AND ELEVATOR)

○ FUTURE SECONDARY ACCESS LOCATIONS (STAIRS)

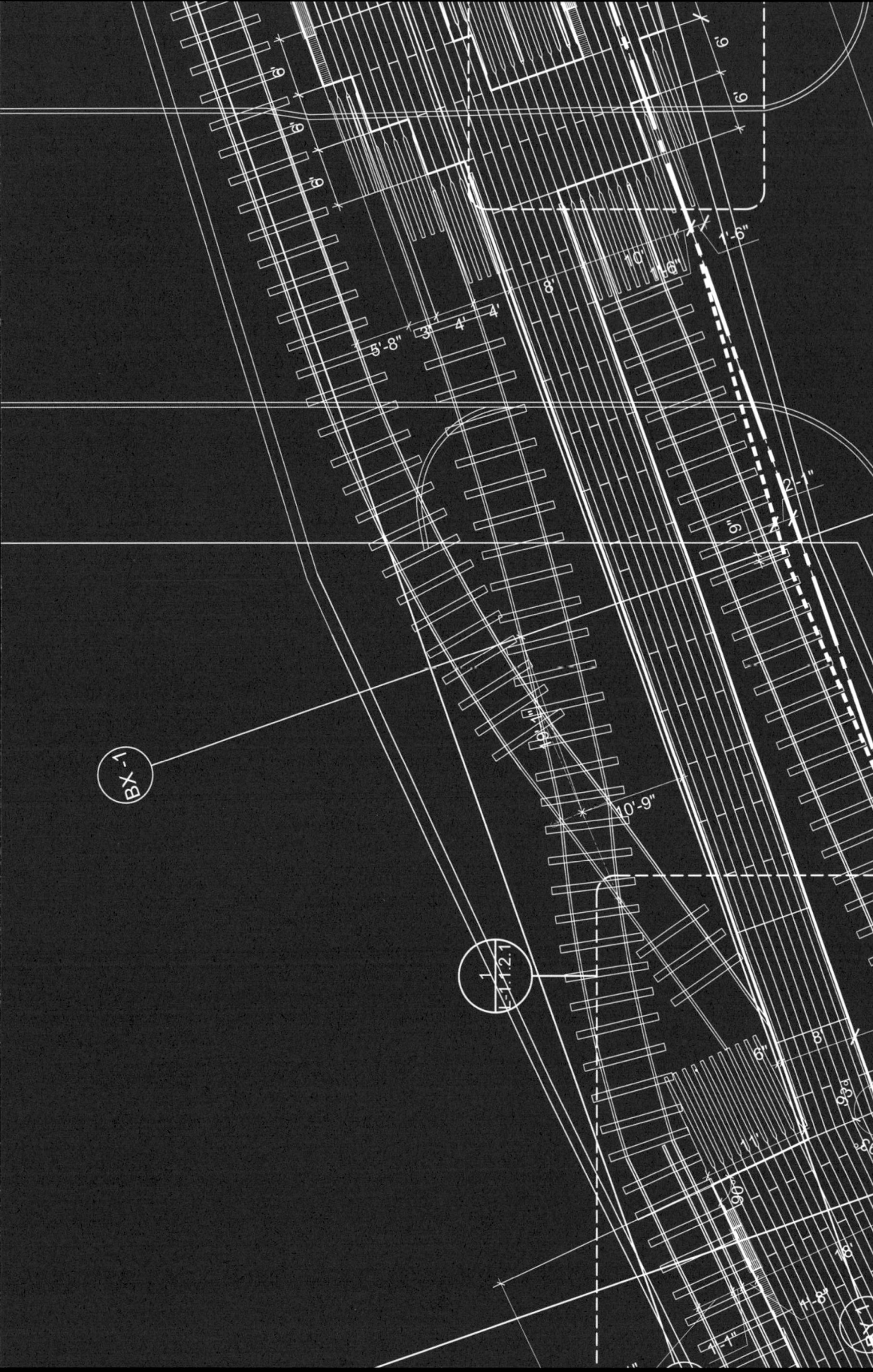

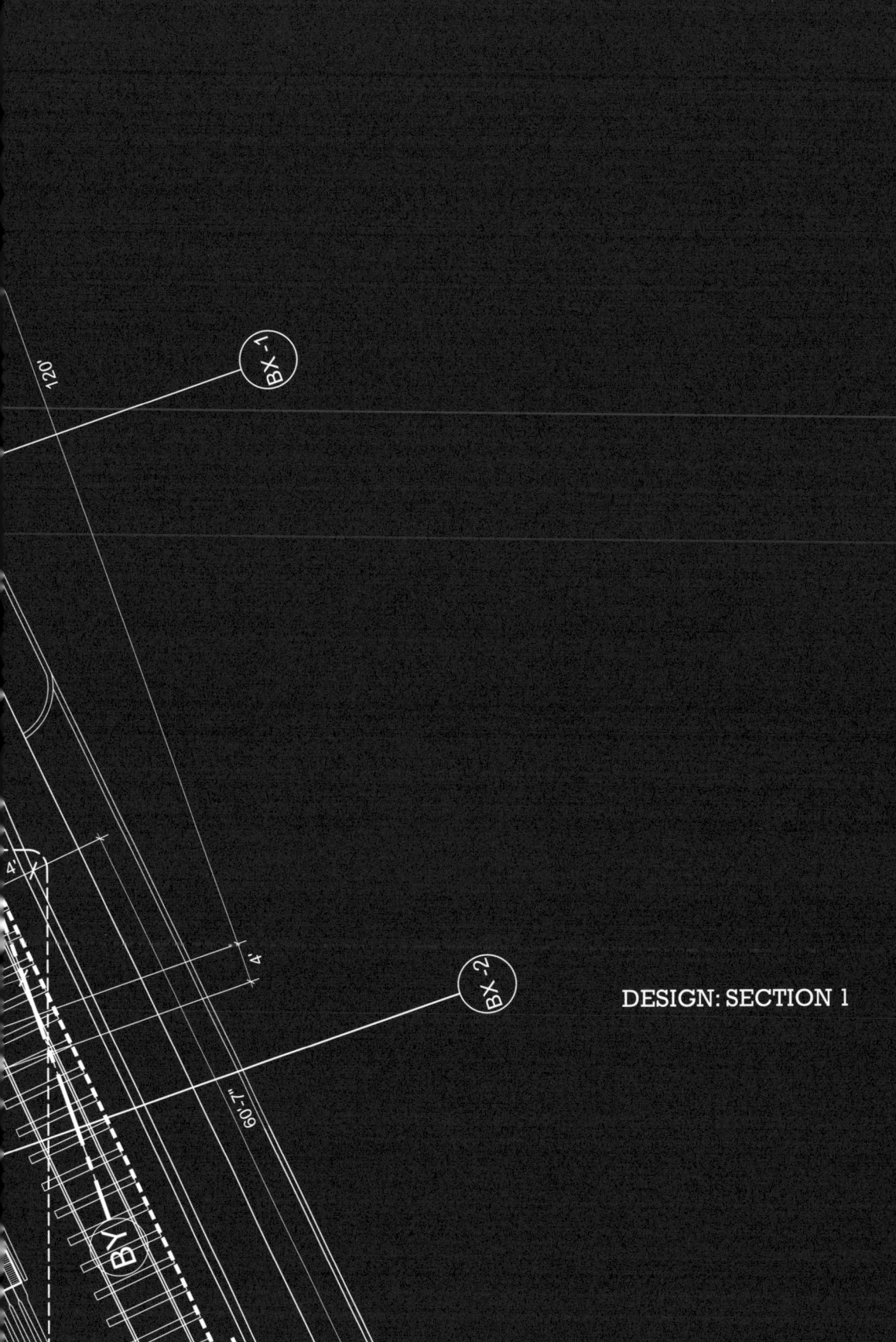

DESIGN: SECTION 1

Gansevoort Street / 13th Street

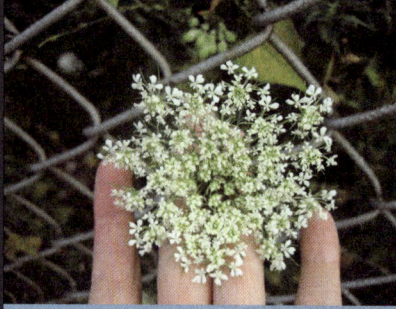

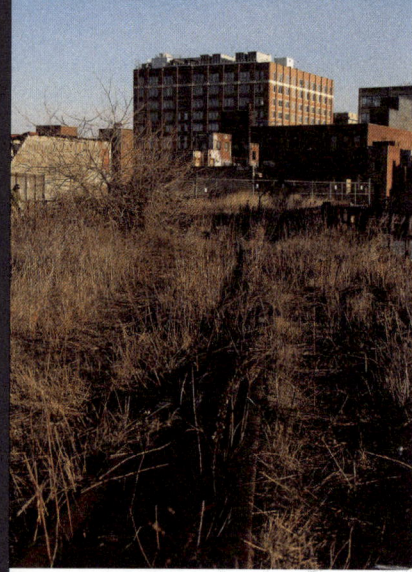

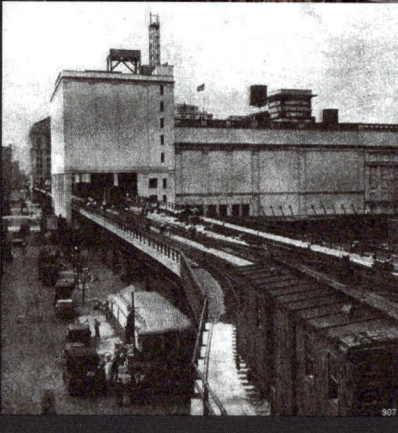

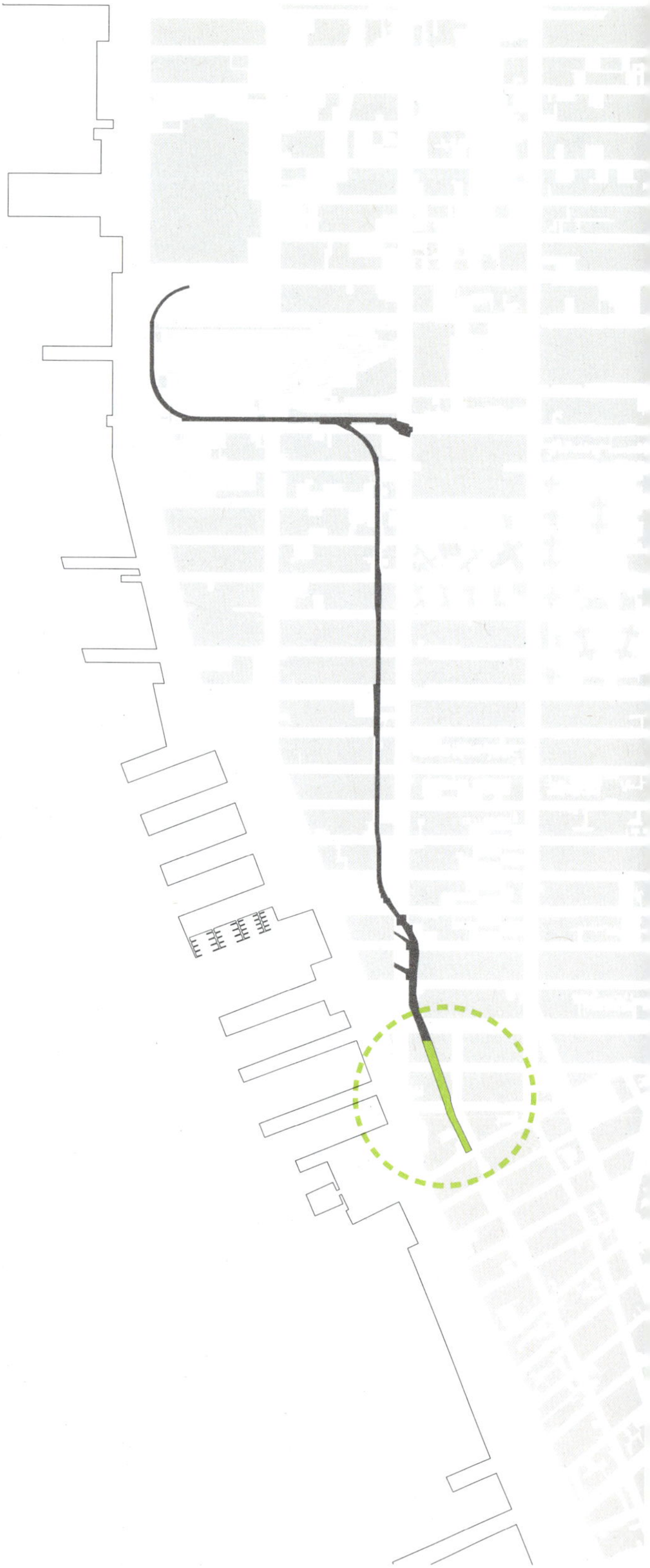

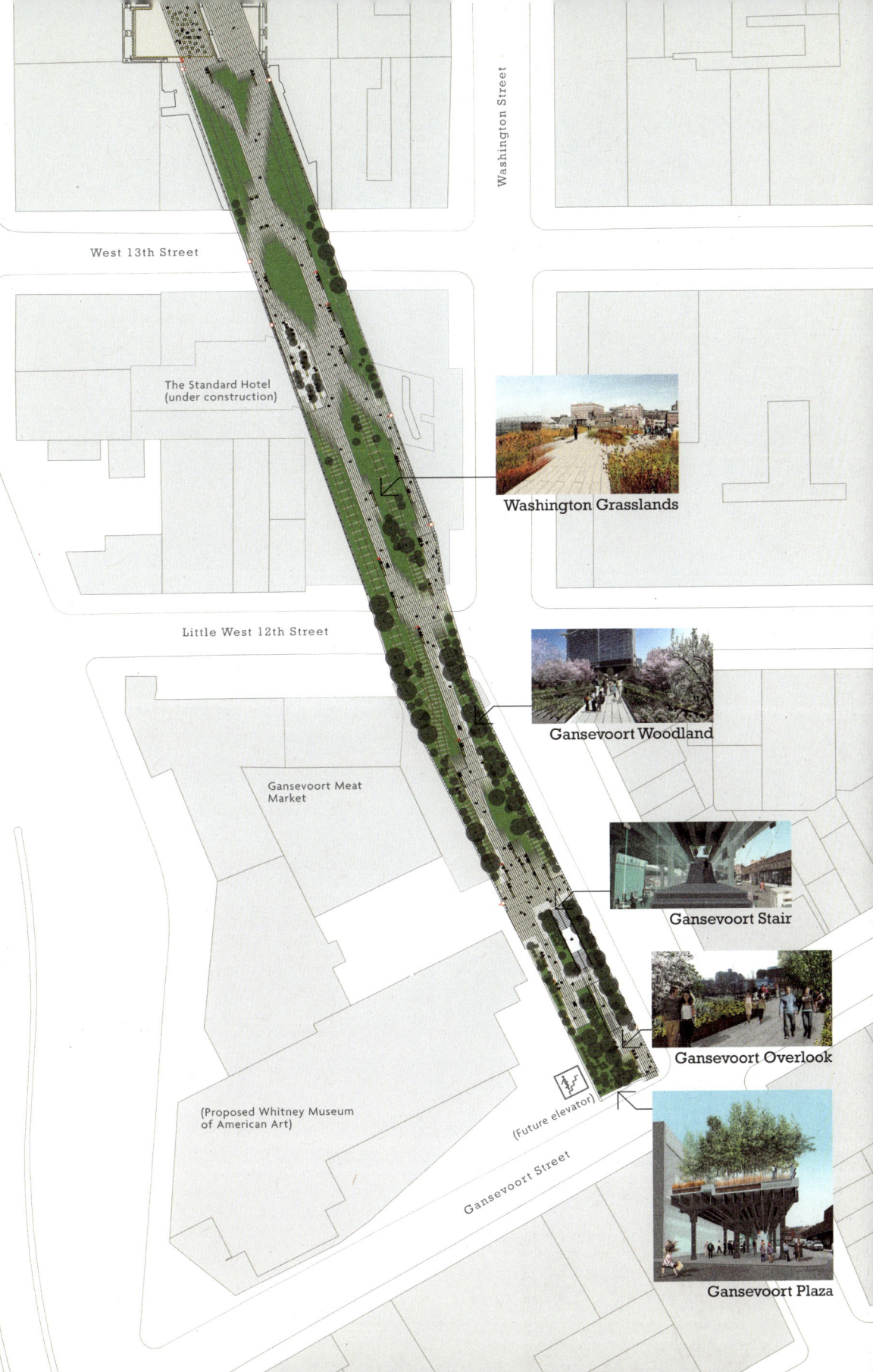

Washington Street

West 13th Street

The Standard Hotel
(under construction)

Washington Grasslands

Little West 12th Street

Gansevoort Woodland

Gansevoort Meat
Market

Gansevoort Stair

Gansevoort Overlook

(Proposed Whitney Museum
of American Art)

(Future elevator)

Gansevoort Street

Gansevoort Plaza

Gansevoort Plaza

A major access point occupies the corner of Gansevoort and Washington Streets, complemented by a street-level public plaza and the High Line-level Gansevoort Overlook.

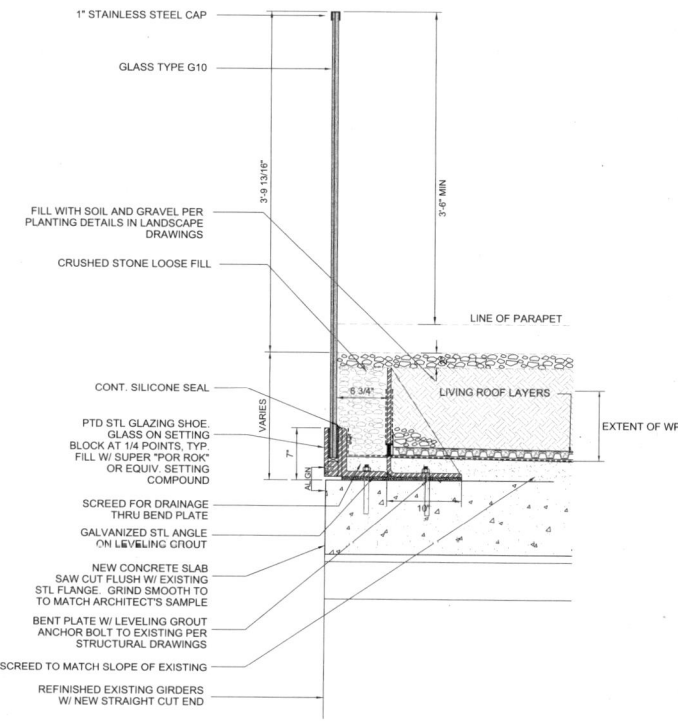

1" STAINLESS STEEL CAP

GLASS TYPE G10

FILL WITH SOIL AND GRAVEL PER PLANTING DETAILS IN LANDSCAPE DRAWINGS

CRUSHED STONE LOOSE FILL

LINE OF PARAPET

LIVING ROOF LAYERS

EXTENT OF WP

CONT. SILICONE SEAL

PTD STL GLAZING SHOE. GLASS ON SETTING BLOCK AT 1/4 POINTS, TYP. FILL W/ SUPER "POR ROK" OR EQUIV. SETTING COMPOUND

SCREED FOR DRAINAGE THRU BEND PLATE

GALVANIZED STL ANGLE ON LEVELING GROUT

NEW CONCRETE SLAB SAW CUT FLUSH W/ EXISTING STL FLANGE. GRIND SMOOTH TO TO MATCH ARCHITECT'S SAMPLE

BENT PLATE W/ LEVELING GROUT ANCHOR BOLT TO EXISTING PER STRUCTURAL DRAWINGS

SCREED TO MATCH SLOPE OF EXISTING

REFINISHED EXISTING GIRDERS W/ NEW STRAIGHT CUT END

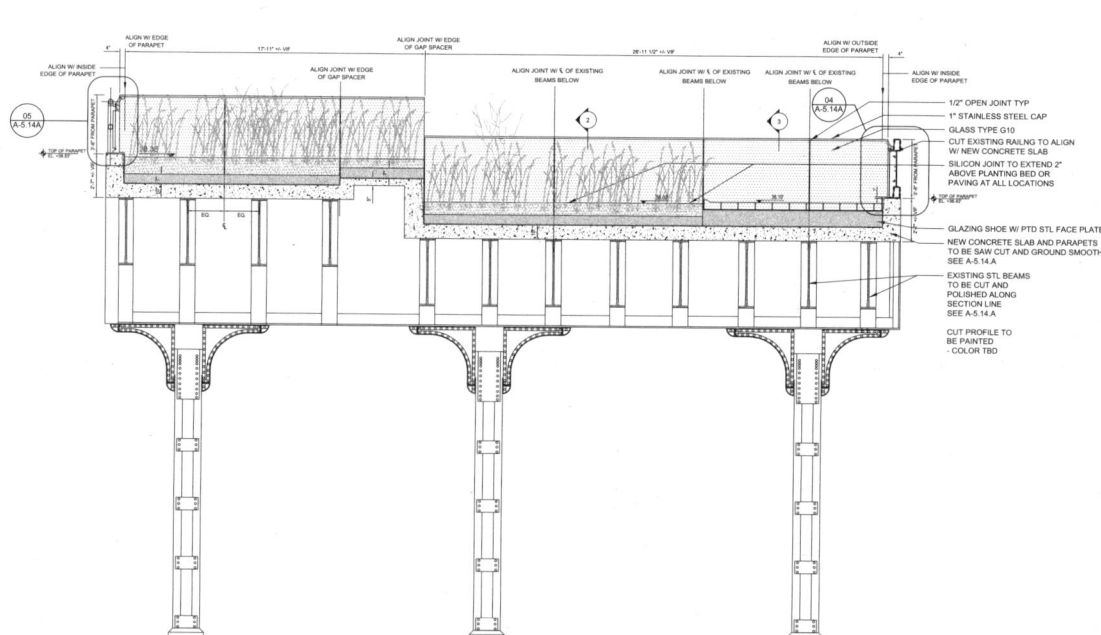

ALIGN W/ EDGE OF PARAPET

ALIGN JOINT W/ EDGE OF GAP SPACER

ALIGN W/ OUTSIDE EDGE OF PARAPET

ALIGN W/ INSIDE EDGE OF PARAPET

ALIGN JOINT W/ EDGE OF GAP SPACER

ALIGN JOINT W/ ℄ OF EXISTING BEAMS BELOW

ALIGN JOINT W/ ℄ OF EXISTING BEAMS BELOW

ALIGN JOINT W/ ℄ OF EXISTING BEAMS BELOW

ALIGN W/ INSIDE EDGE OF PARAPET

1/2" OPEN JOINT TYP

1" STAINLESS STEEL CAP

GLASS TYPE G10

CUT EXISTING RAILING TO ALIGN W/ NEW CONCRETE SLAB

SILICON JOINT TO EXTEND 2" ABOVE PLANTING BED OR PAVING AT ALL LOCATIONS

GLAZING SHOE W/ PTD STL FACE PLATE

NEW CONCRETE SLAB AND PARAPETS TO BE SAW CUT AND GROUND SMOOTH SEE A-5.14.A

EXISTING STL BEAMS TO BE CUT AND POLISHED ALONG SECTION LINE SEE A-5.14.A

CUT PROFILE TO BE PAINTED - COLOR TBD

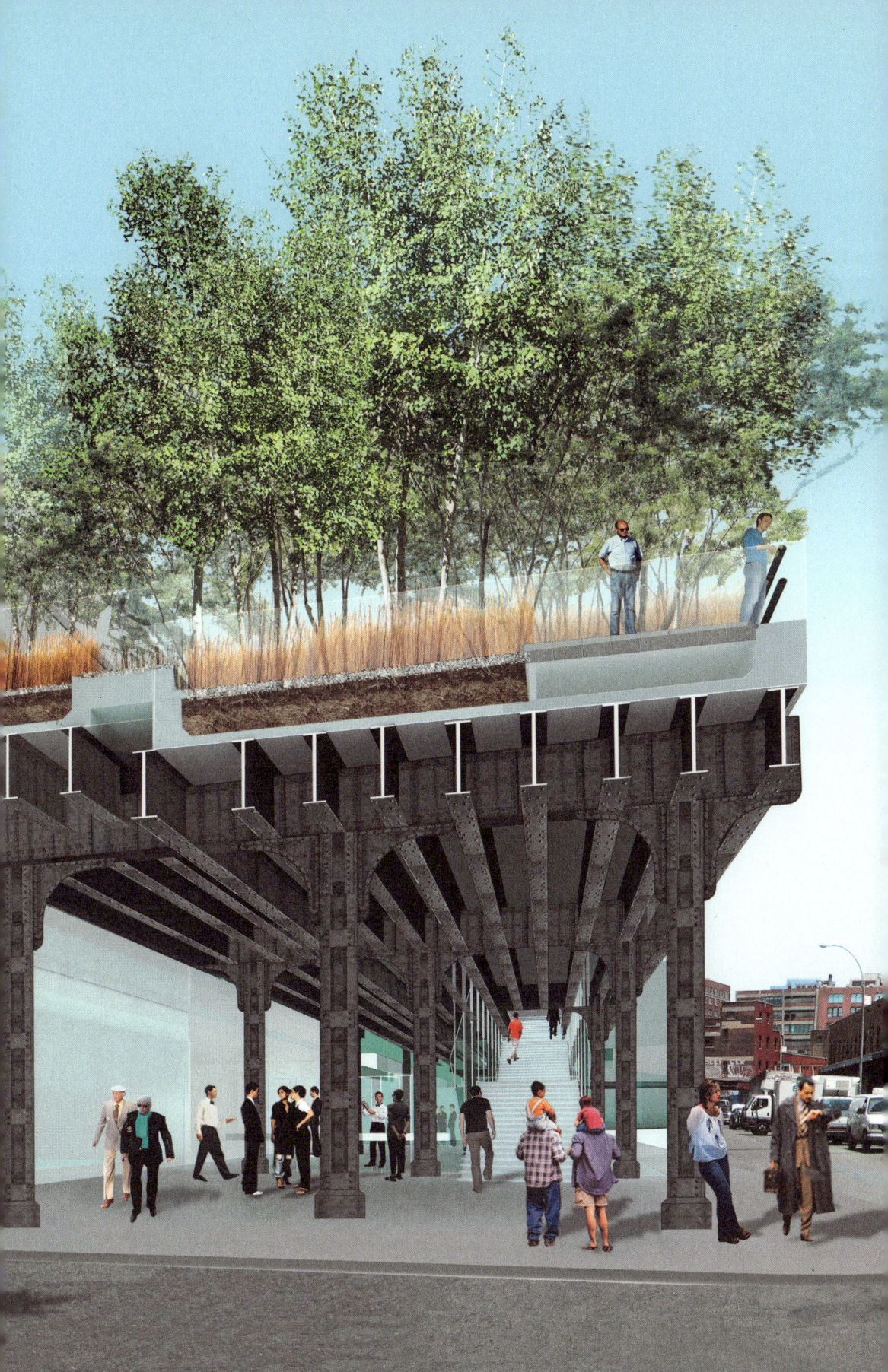

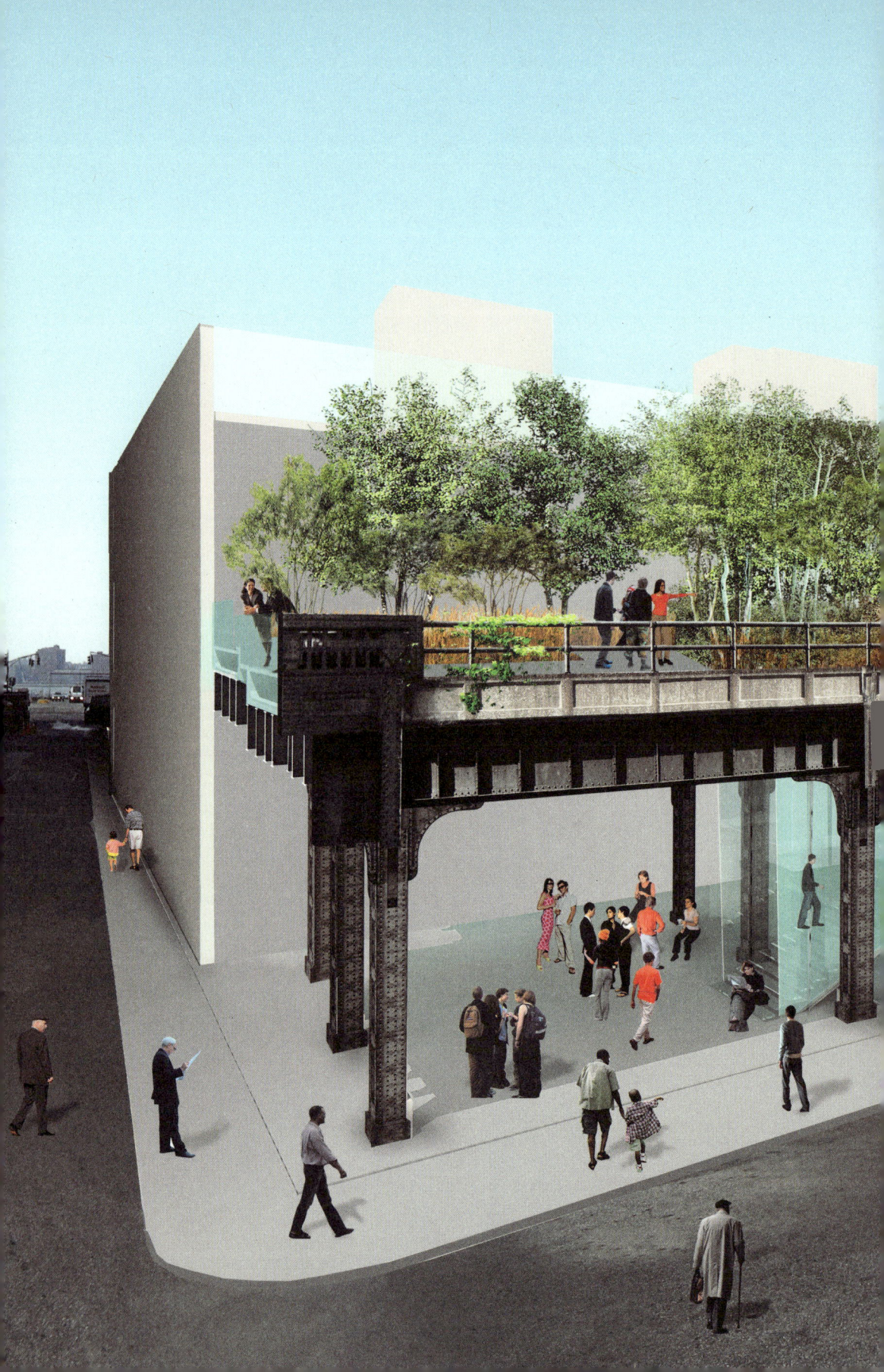

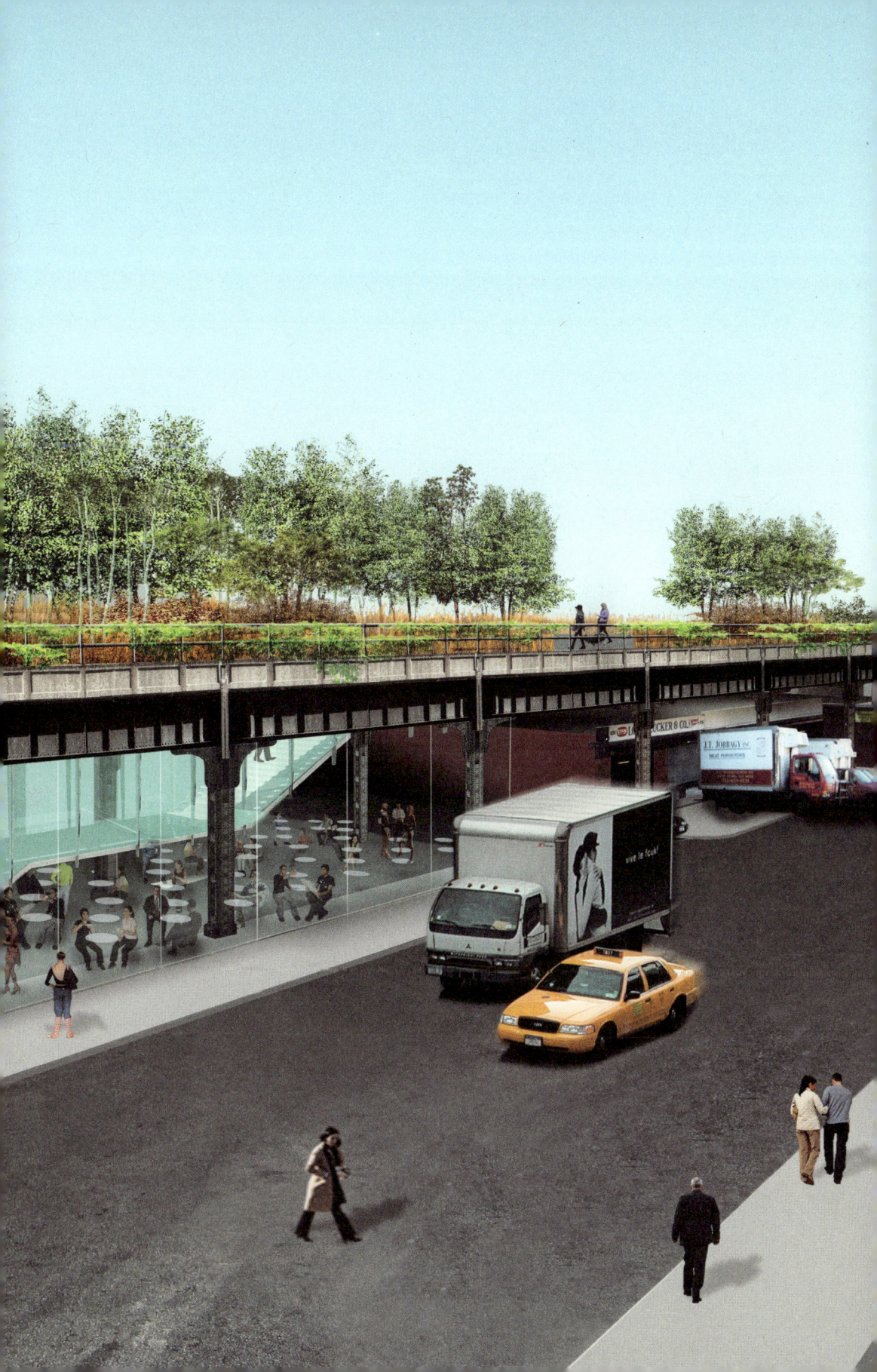

Gansevoort Stair

Whenever possible, stairs are brought up between the existing beams, through openings cut into the structure. These "slow stairs" signal a gradual transition from the busy street below to the quiet, elevated landscape on the High Line.

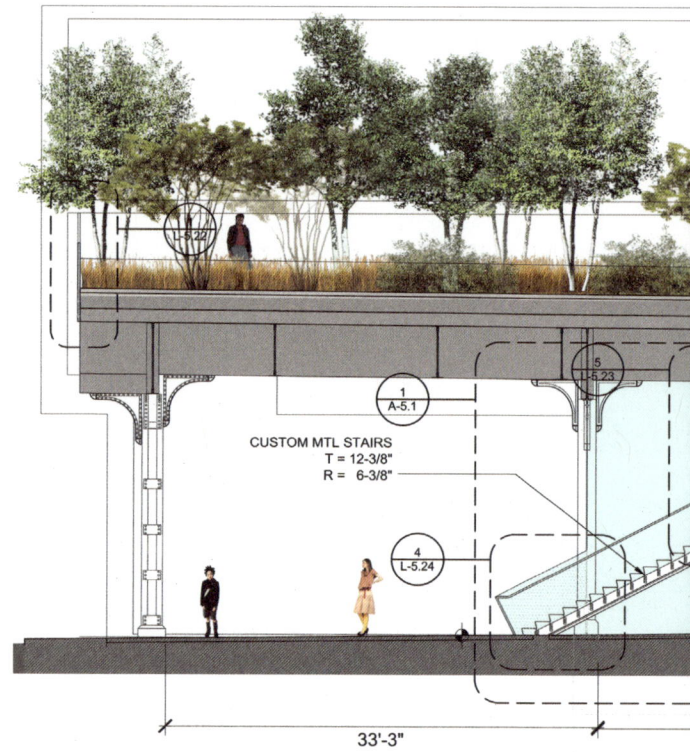

CUSTOM MTL STAIRS
T = 12-3/8"
R = 6-3/8"

1
A-5.1

4
L-5.24

5
L-5.23

33'-3"

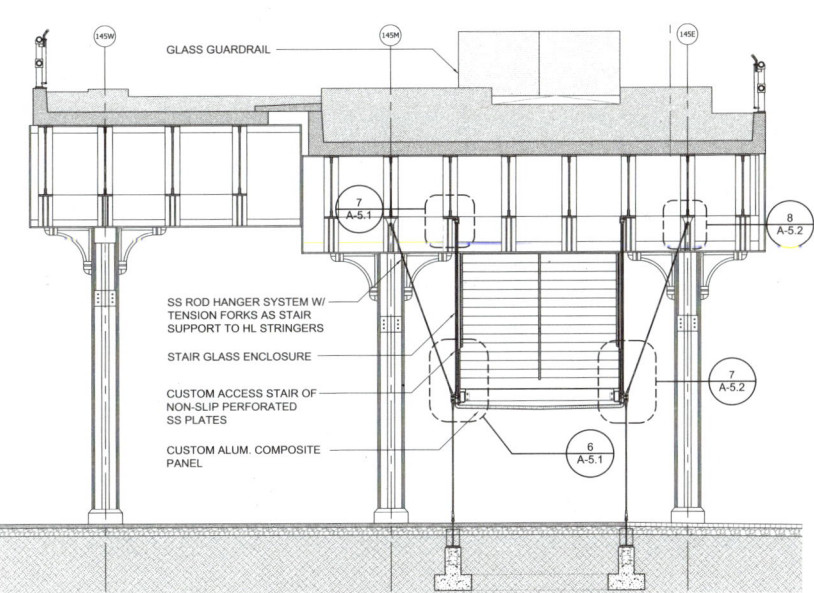

GLASS GUARDRAIL

145W   145M   145E

7
A-5.1

8
A-5.2

SS ROD HANGER SYSTEM W/
TENSION FORKS AS STAIR
SUPPORT TO HL STRINGERS

STAIR GLASS ENCLOSURE

CUSTOM ACCESS STAIR OF
NON-SLIP PERFORATED
SS PLATES

CUSTOM ALUM. COMPOSITE
PANEL

7
A-5.2

6
A-5.1

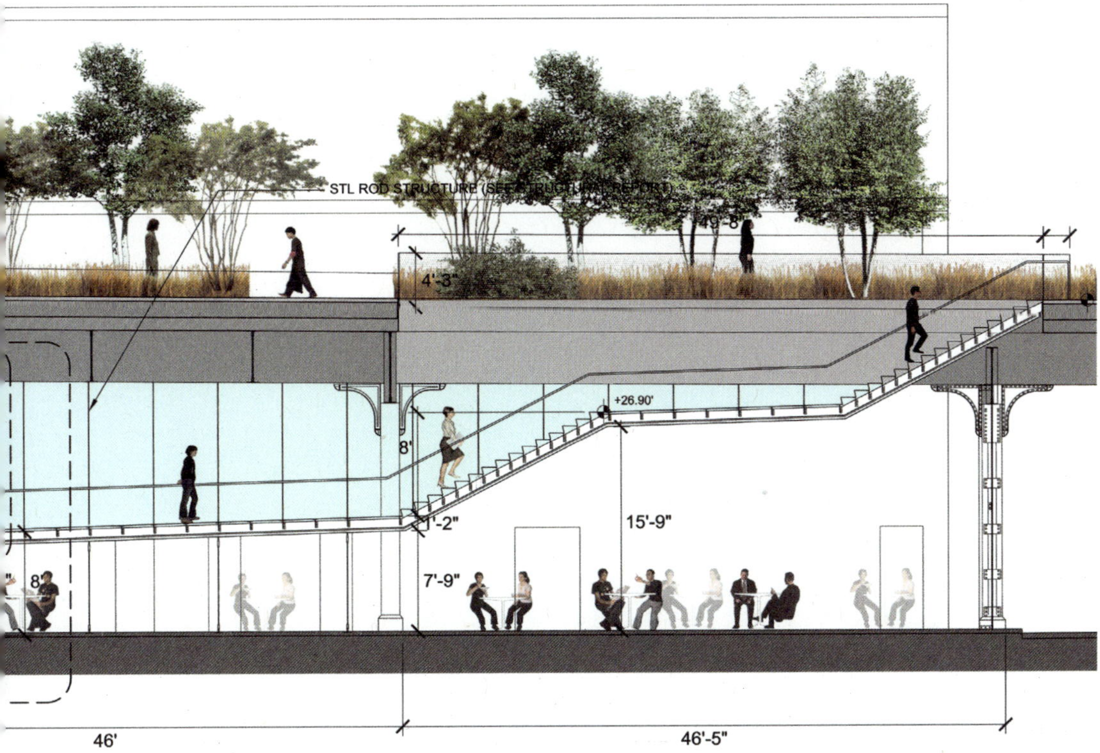

STL ROD STRUCTURE (SEE STRUCTURAL DRAWINGS)

4'-8"

4'-3"

+26.90'

8'

1'-2"

15'-9"

7'-9"

8'

46'

46'-5"

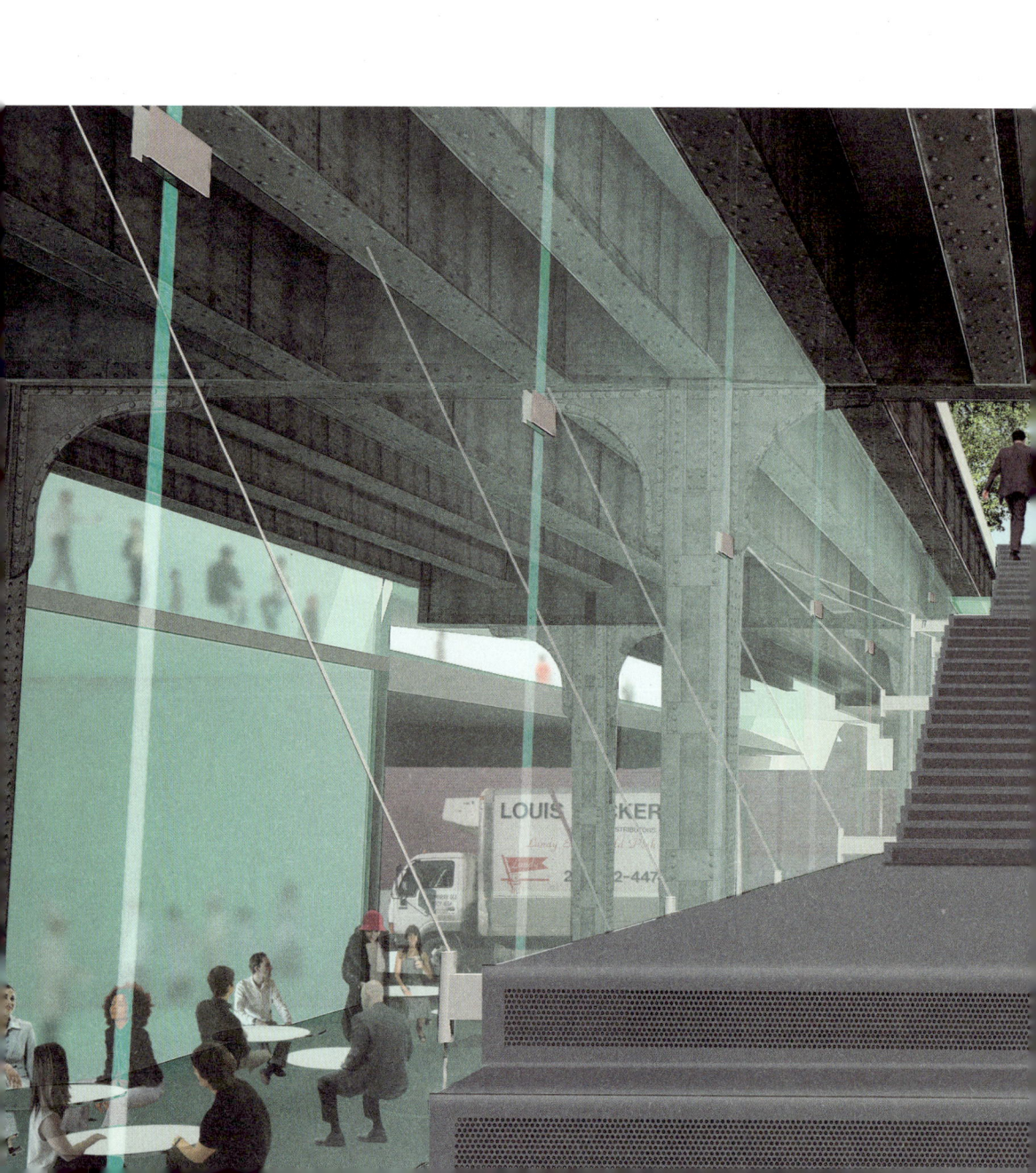

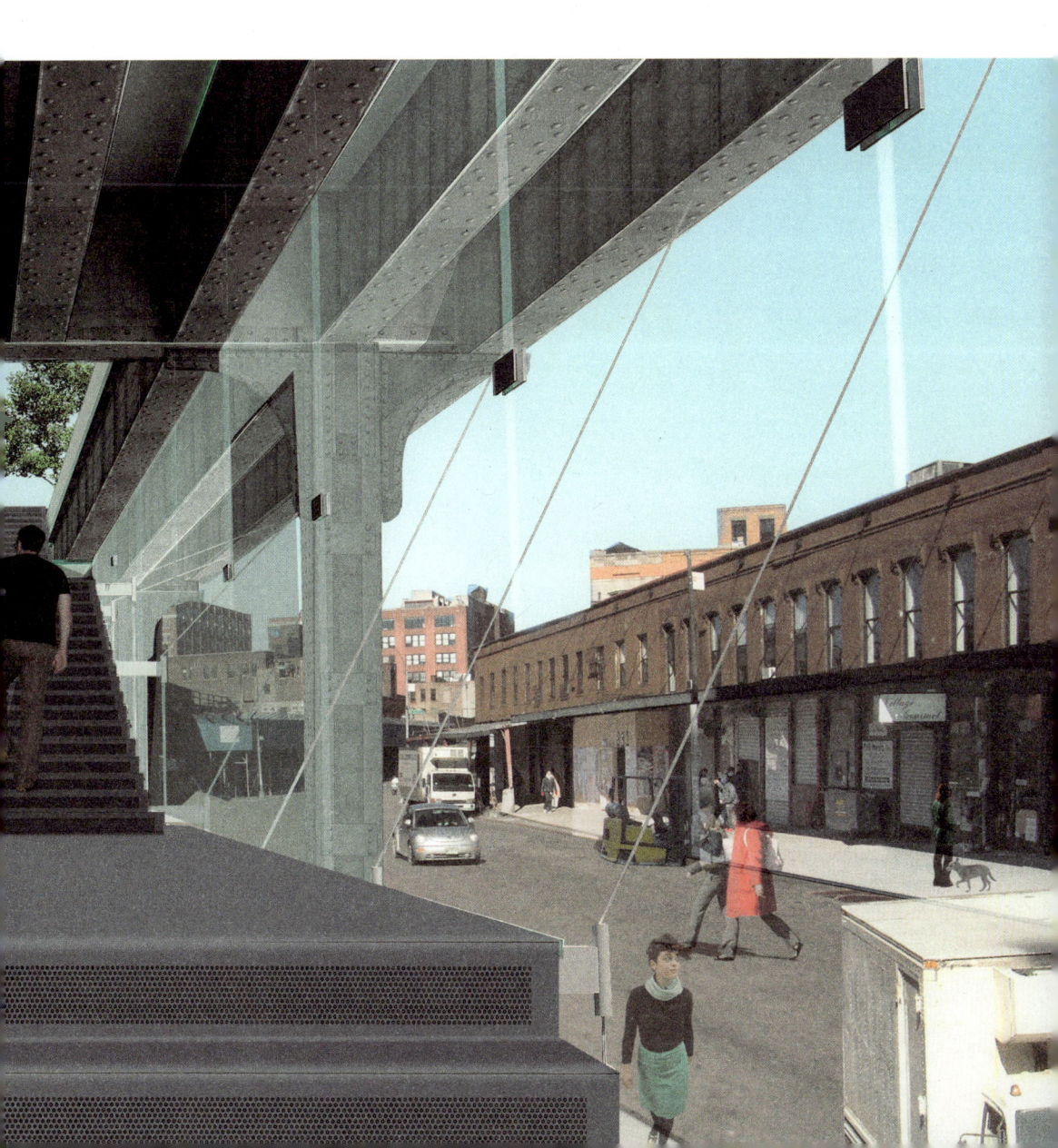

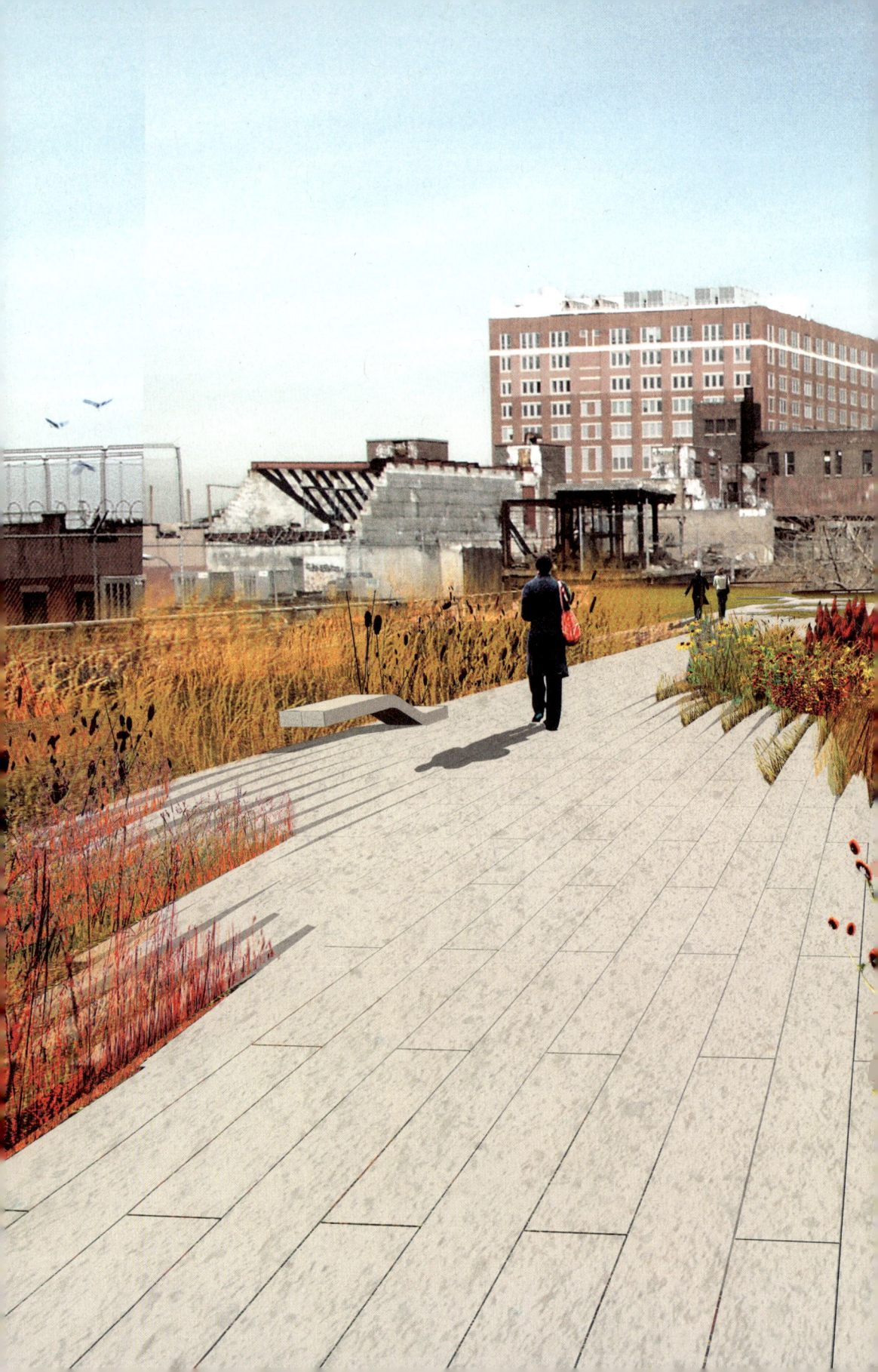

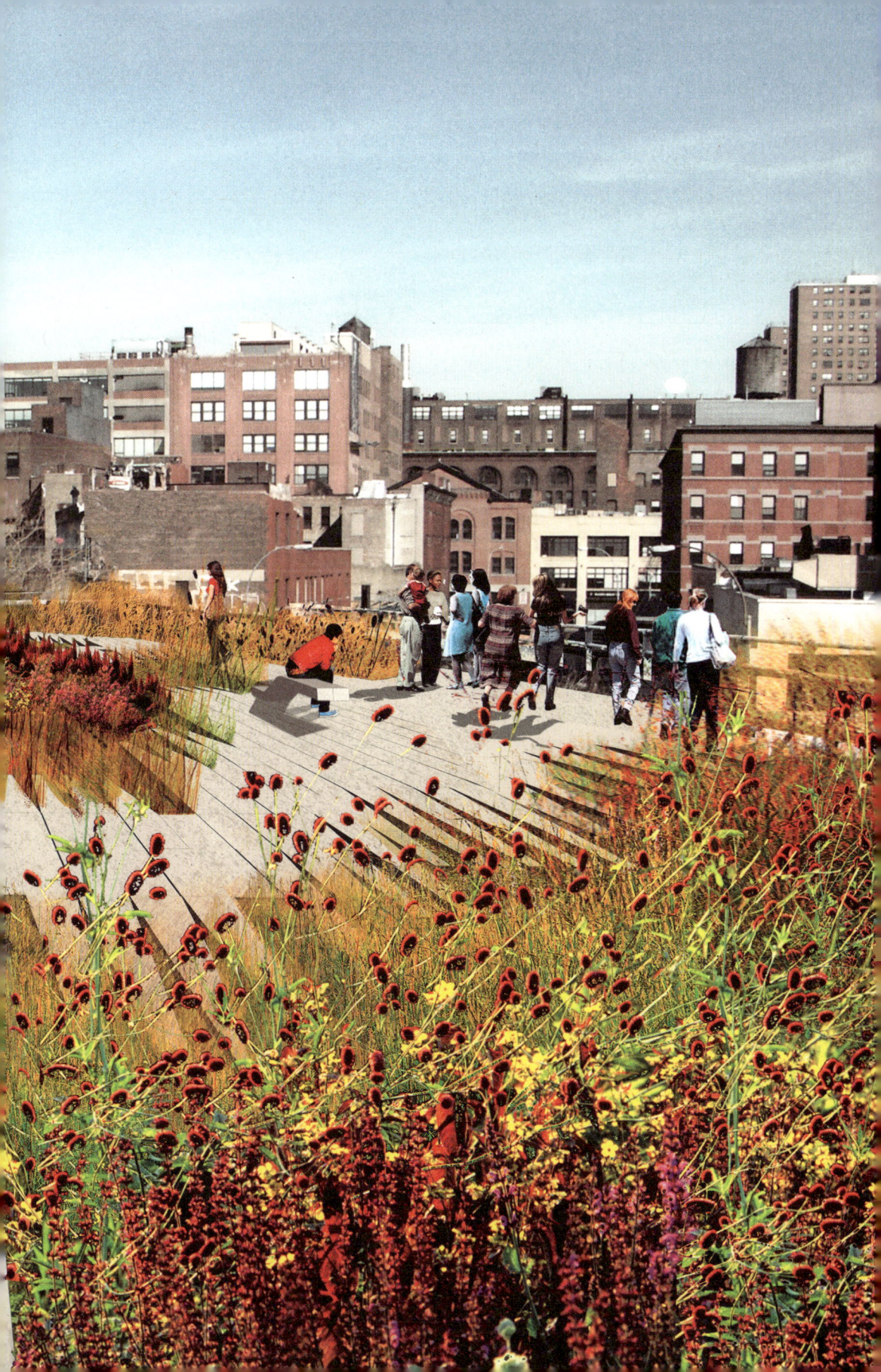

Gansevoort Overlook

A wooded terrace at the southeast corner of the High Line offers views down Gansevoort and Washington Streets.

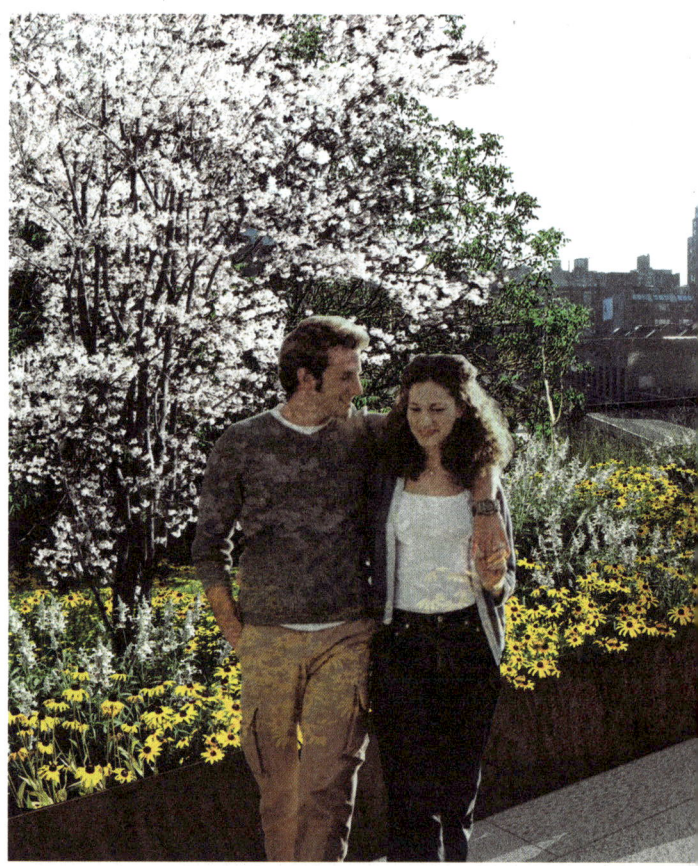

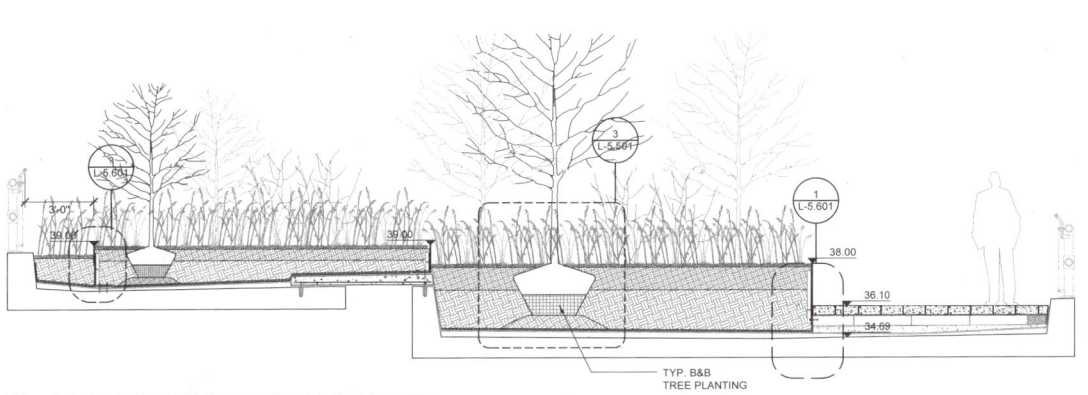

3-01

39.00

3
L-6.601

3
L-5.561

39.00

1
L-5.601

38.00

38.00

36.10

34.69

TYP. B&B
TREE PLANTING

1 GANSEVOORT ENTRY SECTION 1 @OVERLOOK

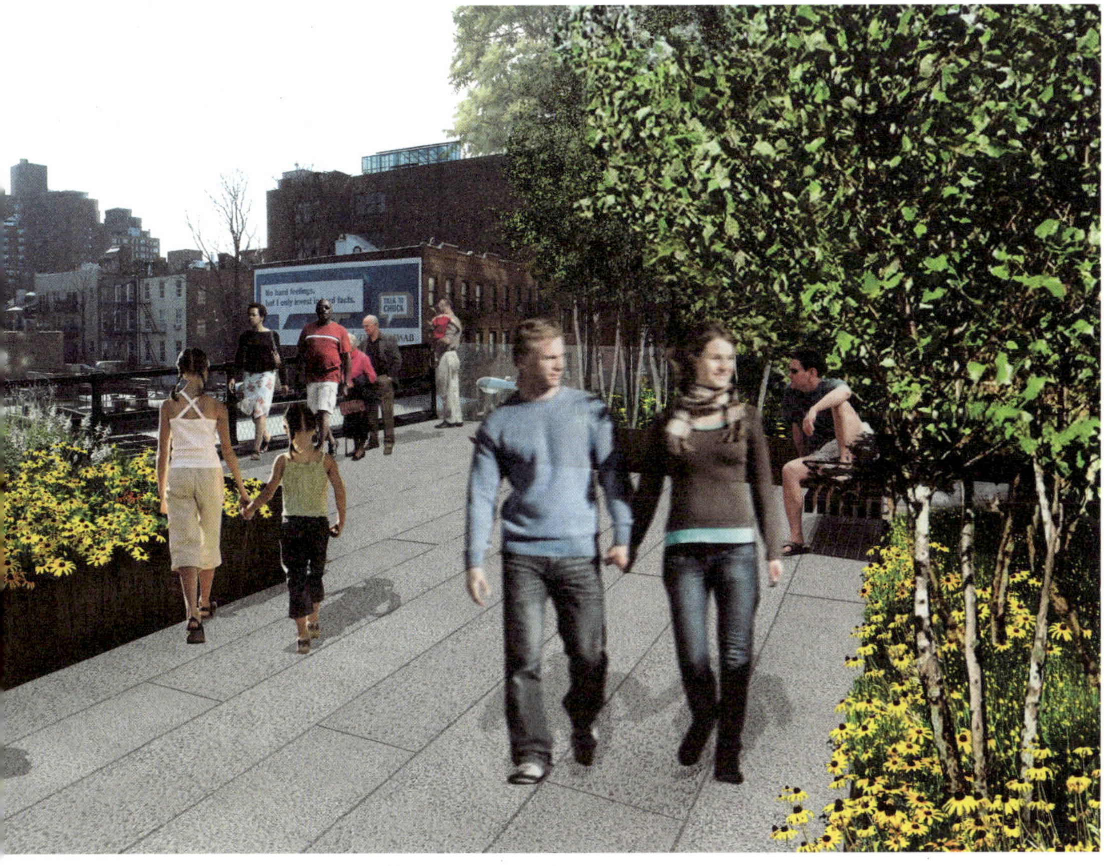

Gansevoort Woodland and Washington Grasslands

Moving to the north, the Washington Grasslands, between Little West 12th and 13th Streets, leads visitors to pass under The Standard, a new hotel that bridges over the High Line. At the top of the Gansevoort Stair, the Gansevoort Woodland provides dense plantings and trees at the edge of the High Line, welcoming visitors into thick greenery. The Gansevoort Woodland is made possible by Donald Pels and Wendy Keys.

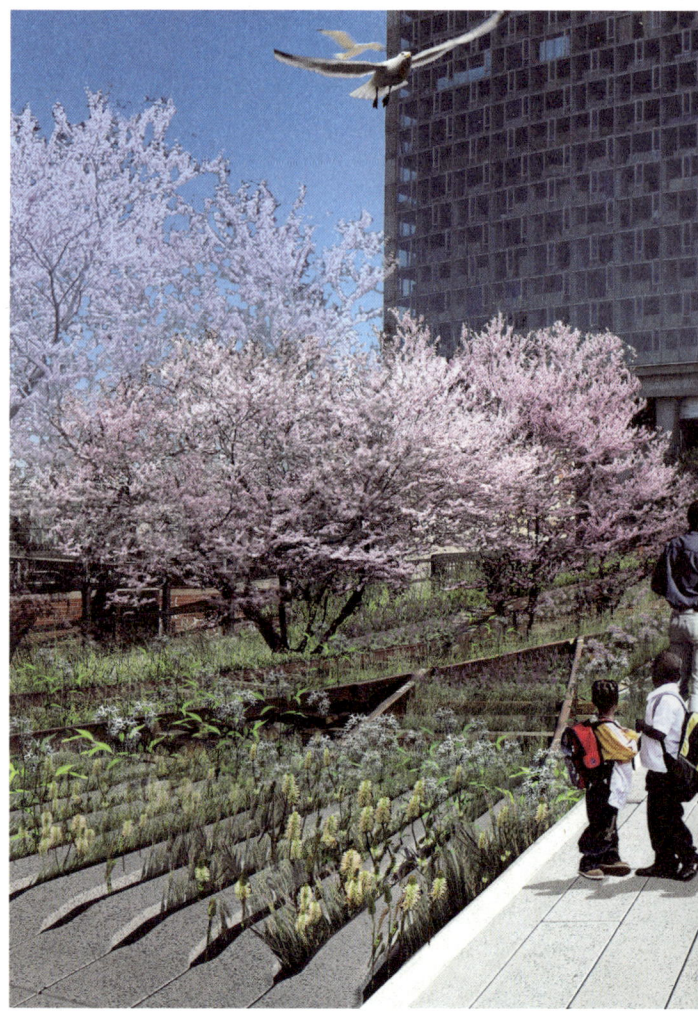

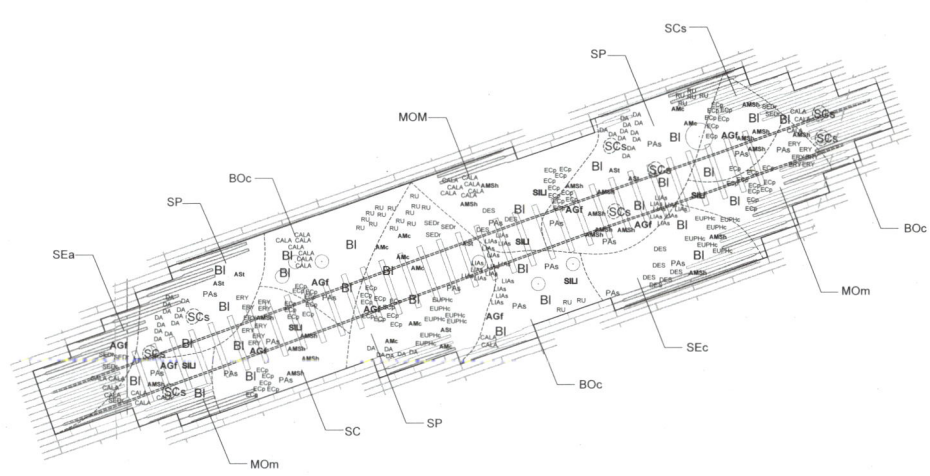

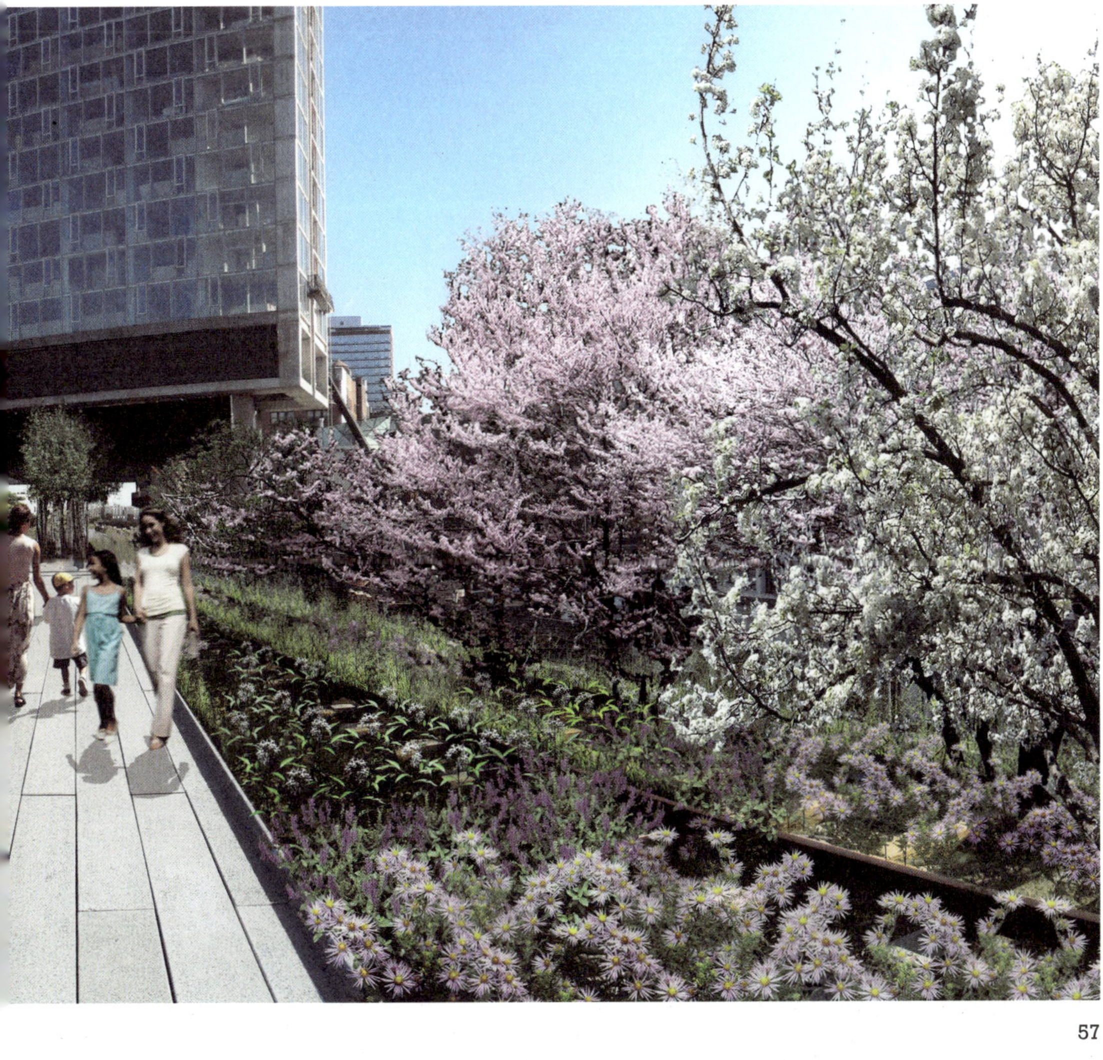

13th Street /
17th Street

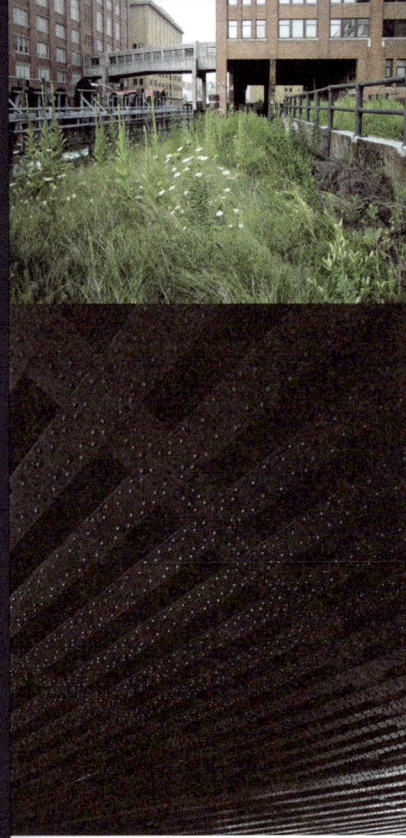

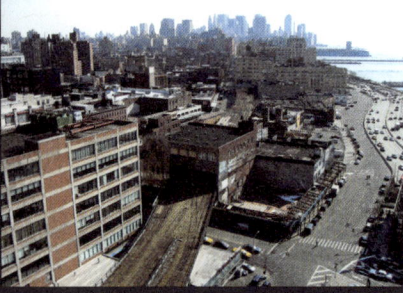

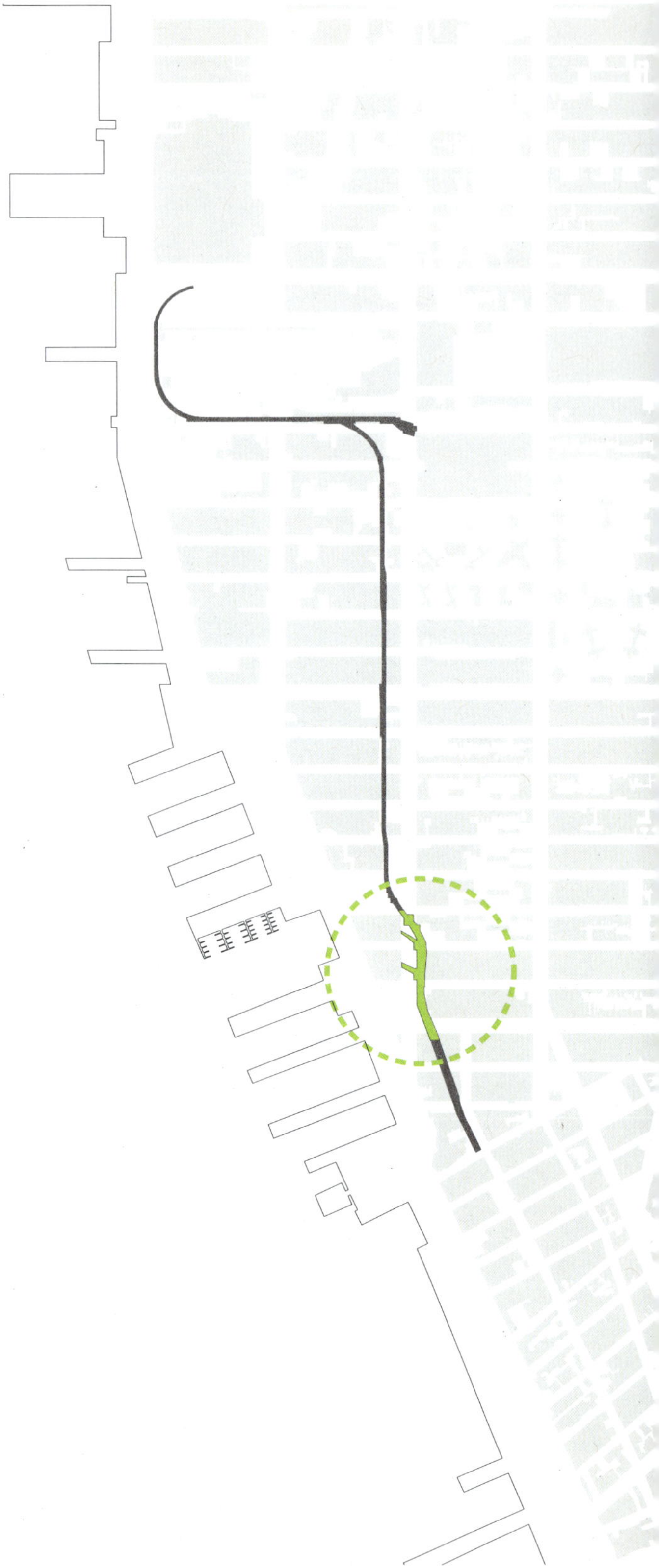

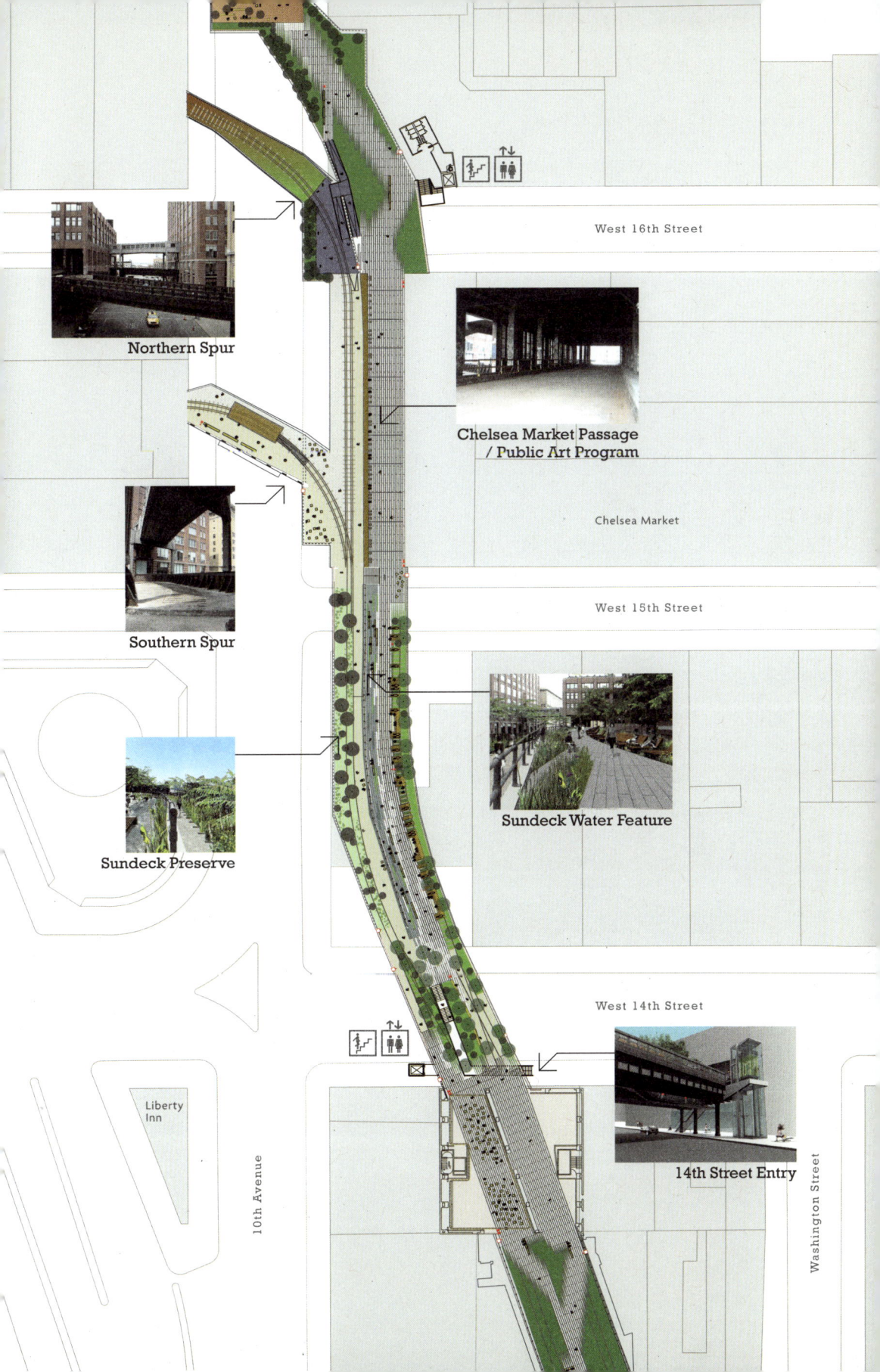

Northern Spur

Chelsea Market Passage
/ Public Art Program

Chelsea Market

Southern Spur

Sundeck Water Feature

Sundeck Preserve

West 16th Street

West 15th Street

West 14th Street

14th Street Entry

Liberty
Inn

10th Avenue

Washington Street

14th Street Entry

"Slow stairs" rise from the 14th Street sidewalk, supplemented by an elevator. Where the stairs turn to pass over the street and through the steel beams, glimpses of visitors' legs and feet are visible to observers below. The 14th Street Stairs are made possible by Philip and Lisamaria Falcone.

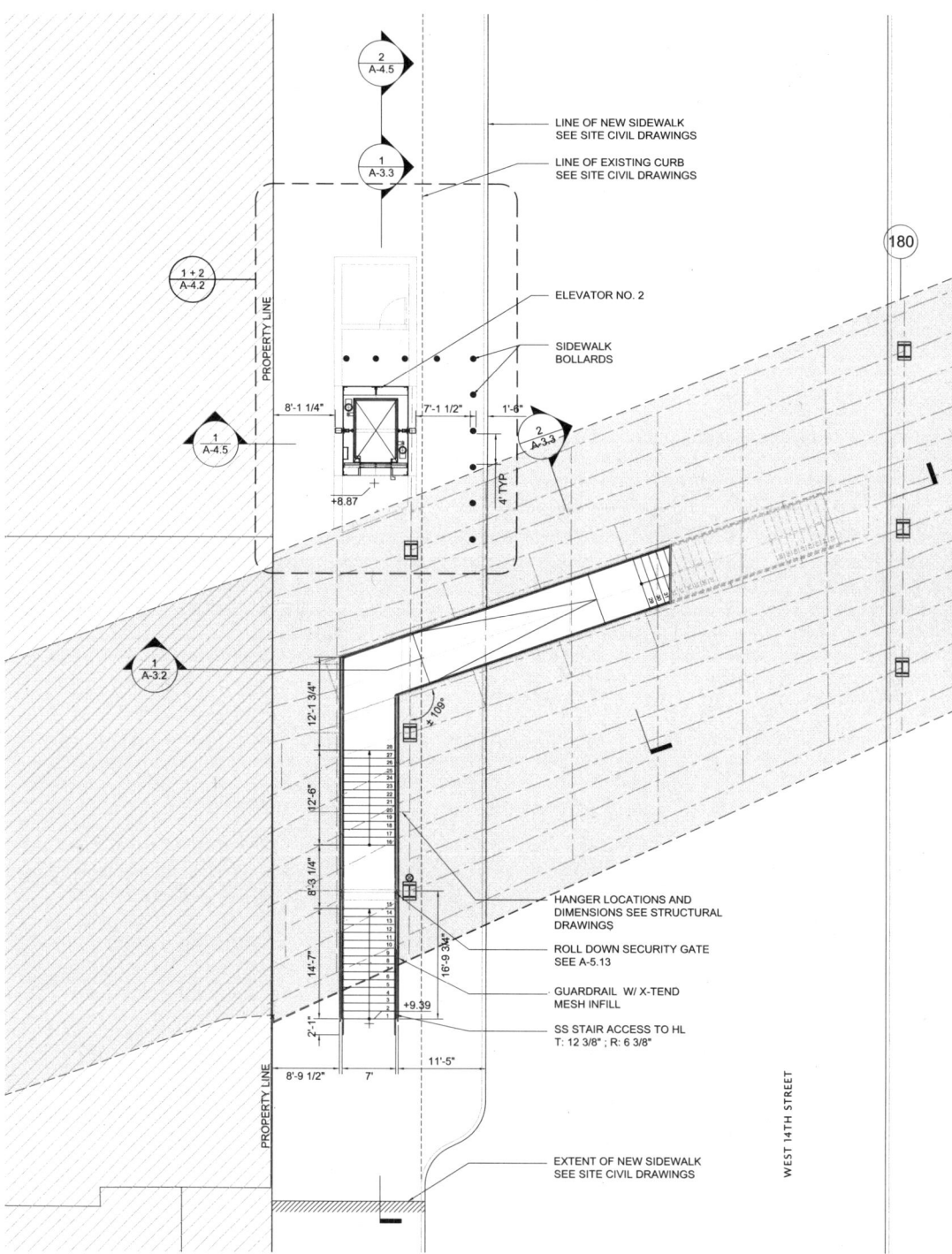

LINE OF NEW SIDEWALK
SEE SITE CIVIL DRAWINGS

LINE OF EXISTING CURB
SEE SITE CIVIL DRAWINGS

ELEVATOR NO. 2

SIDEWALK
BOLLARDS

PROPERTY LINE

HANGER LOCATIONS AND
DIMENSIONS SEE STRUCTURAL
DRAWINGS

ROLL DOWN SECURITY GATE
SEE A-5.13

GUARDRAIL W/ X-TEND
MESH INFILL

SS STAIR ACCESS TO HL
T: 12 3/8" ; R: 6 3/8"

EXTENT OF NEW SIDEWALK
SEE SITE CIVIL DRAWINGS

WEST 14TH STREET

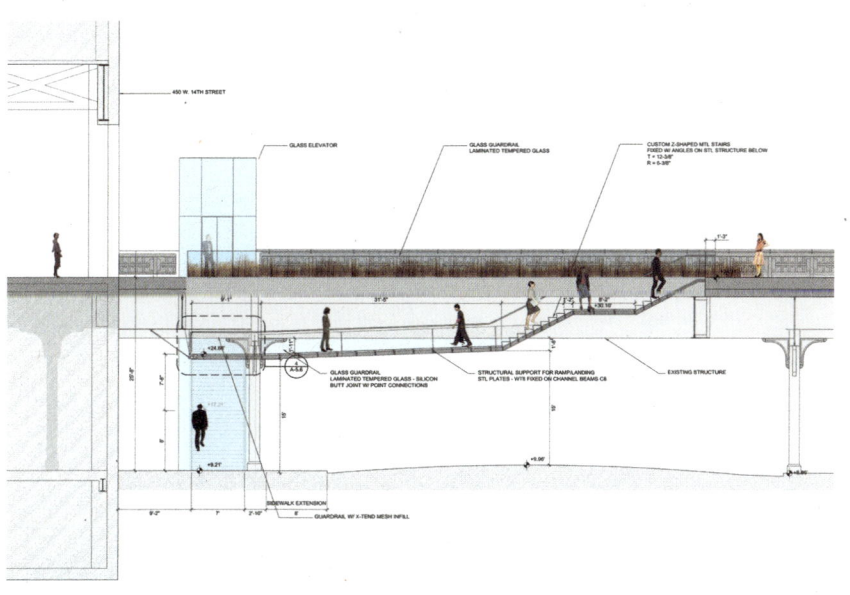

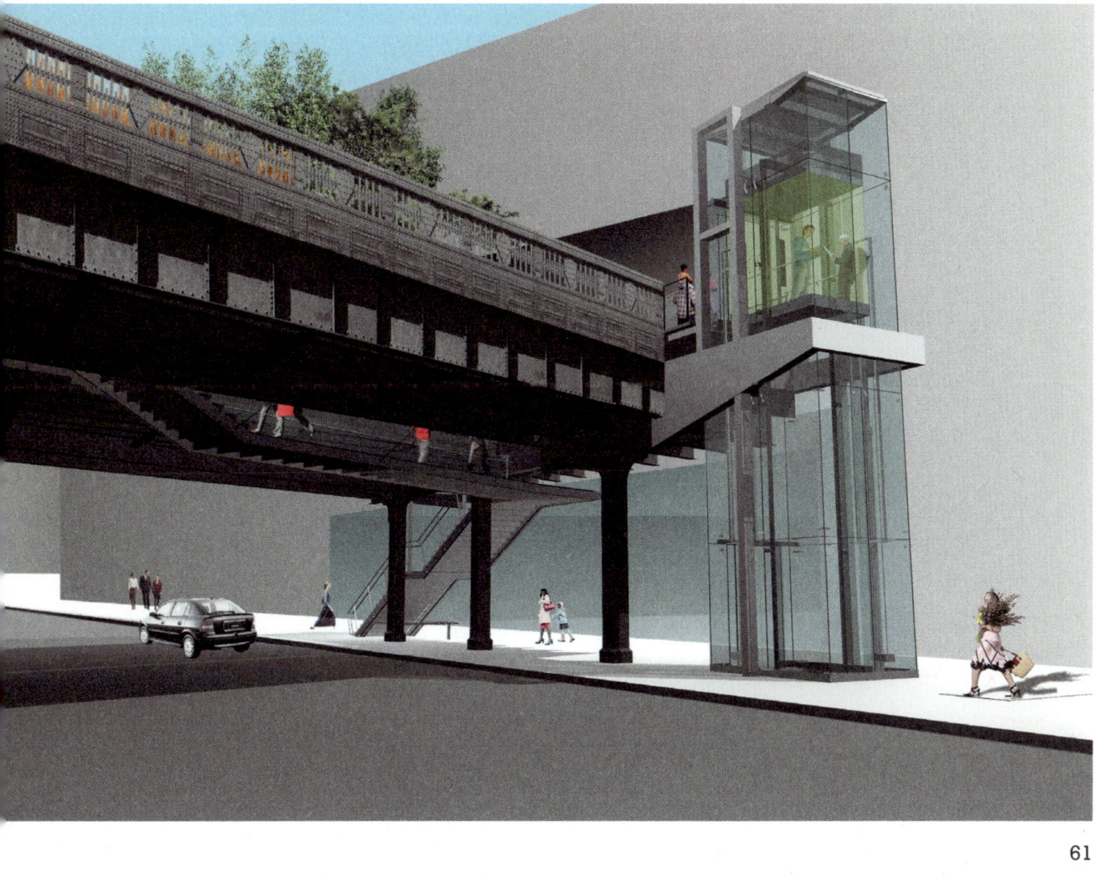

Sundeck Water Feature / Sundeck Preserve

The Sundeck (between 14th and 15th Streets) offers unobstructed sun and views over the Hudson River. Water skims the upper walkway, providing visitors the opportunity to wade barefoot. Rail tracks in the Sundeck Preserve, on the lower level, are reinstalled in plantings derived from the High Line's self-sown landscape. The Sundeck Water Feature is made possible by the Diller-von Furstenberg Family Foundation.

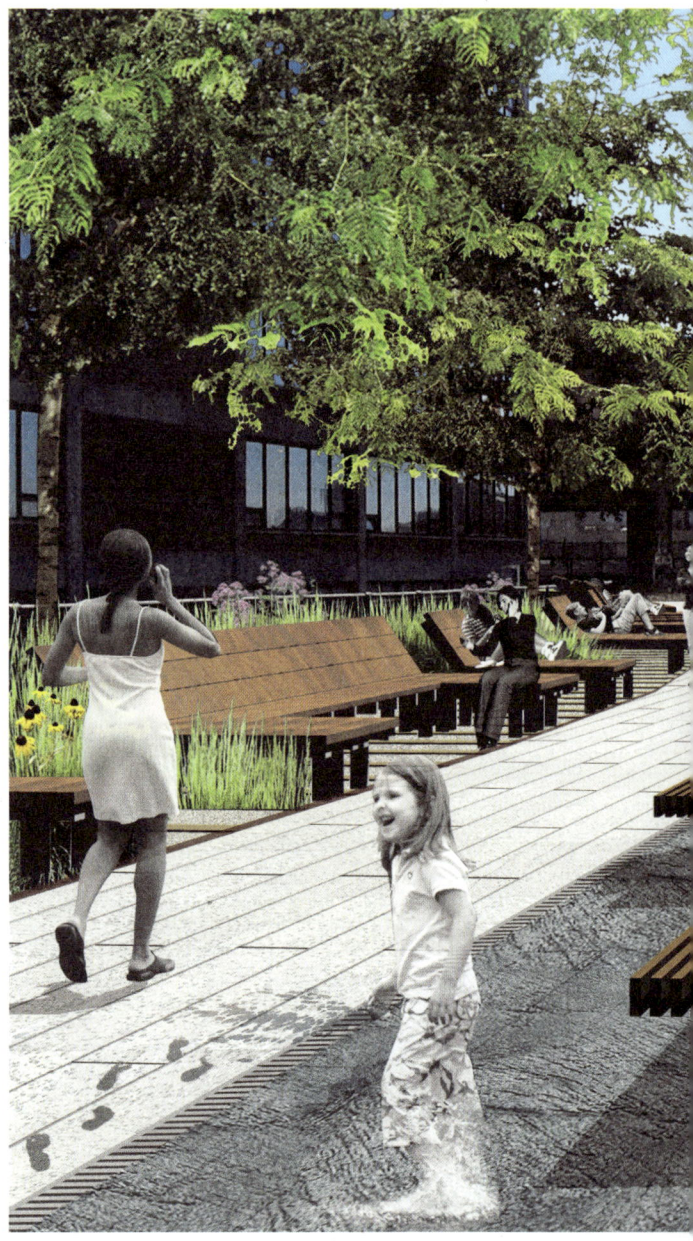

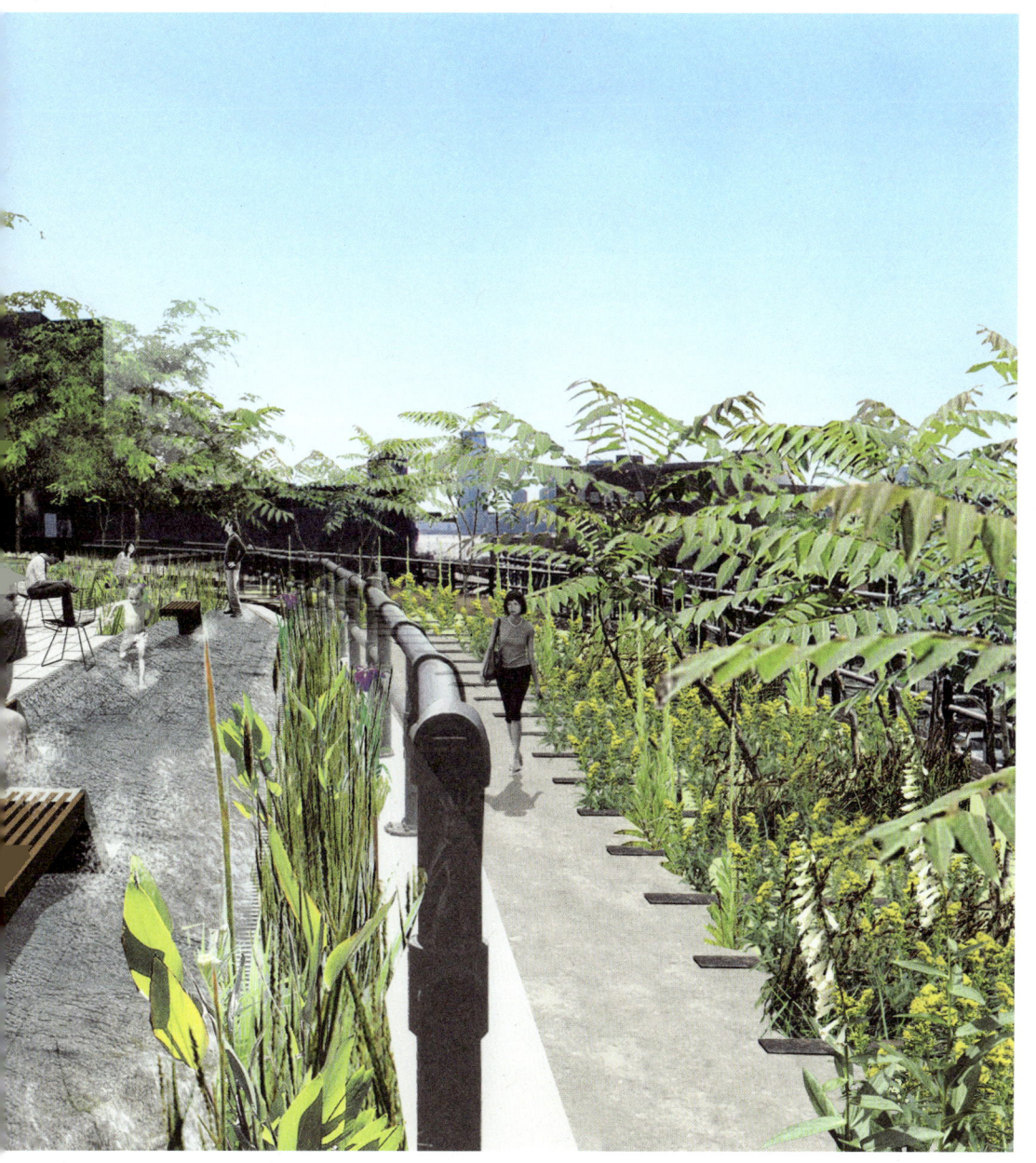

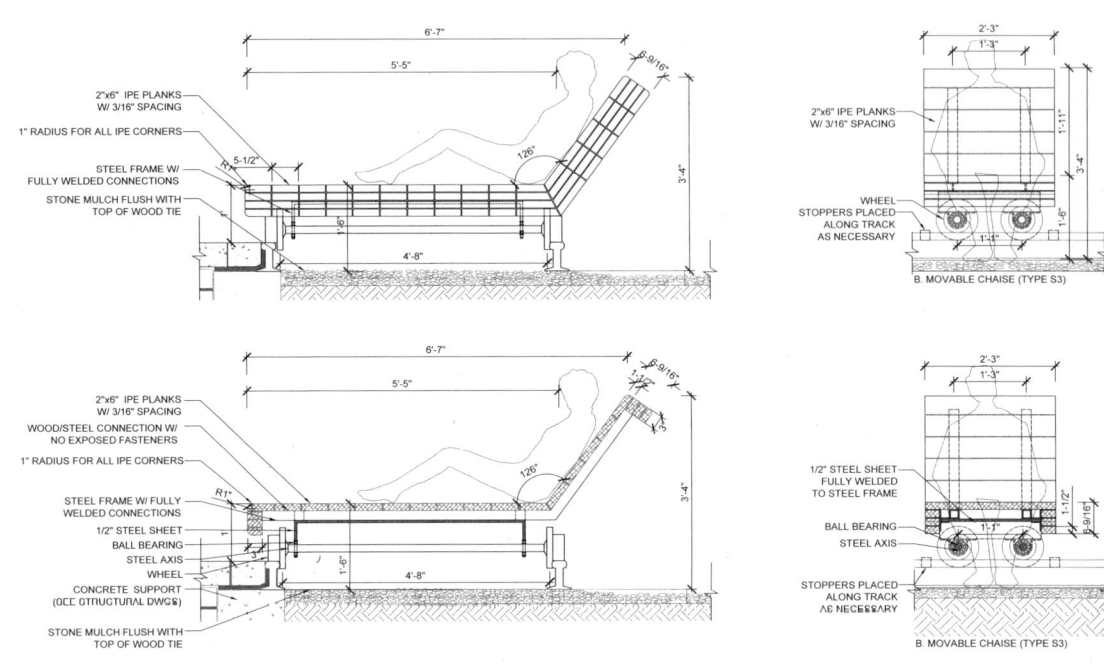

Top-left diagram (fixed chaise section):

- 2"x6" IPE PLANKS W/ 3/16" SPACING
- 1" RADIUS FOR ALL IPE CORNERS
- STEEL FRAME W/ FULLY WELDED CONNECTIONS
- STONE MULCH FLUSH WITH TOP OF WOOD TIE

Dimensions: 6'-7", 5'-5", 8-9/16", 126°, 3'-4", 5-1/2", R1", 4'-8"

Top-right diagram:

- 2"x6" IPE PLANKS W/ 3/16" SPACING
- WHEEL
- STOPPERS PLACED ALONG TRACK AS NECESSARY

Dimensions: 2'-3", 1'-3", 1'-11", 3'-4", 1'-6", 1'-1"

B. MOVABLE CHAISE (TYPE S3)

Bottom-left diagram (movable chaise section):

- 2"x6" IPE PLANKS W/ 3/16" SPACING
- WOOD/STEEL CONNECTION W/ NO EXPOSED FASTENERS
- 1" RADIUS FOR ALL IPE CORNERS
- STEEL FRAME W/ FULLY WELDED CONNECTIONS
- 1/2" STEEL SHEET
- BALL BEARING
- STEEL AXIS
- WHEEL
- CONCRETE SUPPORT (SEE STRUCTURAL DWGS)
- STONE MULCH FLUSH WITH TOP OF WOOD TIE

Dimensions: 6'-7", 5'-5", 8-9/16", 3", 126°, 3'-4", R1", 3", 1'-6", 4'-8"

Bottom-right diagram:

- 1/2" STEEL SHEET FULLY WELDED TO STEEL FRAME
- BALL BEARING
- STEEL AXIS
- STOPPERS PLACED ALONG TRACK AS NECESSARY

Dimensions: 2'-3", 1'-3", 1-1/2", 8-9/16"

B. MOVABLE CHAISE (TYPE S3)

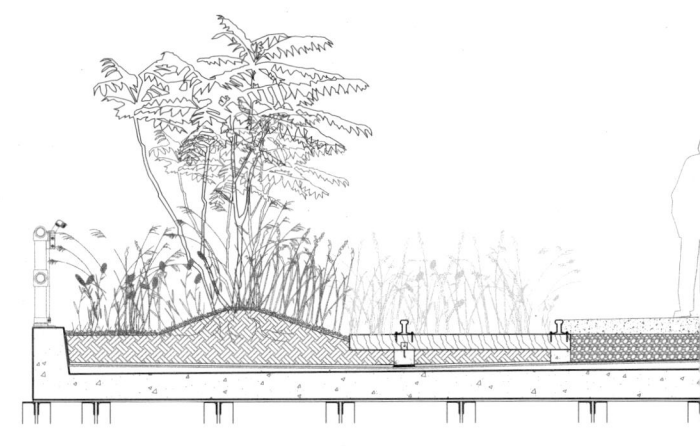

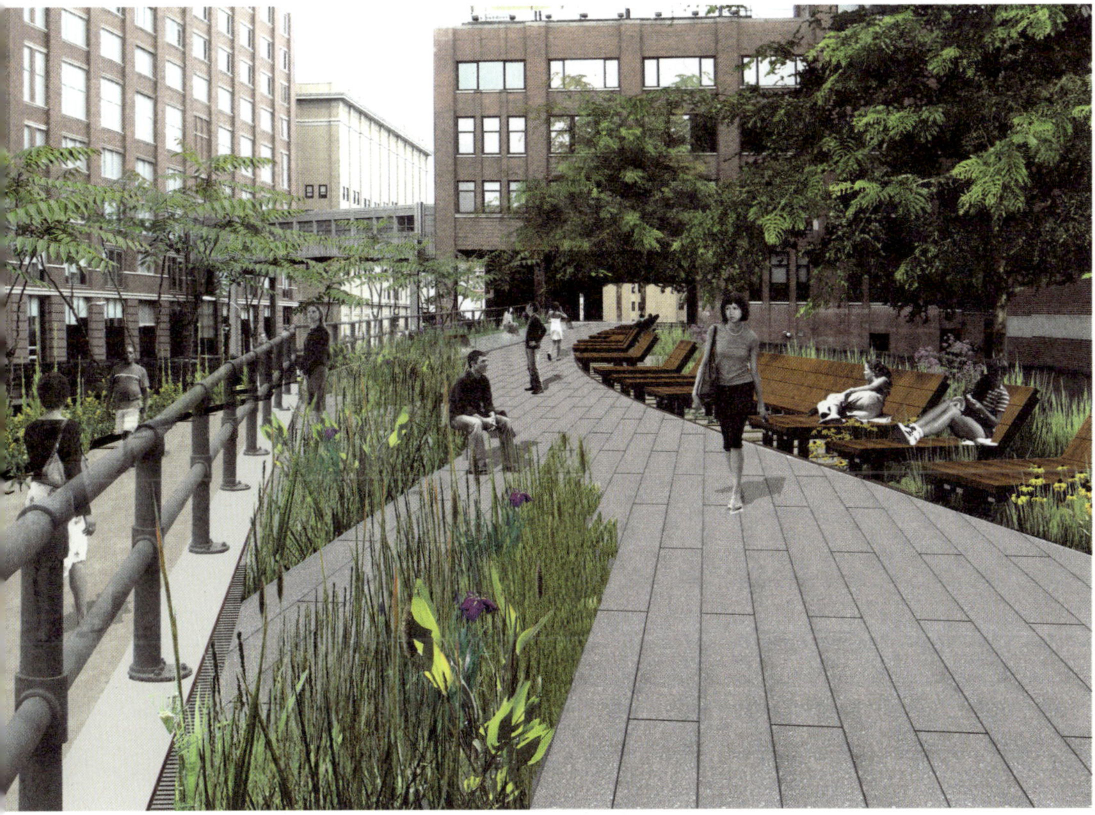

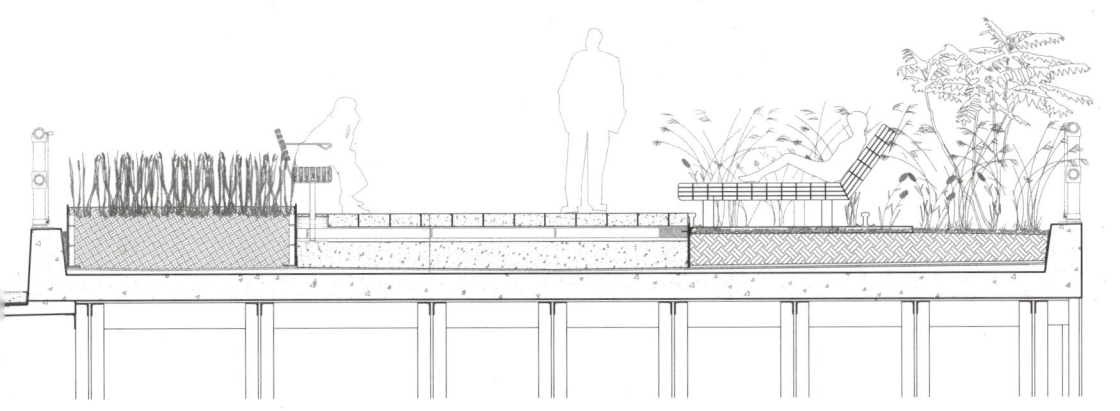

Chelsea Market Passage / Public Art Program

The space where the High Line cuts through the Chelsea Market building, formerly a Nabisco factory, will be a site for public art. "The River That Flows Both Ways," by Spencer Finch, is the public art program's inaugural work. Finch was recently the subject of a retrospective at Mass MoCA (below). For the High Line project, Finch installs panes of glass in the casement windows of this towering, semi-enclosed industrial space (bottom). The color and translucency of each pane is derived from studies of 700 minutes on the Hudson River. The program is presented by Friends of the High Line, Creative Time, and the Department of Parks & Recreation, and is made possible by the Rockefeller Foundation's New York City Cultural Innovation Fund.

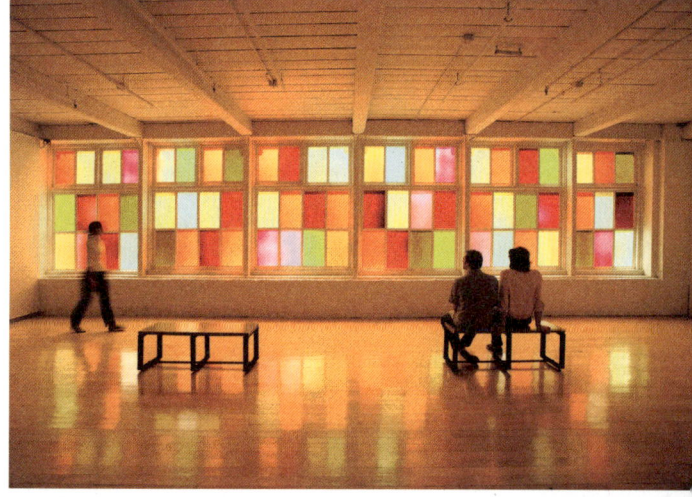

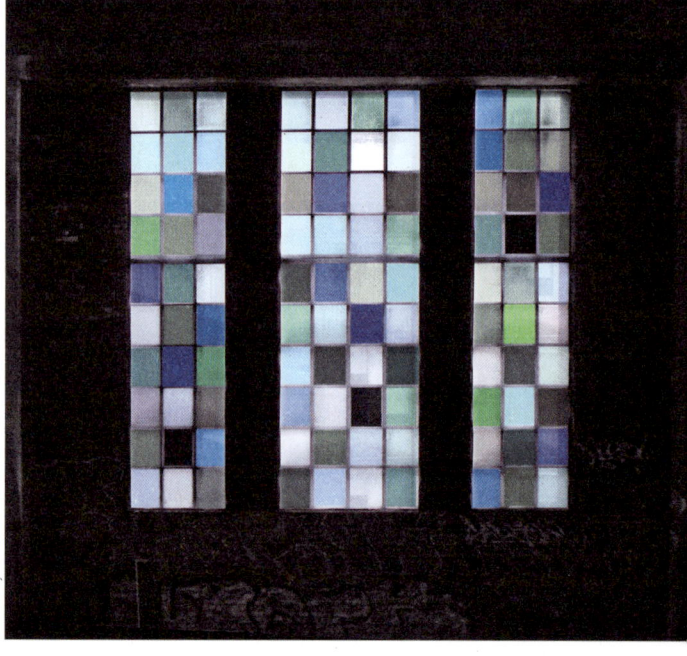

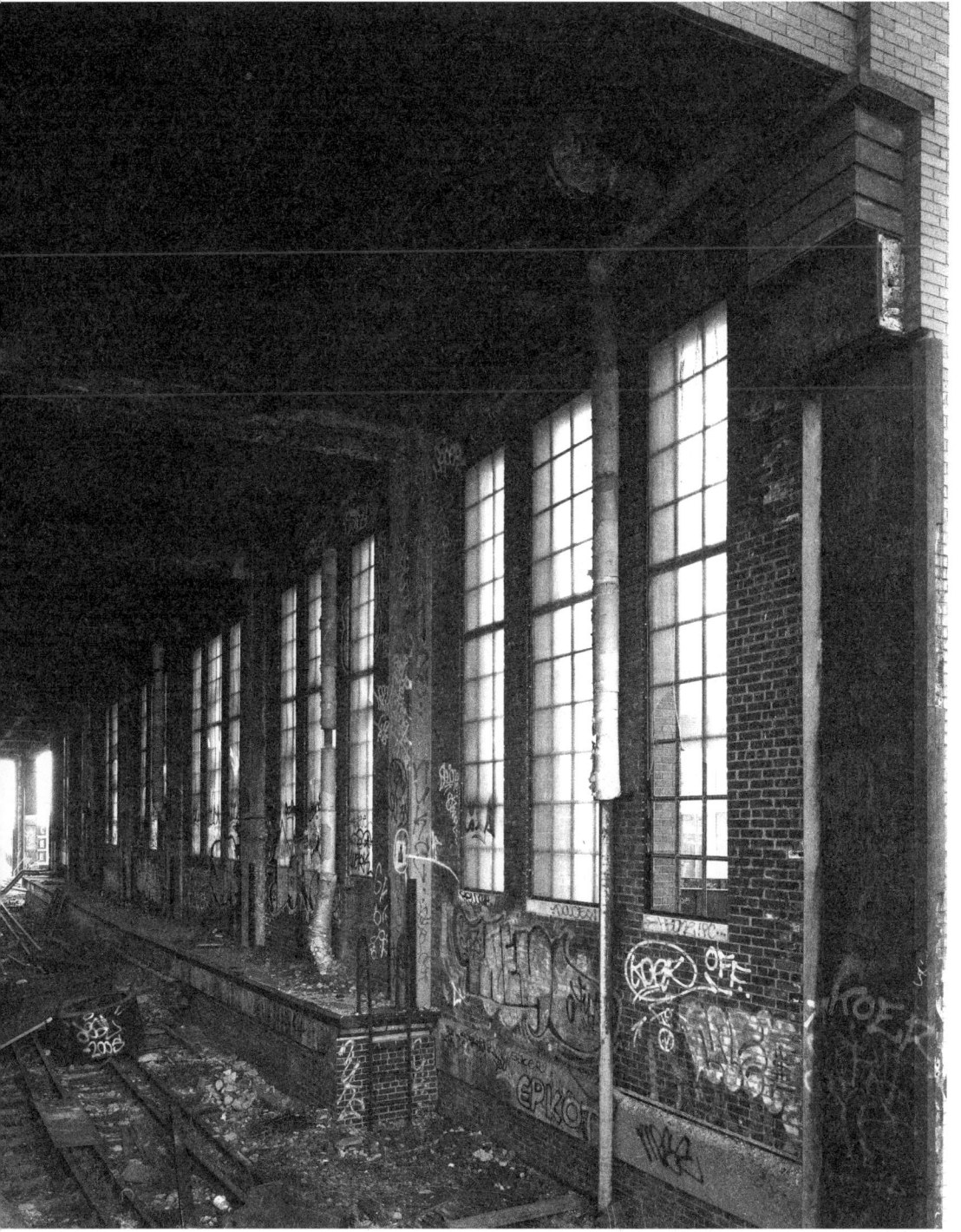

17th Street /
20th Street

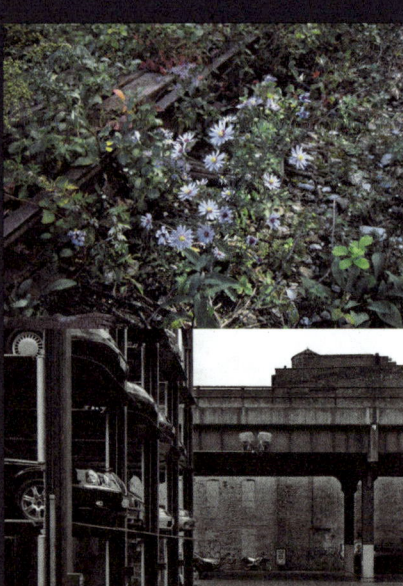

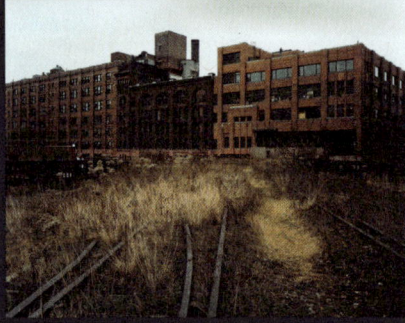

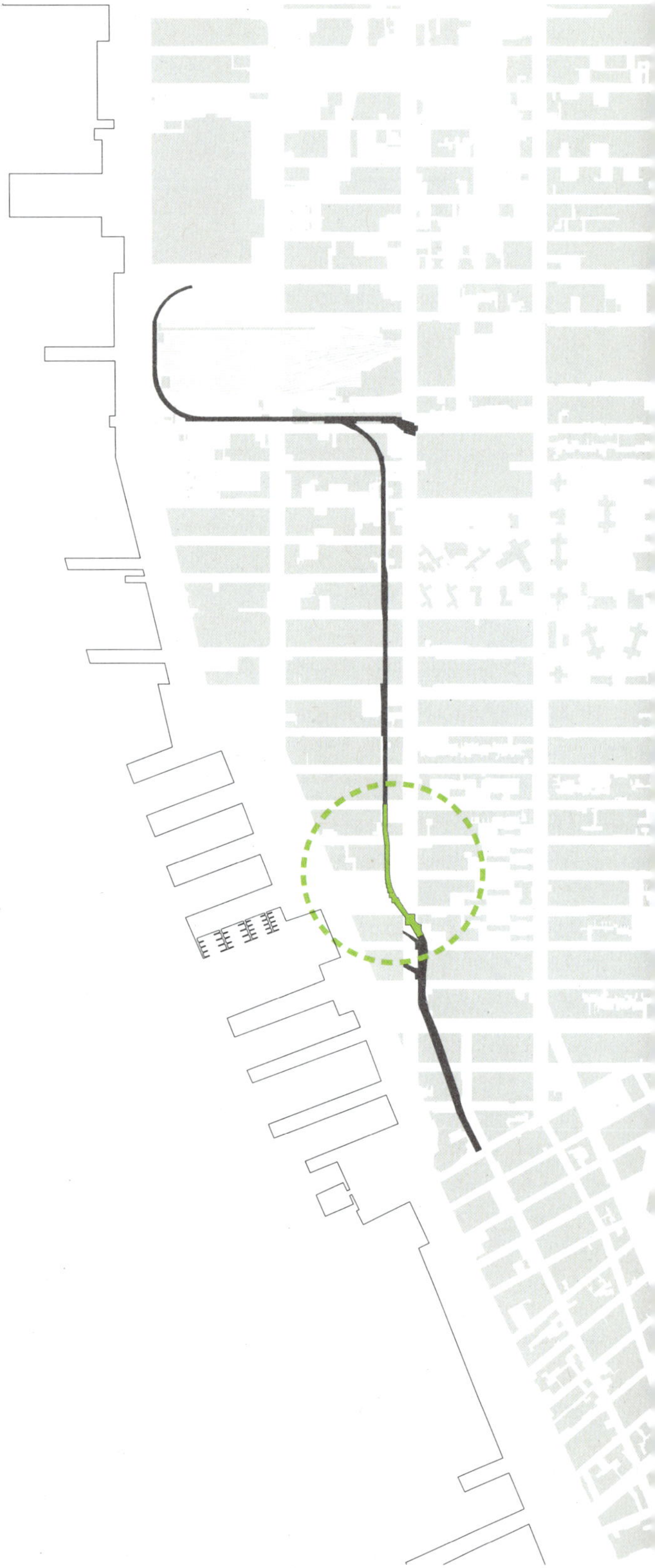

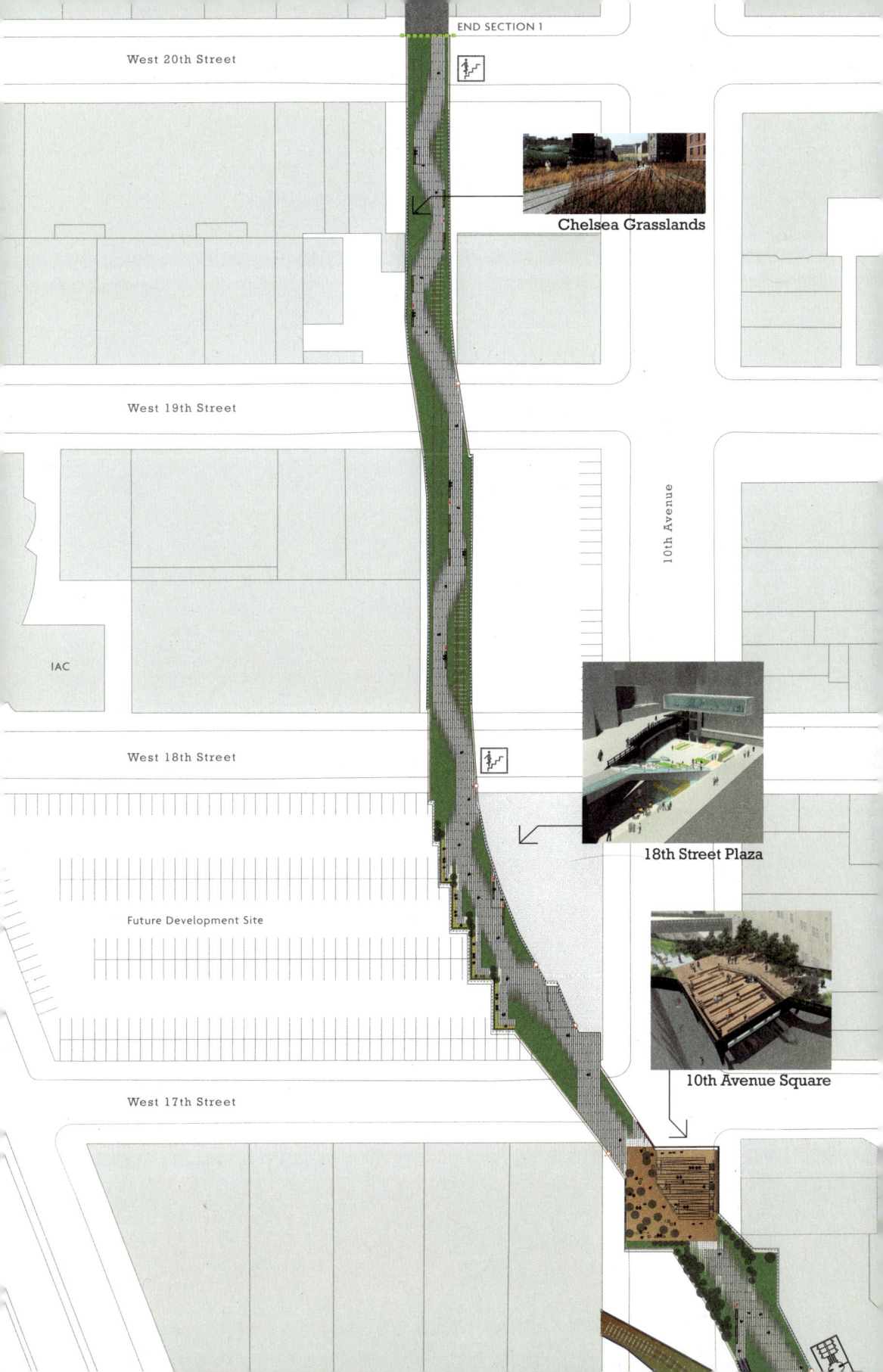

END SECTION 1

West 20th Street

Chelsea Grasslands

West 19th Street

10th Avenue

IAC

West 18th Street

18th Street Plaza

Future Development Site

10th Avenue Square

West 17th Street

10th Avenue Square

An elevated square is formed by the High Line's crossing of 10th Avenue at 17th Street. By cutting down into the High Line's deck, steps and ramps allow visitors to inhabit the structure. Views of midtown and the Statue of Liberty can be enjoyed at this location. The 10th Avenue Square is made possible by Hermine Riegerl Heller and David Heller, and Sukey and Mike Novogratz.

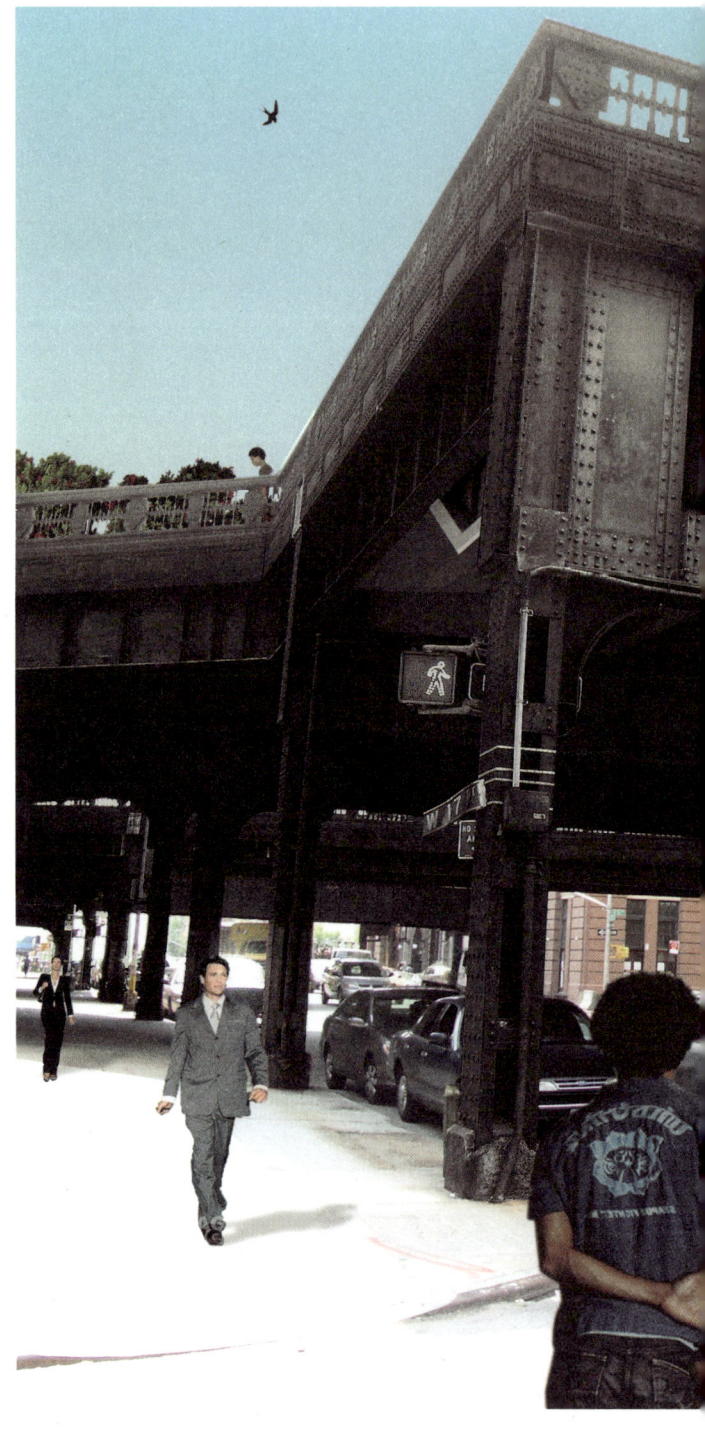

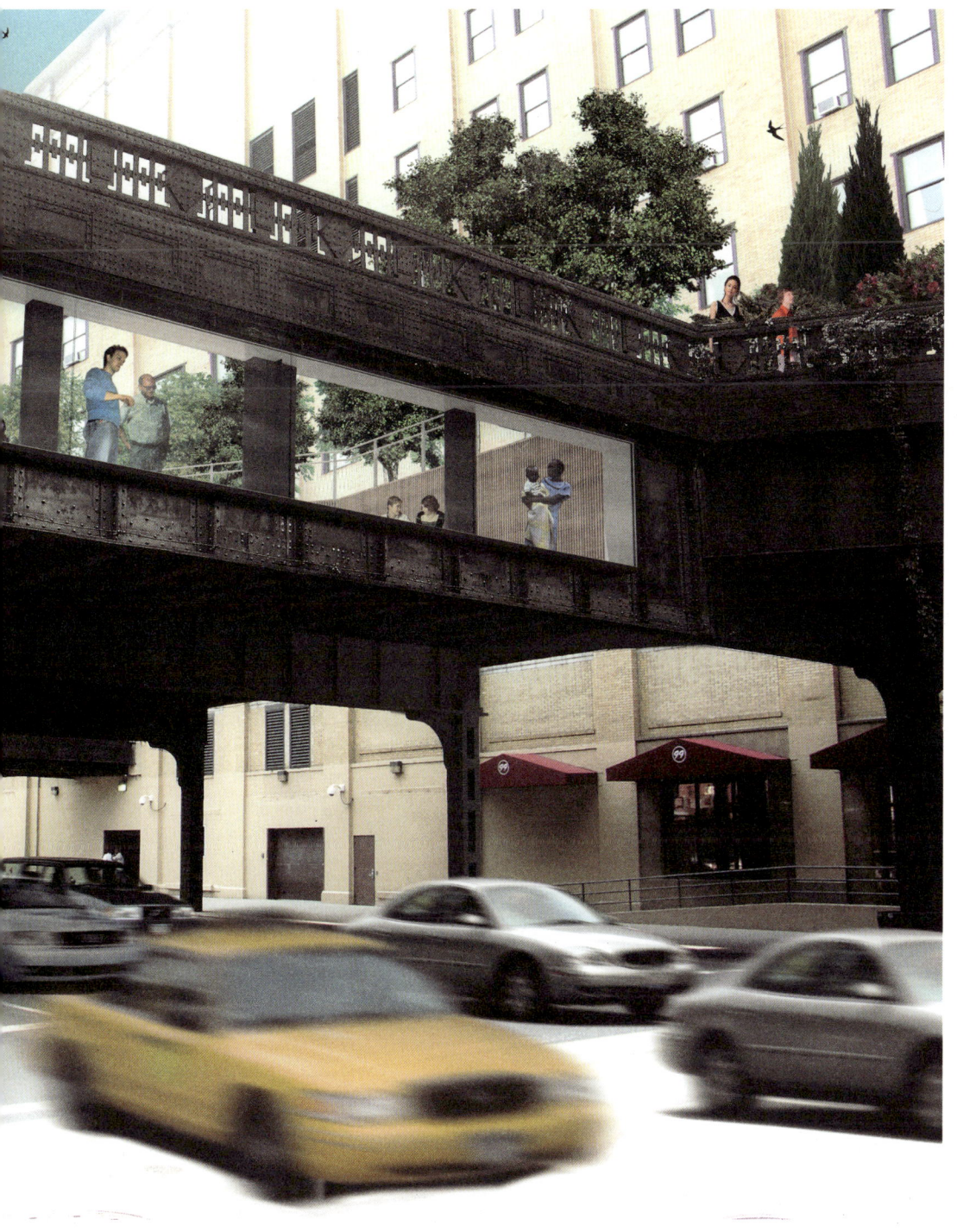

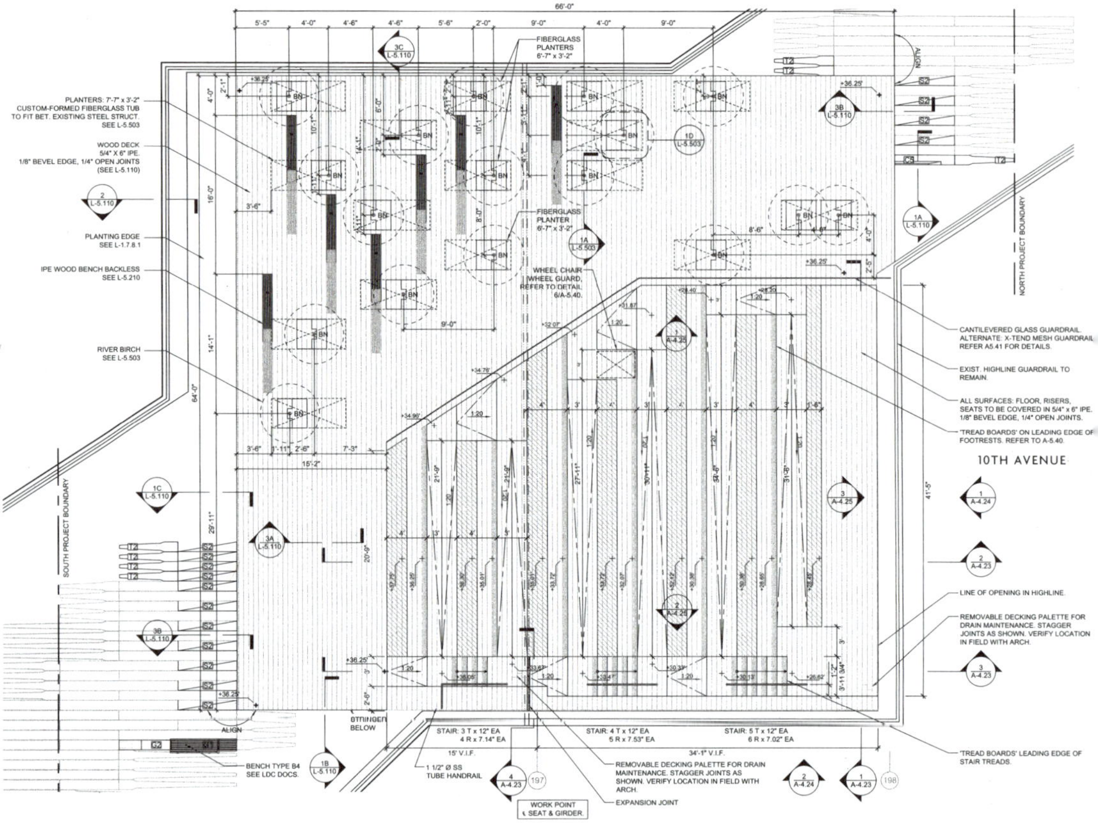

PLANTERS: 7'-7" x 3'-2"
CUSTOM-FORMED FIBERGLASS TUB
TO FIT BET. EXISTING STEEL STRUCT.
SEE L-5.503

WOOD DECK
5/4" X 6" IPE.
1/8" BEVEL EDGE, 1/4" OPEN JOINTS.
(SEE L-5.110)

PLANTING EDGE
SEE L-1.7.8.1

IPE WOOD BENCH BACKLESS
SEE L-5.210

RIVER BIRCH
SEE L-5.503

FIBERGLASS
PLANTERS
6'-7" X 3'-2"

FIBERGLASS
PLANTER
6'-7" X 3'-2"

WHEEL CHAIR
[WHEEL GUARD].
REFER TO DETAIL
6/A-5.40.

NORTH PROJECT BOUNDARY
SOUTH PROJECT BOUNDARY

10TH AVENUE

CANTILEVERED GLASS GUARDRAIL.
ALTERNATE: X-TEND MESH GUARDRAIL.
REFER AS.41 FOR DETAILS

EXIST. HIGHLINE GUARDRAIL TO
REMAIN.

ALL SURFACES: FLOOR, RISERS,
SEATS TO BE COVERED IN 5/4" x 6" IPE.
1/8" BEVEL EDGE, 1/4" OPEN JOINTS.

'TREAD BOARDS' ON LEADING EDGE OF
FOOTRESTS. REFER TO A-5.40

LINE OF OPENING IN HIGHLINE

REMOVABLE DECKING PALETTE FOR
DRAIN MAINTENANCE. STAGGER
JOINTS AS SHOWN. VERIFY LOCATION
IN FIELD WITH ARCH.

'TREAD BOARDS' LEADING EDGE OF
STAIR TREADS.

STRINGER
BELOW

STAIR: 3 T x 12" EA
4 R x 7.14" EA

STAIR: 4 T x 12" EA
5 R x 7.53" EA

STAIR: 5 T x 12" EA
6 R x 7.02" EA

15' V.I.F.

34'-1" V.I.F.

1 1/2" Ø SS
TUBE HANDRAIL

REMOVABLE DECKING PALETTE FOR DRAIN
MAINTENANCE. STAGGER JOINTS AS
SHOWN. VERIFY LOCATION IN FIELD WITH
ARCH.

EXPANSION JOINT

WORK POINT
₵ SEAT & GIRDER.

BENCH TYPE B4
SEE LDC DOCS.

ALIGN

66'-0"

64'-0"

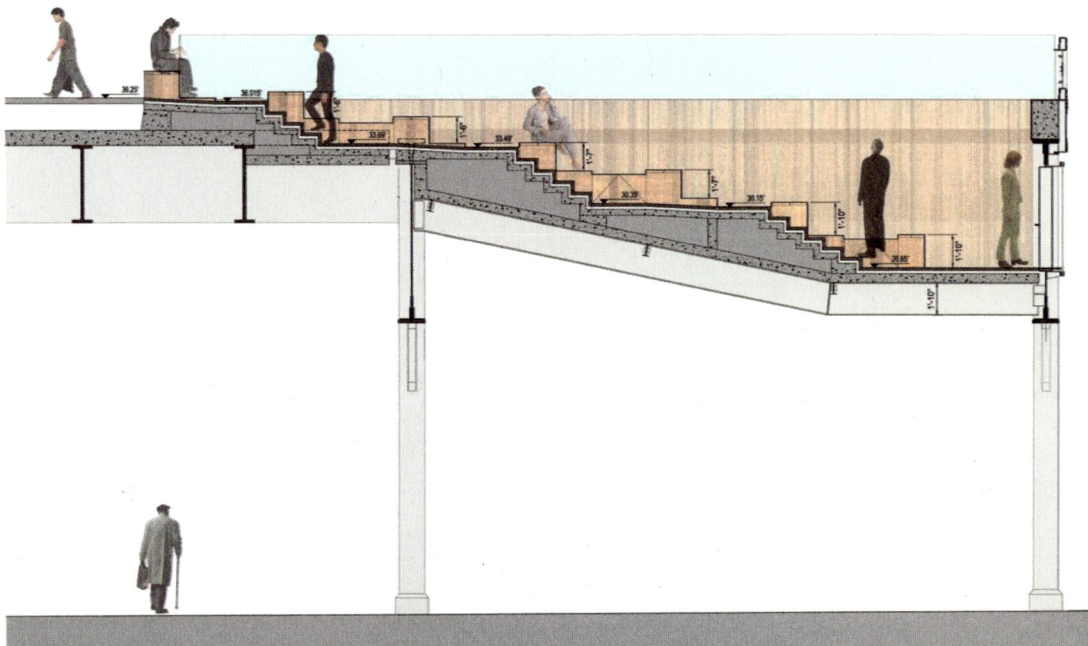

Views north and south from the 10th Avenue Square. Looking south (bottom photo), one can see the Northern and Southern Spurs, which were built to carry trains into adjacent warehouses. The Northern Spur, a horticultural preserve, is made possible by the Mack Family Foundation.

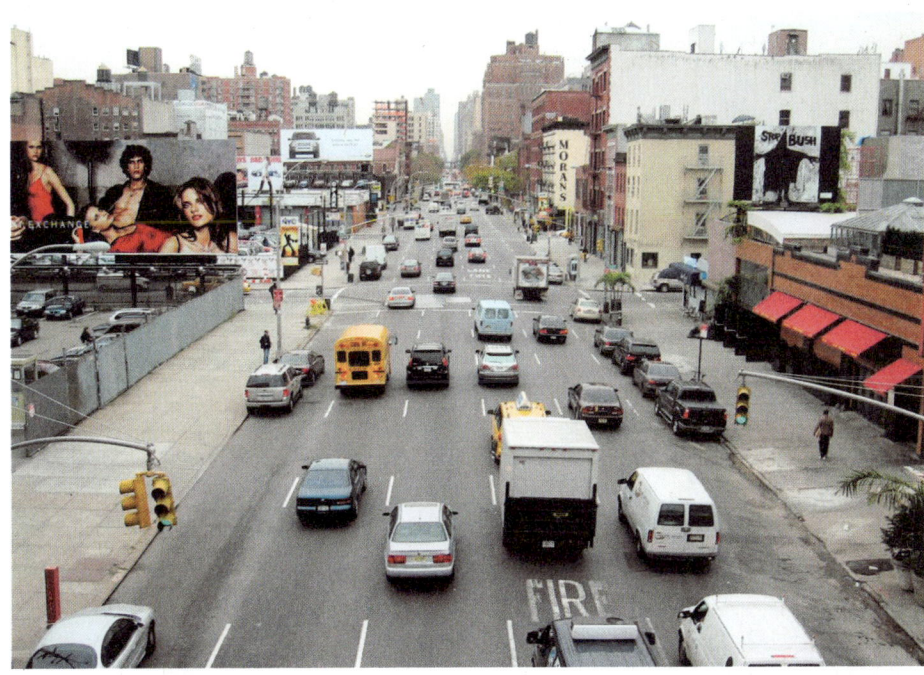

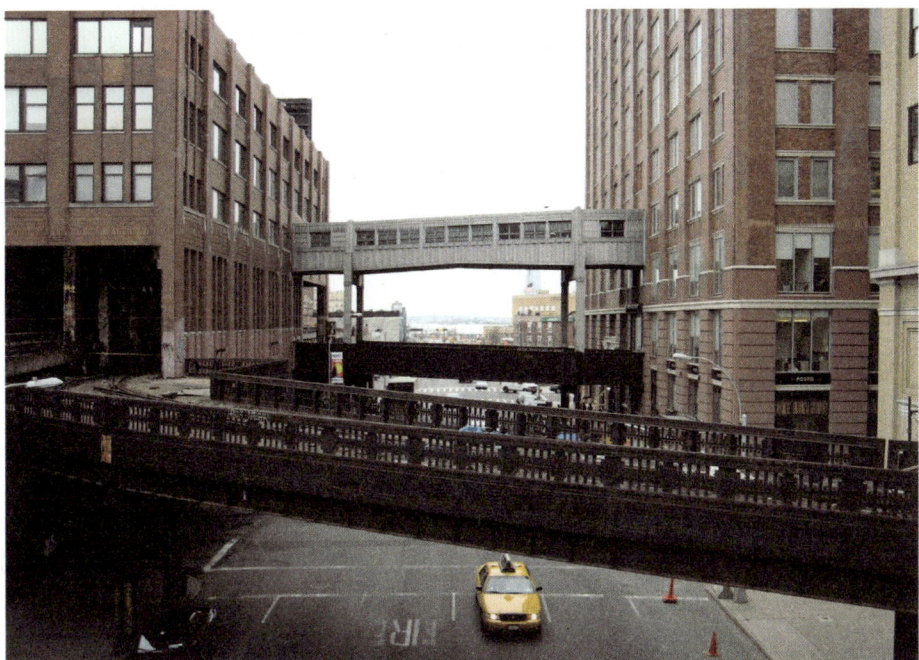

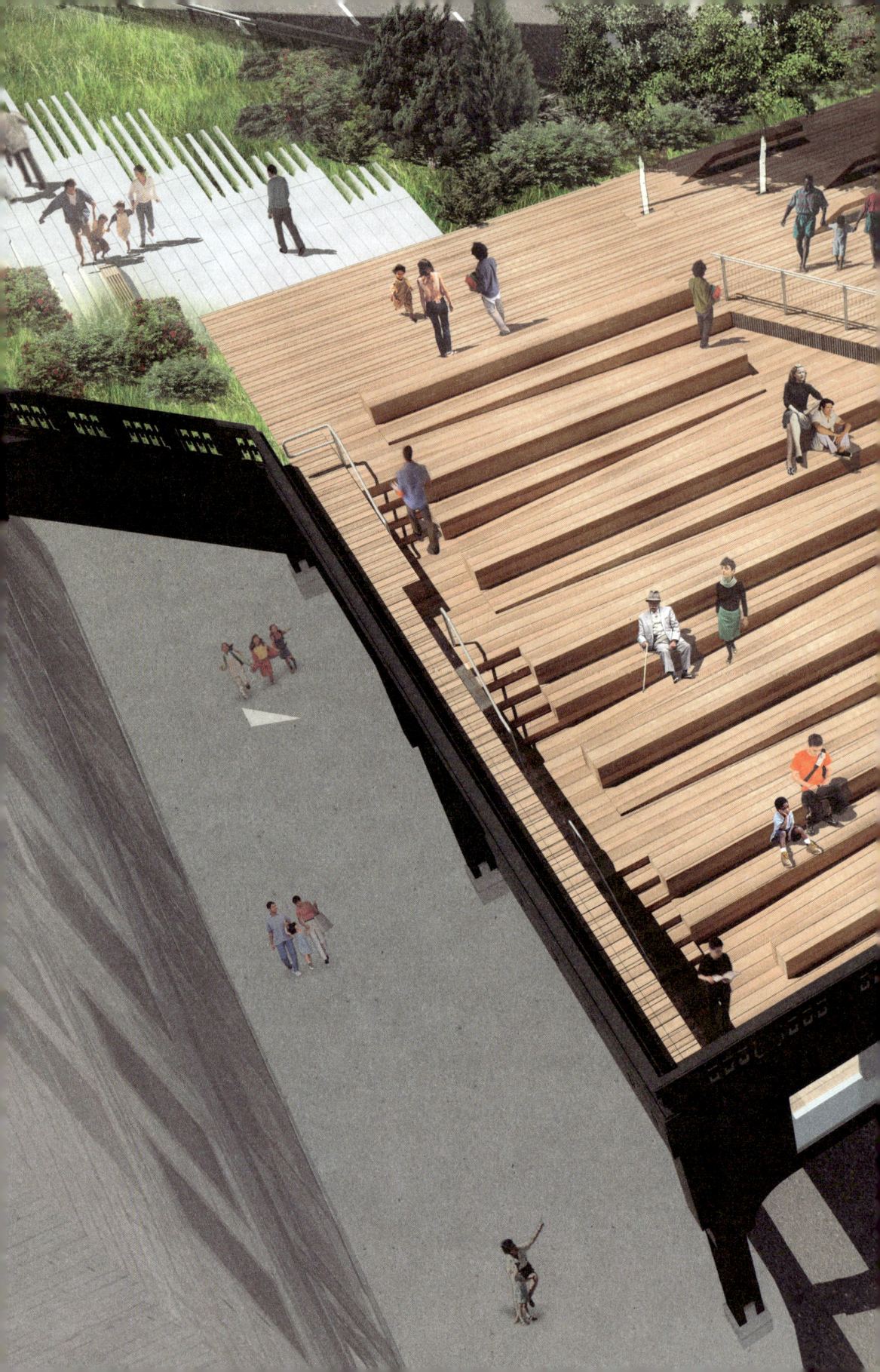

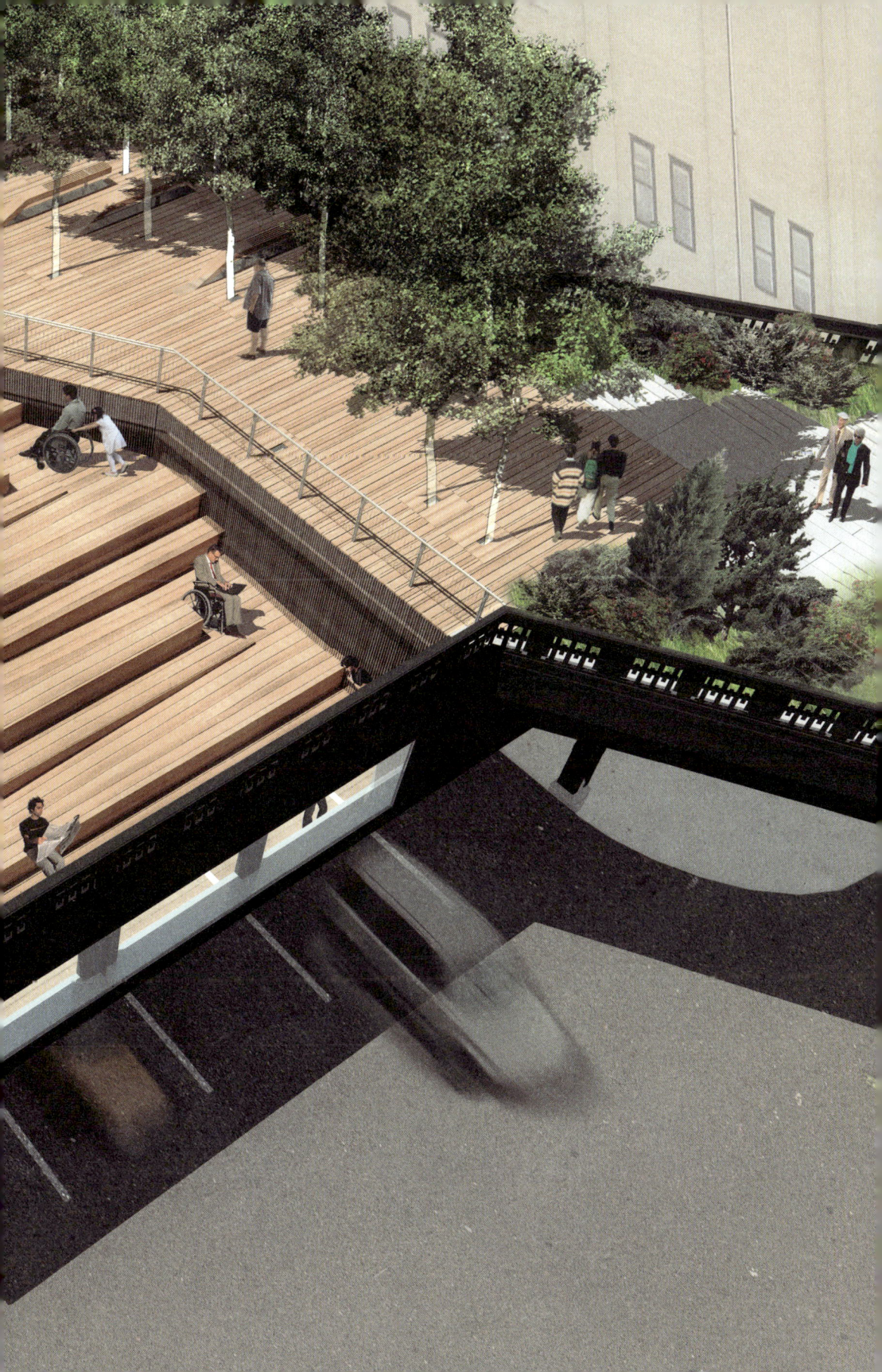

18th Street Plaza

A prominent street-level public plaza will become an iconic hub for the neighborhood, linking the High Line to the life of the street. A grand stair doubles as an inviting seating element, while a new elevated snack bar, cantilevered from the High Line, frames the edge of the site. The 18th Street Plaza will be built subsequent to Section 1, pending funding and approvals.

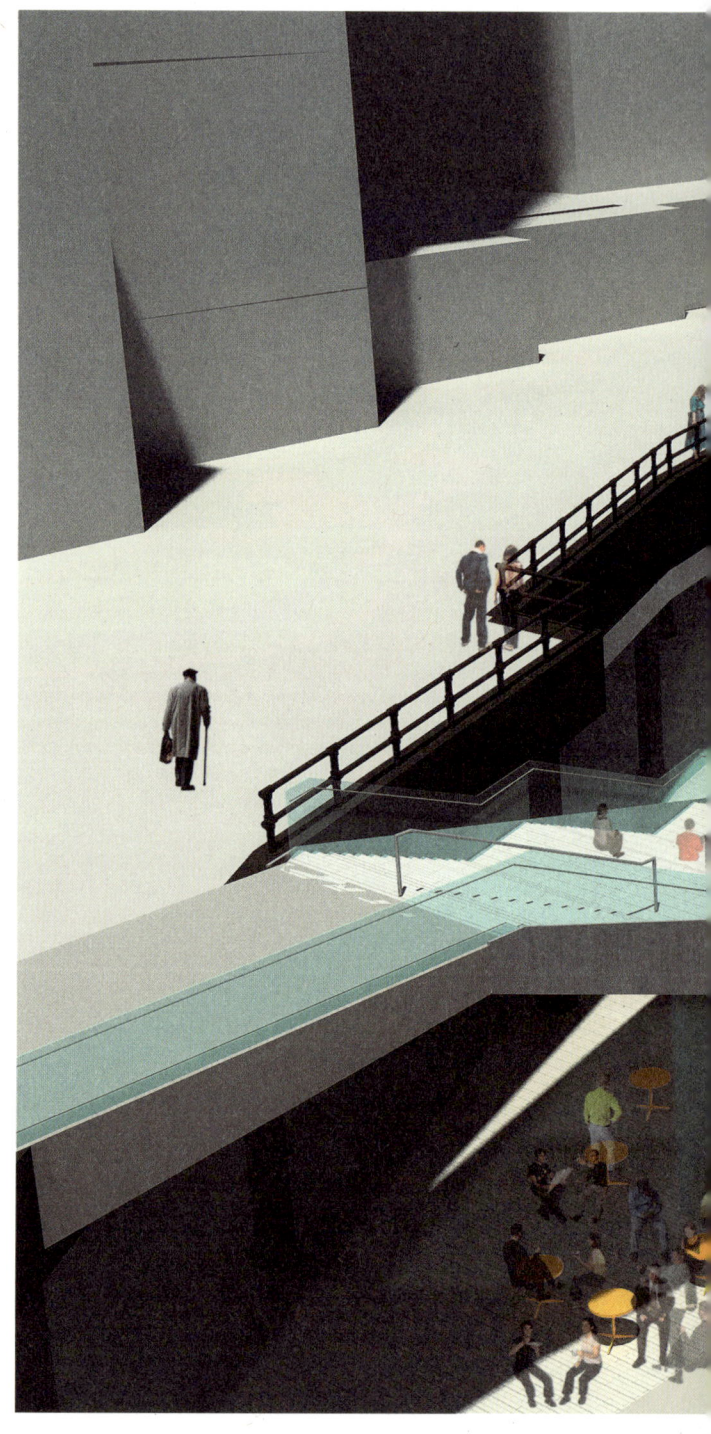

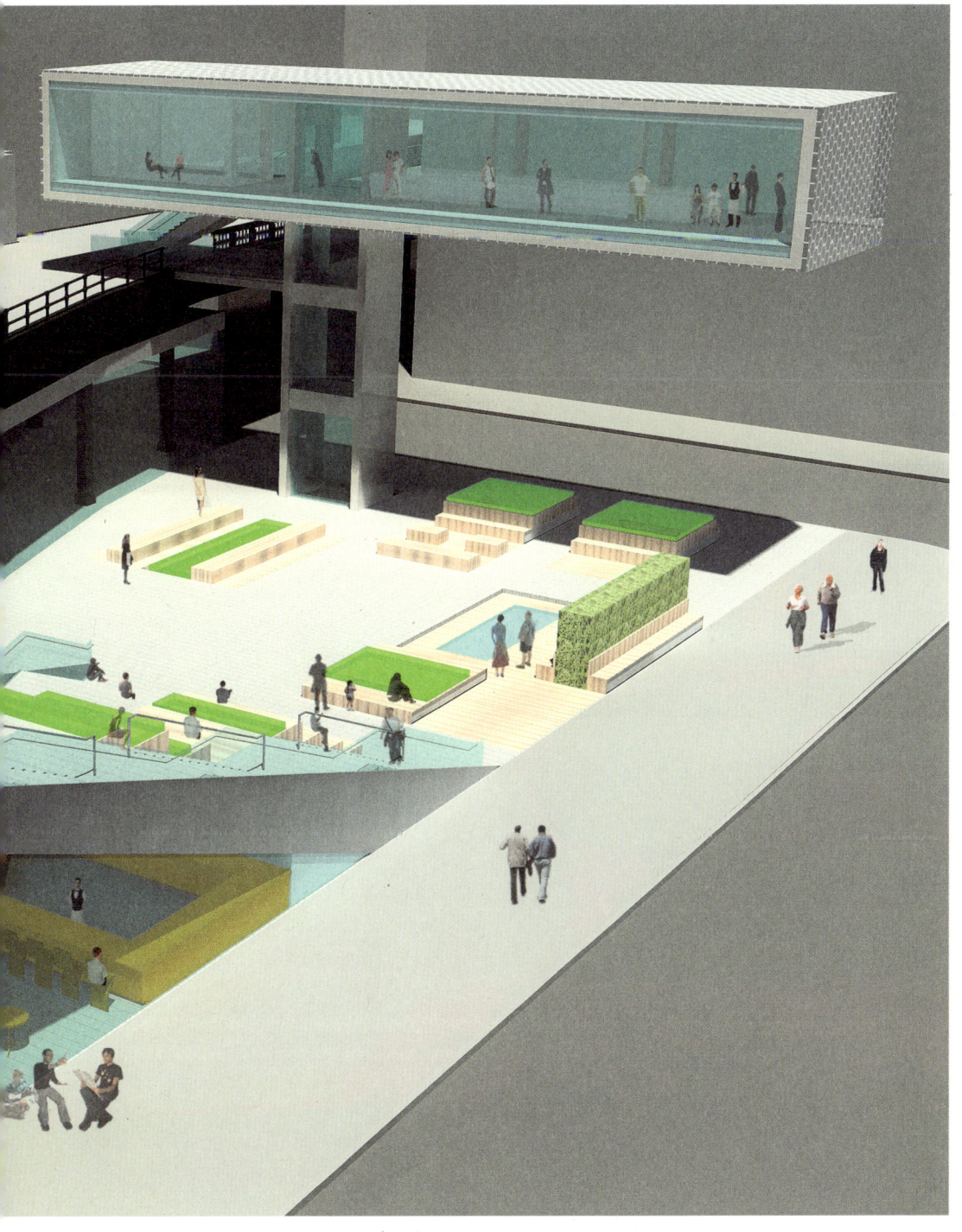

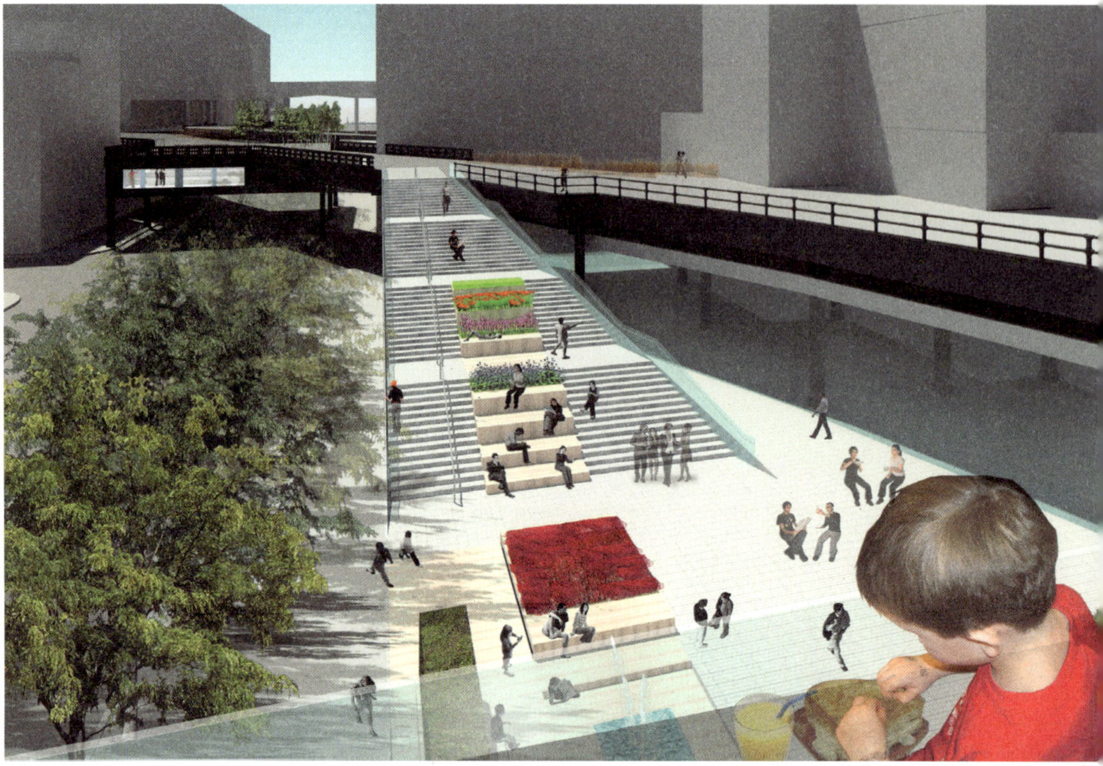

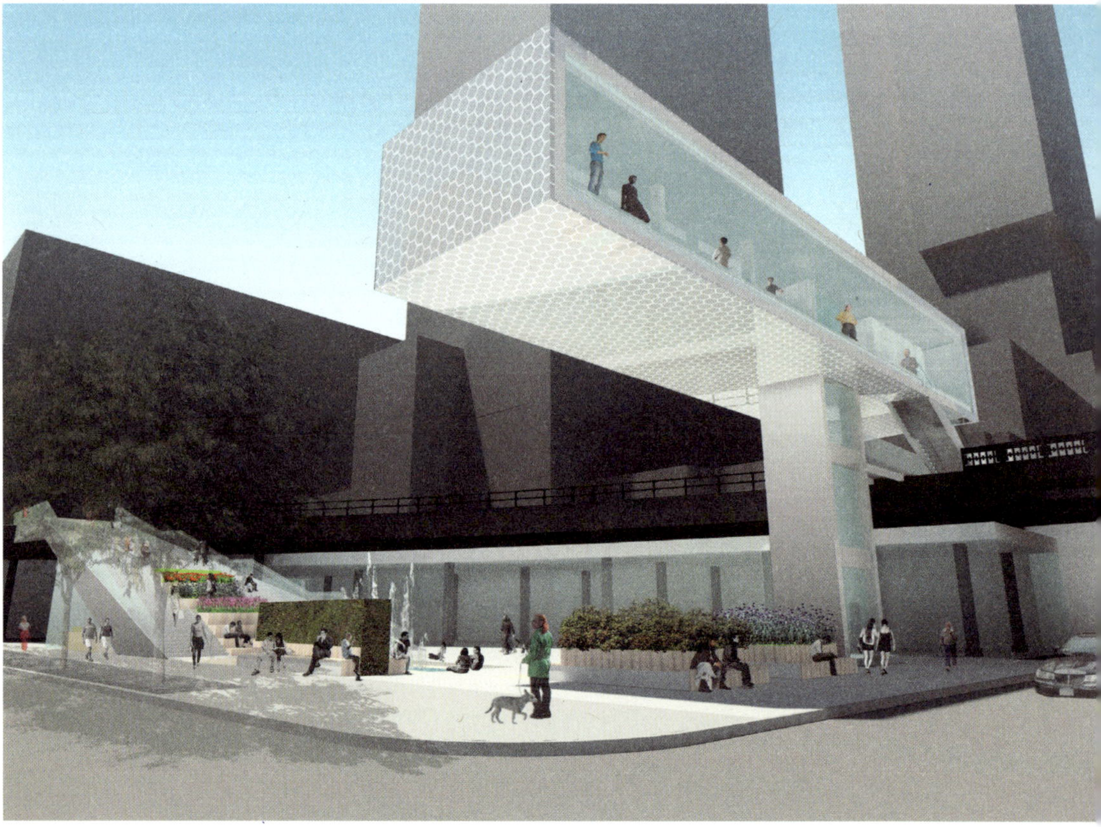

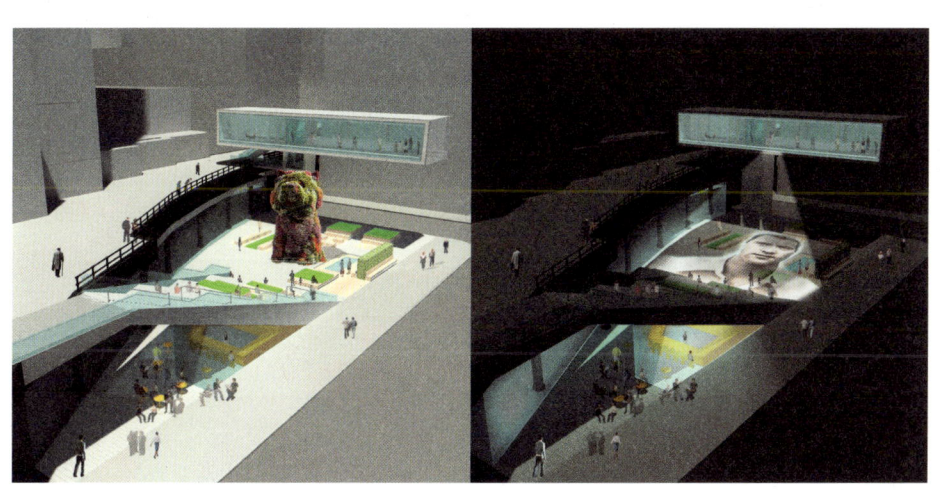

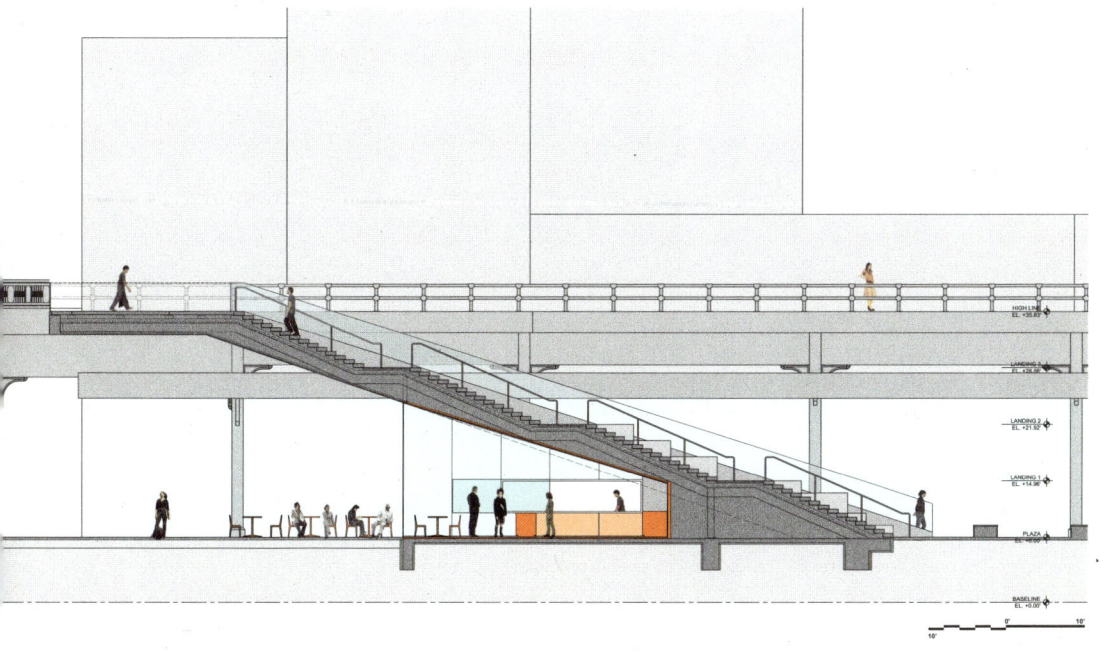

Chelsea Grasslands

Plantings by Piet Oudolf, in collaboration with Field Operations, inspired by the
High Line's self-sown landscape, push up through the tapered edges of the planked
walkways. The Chelsea Grasslands are made possible by the Tiffany & Co. Foundation.

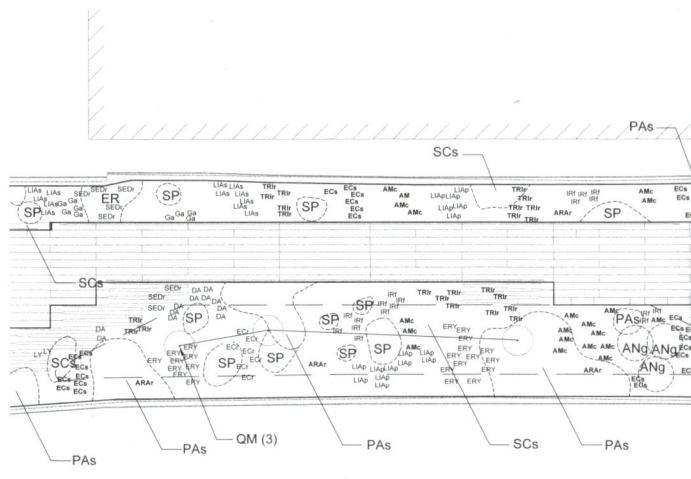

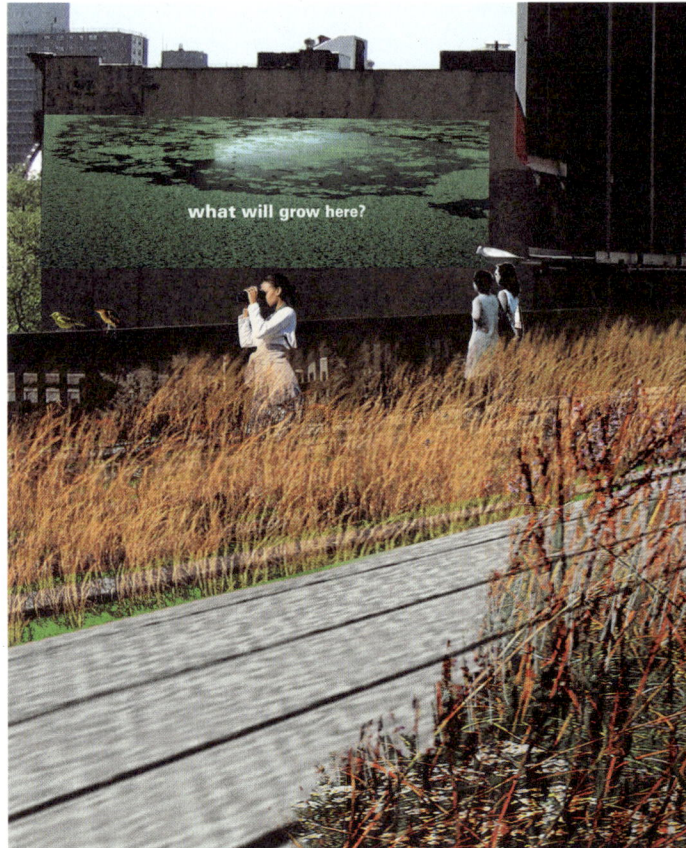

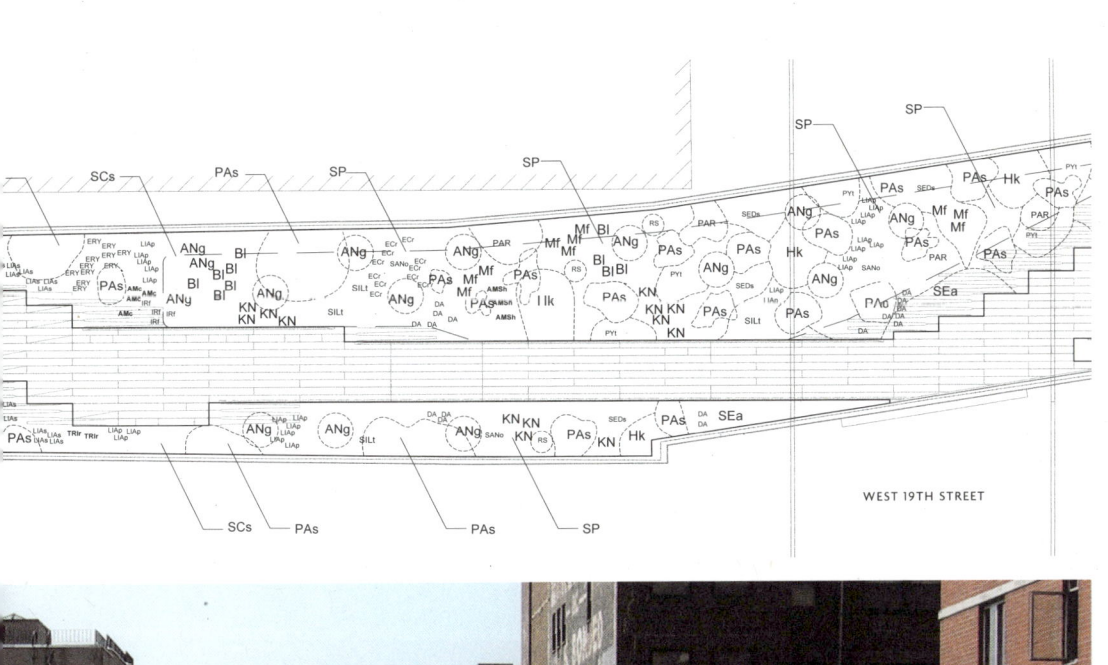

SCs PAs SP SP SP SP PAs PAs Hk PYl

ERY ERY ERY LIAp LIAp ANg Bl ANg ANg Mf Bl Mf ANg Mf PAs
LIAs LIAp ERY ERY ERY LIAp LIAp ANg ANg Bl Bl ECr ECr Mf ANg PAs Hk Mf Mf ANg PAs
LIAs LIAp ERY ERY PAs Bl Bl Bl ECr ECr PAR Mf Bl ANg PAs PAs Hk PAR PAs
LIAs PAs ANg Bl Bl ECr SANo Mf PAs Bl Bl KN Hk ANg PAR PAs
AMc ANg KN KN SIL1 ECr PAs Mf Bl Bl PAs SEDs ANg SEa
AMc IRl IRl KN KN KN SIL1 DA I lk AMSh KN KN PAs P Ab DA DA
IRl KN DA DA PAs AMSh KN KN PAs SIL1 PAs DA
PYl KN DA

PAs LIAp LIAp DA DA KN KN SEDs PAs SEa
LIAs LIAp LIAs TRlr TRlr LIAp LIAp ANg ANg ANg KN KN PAs Hk
LIAs LIAp LIAp SIL1 SANo KN KN KN
LIAp RS

SCs PAs PAs SP

WEST 19TH STREET

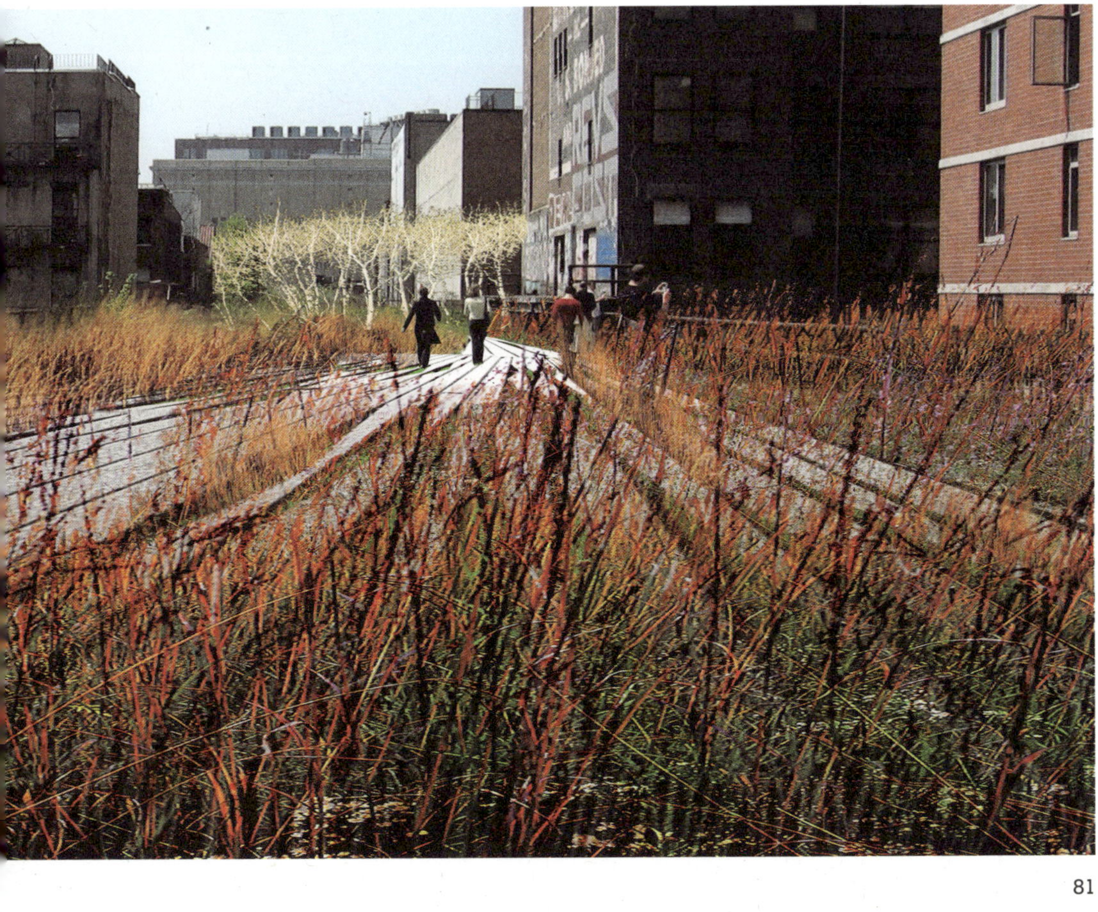

81

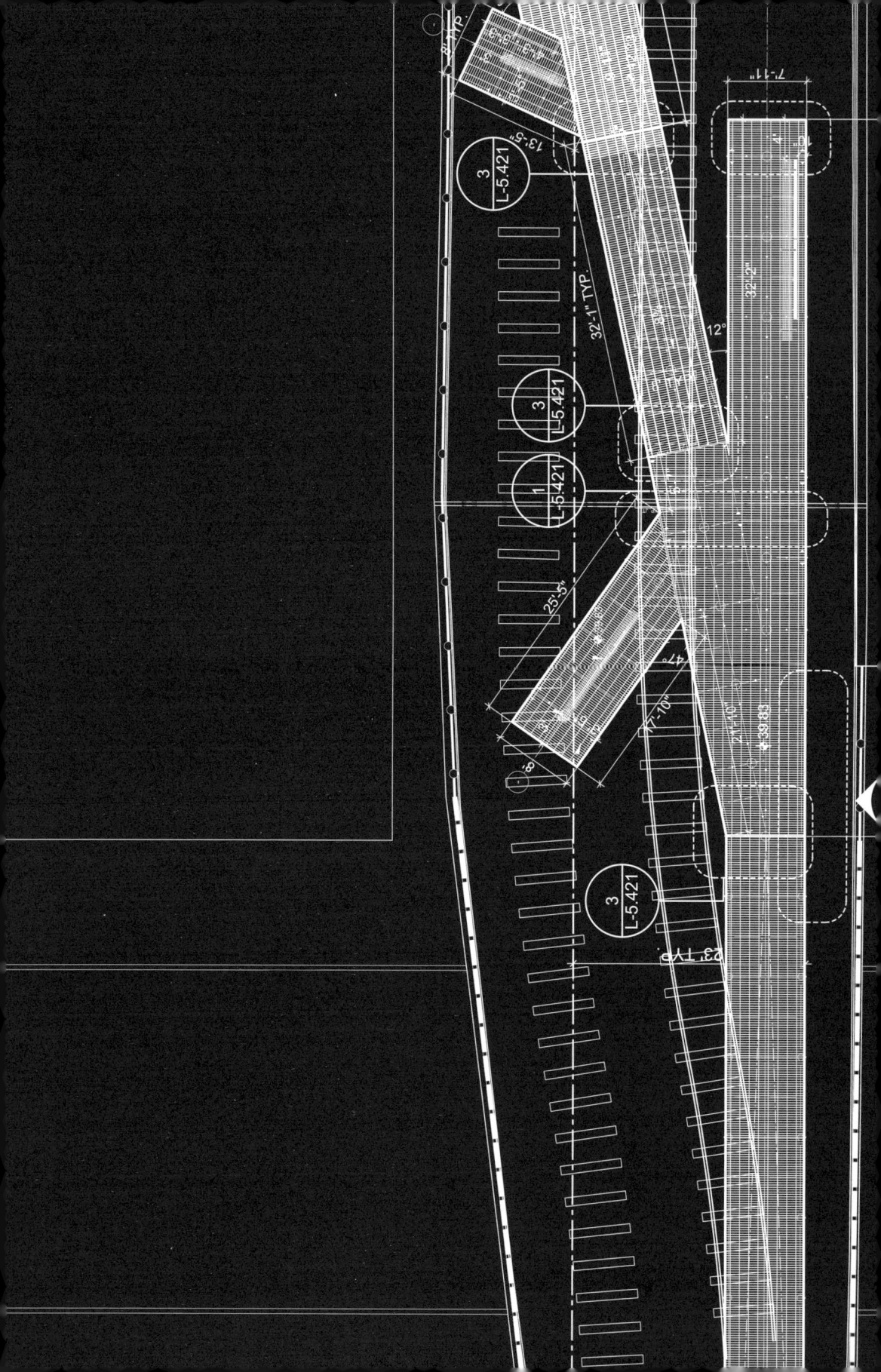

DESIGN: SECTION 2

20th Street /
24th Street

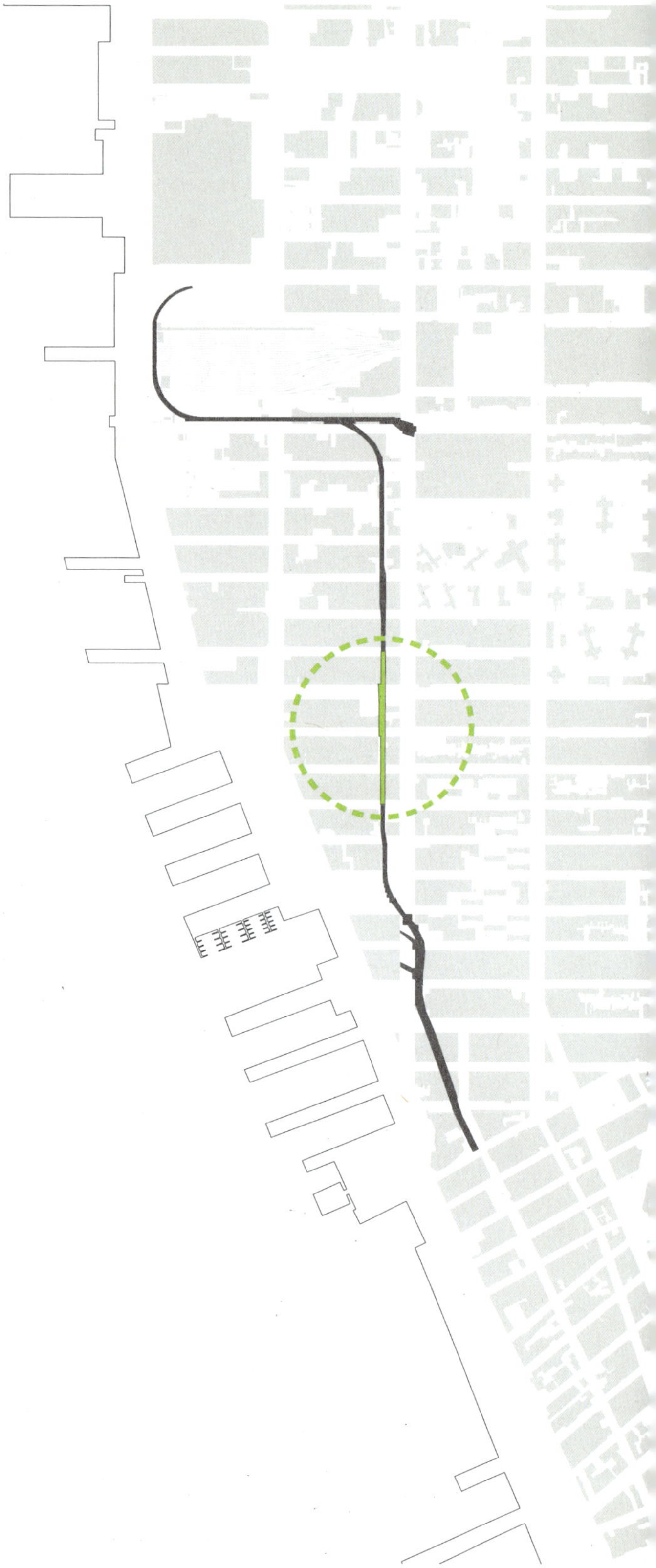

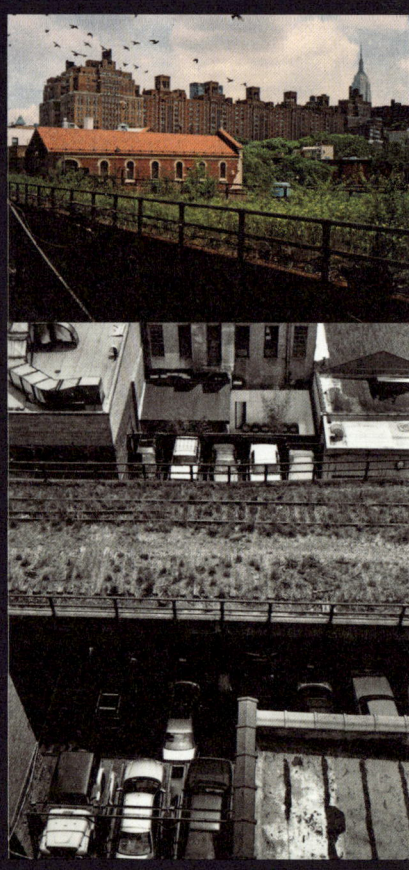

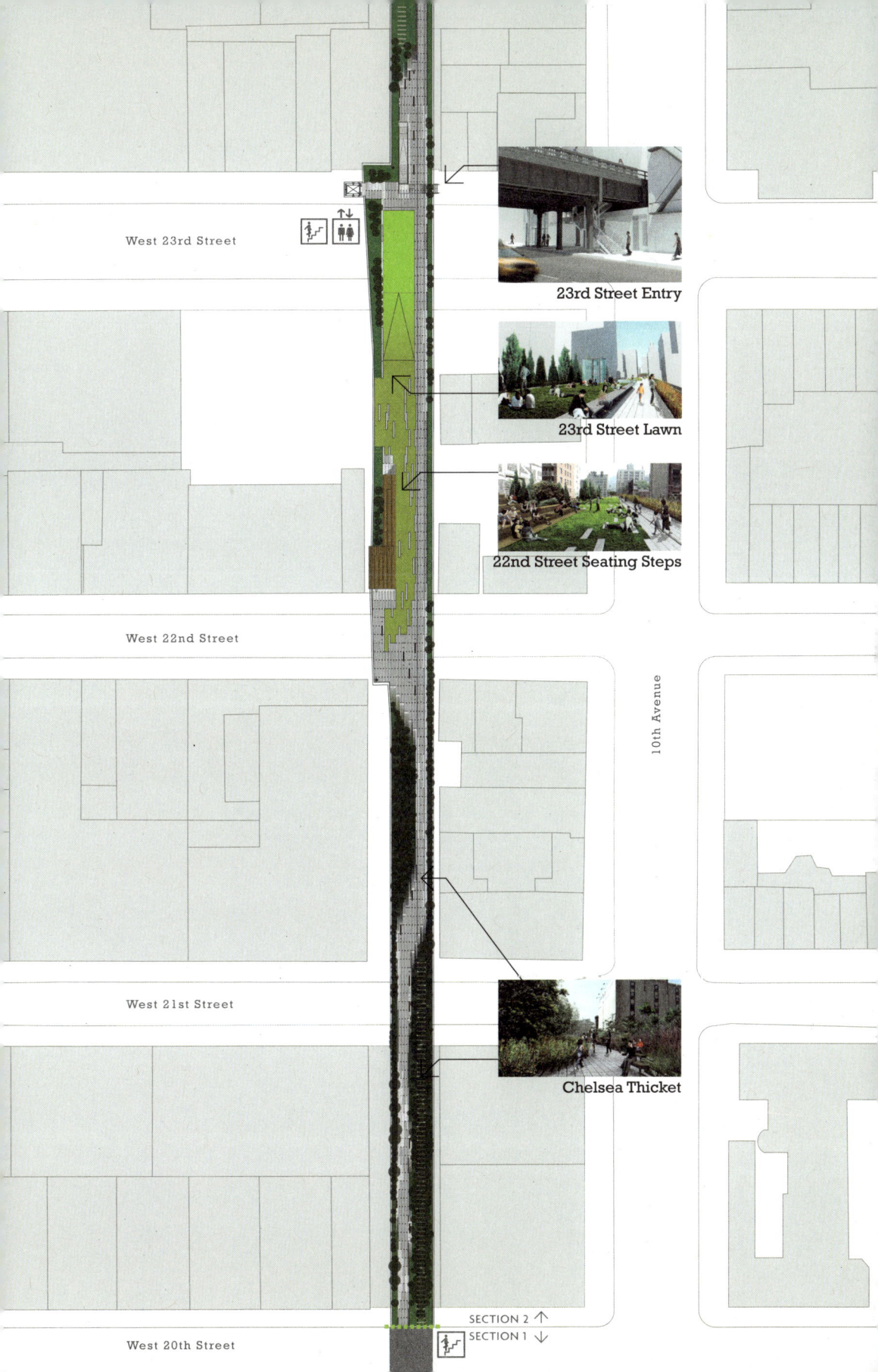

West 23rd Street

23rd Street Entry

23rd Street Lawn

22nd Street Seating Steps

West 22nd Street

10th Avenue

West 21st Street

Chelsea Thicket

West 20th Street

SECTION 2 ↑
SECTION 1 ↓

Chelsea Thicket

As the visitor moves north from the Chelsea Grasslands, the plantings grow denser. Shrubs and small trees add a variety of textures, and seasonal variation in foliage creates an ever-changing color palate.

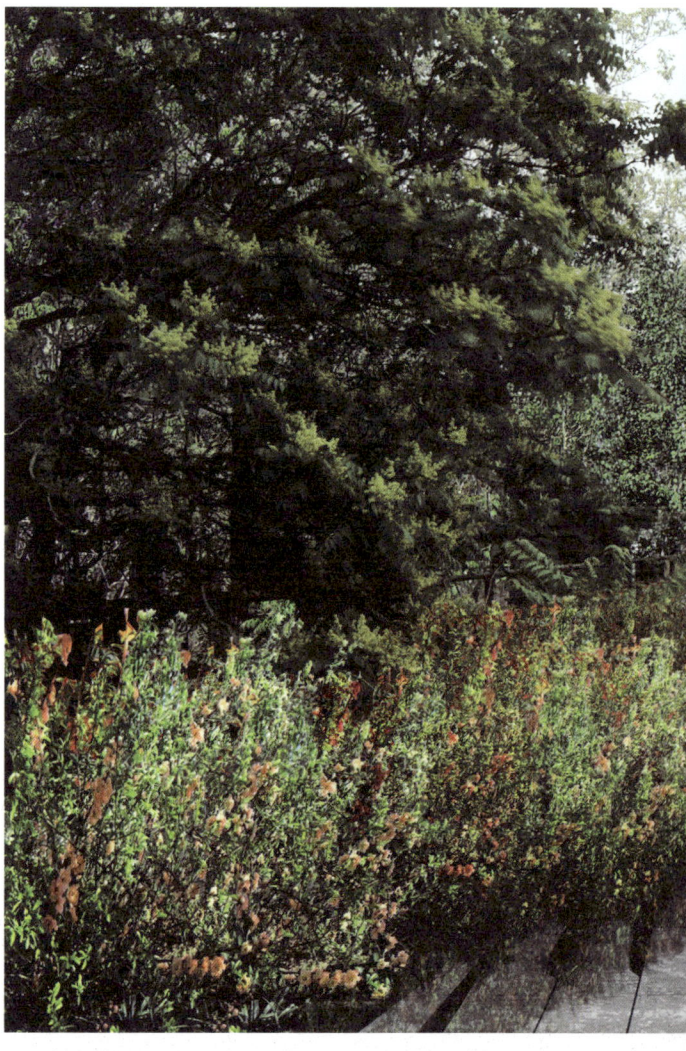

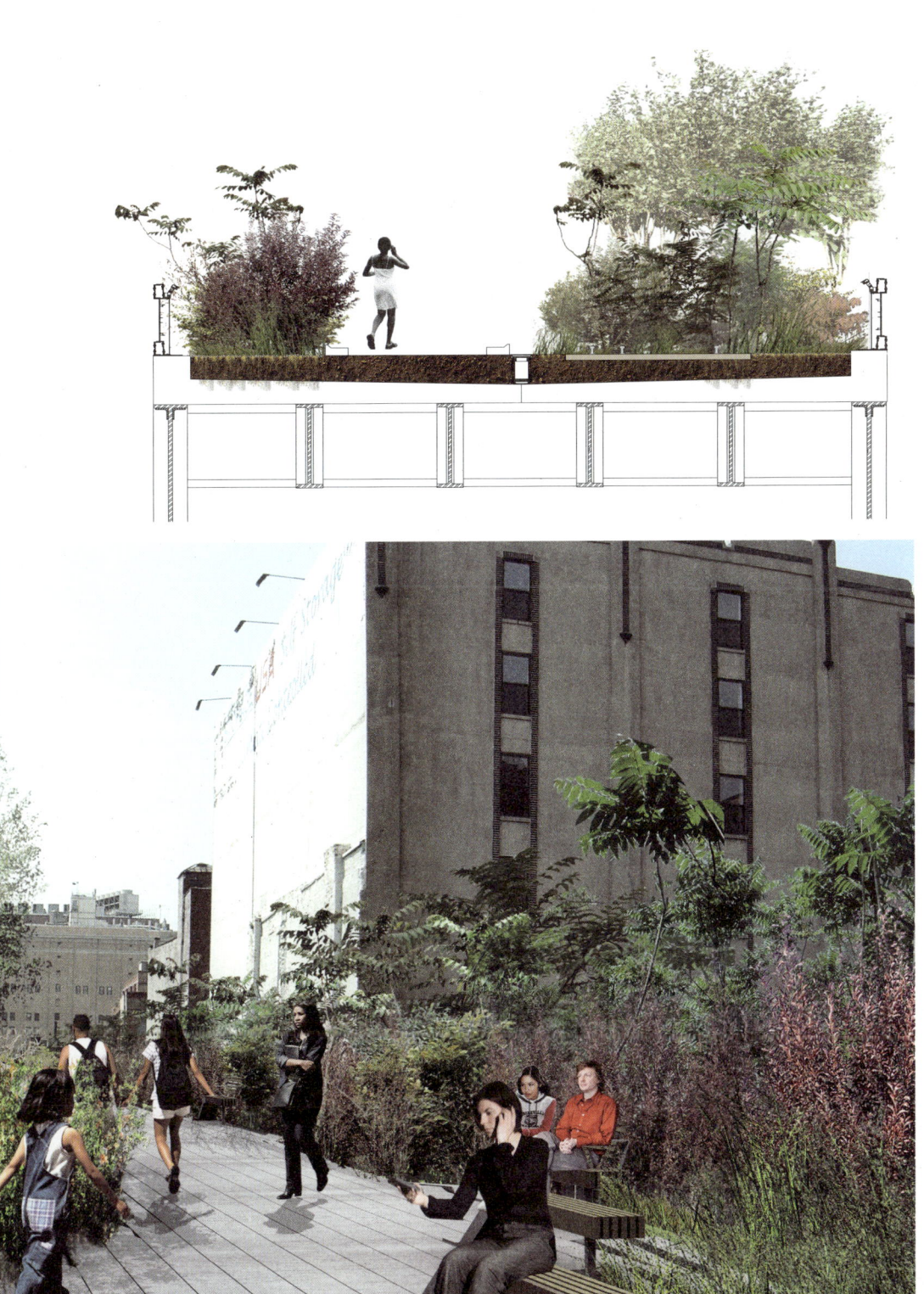

22nd Street Seating Steps / 23rd Street Lawn

The High Line opens to a wider area between 22nd and 23th Streets, where extra tracks once served a siding. The High Line's only lawn "peels up" at this location, lifting seated visitors above the walkway and offering views of the city skyline to the east, and the Hudson River to the west. A stepped seating feature adds another layer of use to this central gathering area.

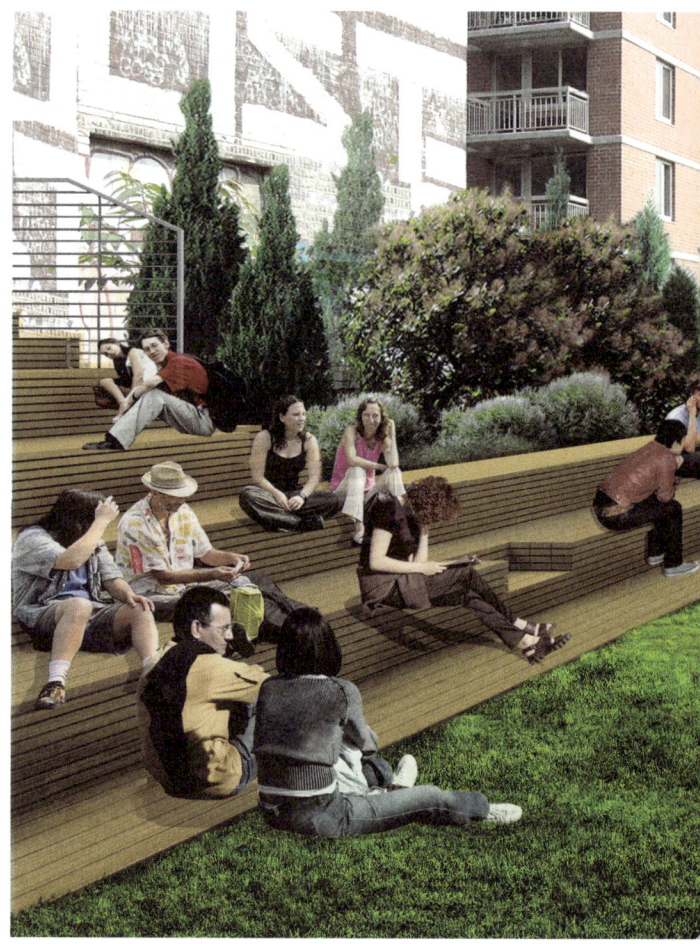

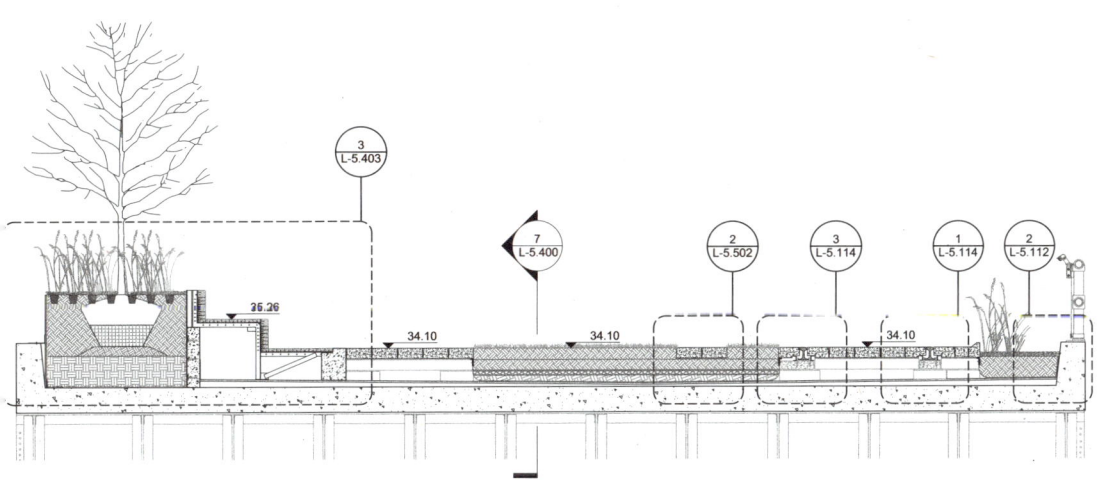

3
L-5.403

7
L-5.400

2
L-5.502

3
L-5.114

1
L-5.114

2
L-5.112

26.26

34.10

34.10

34.10

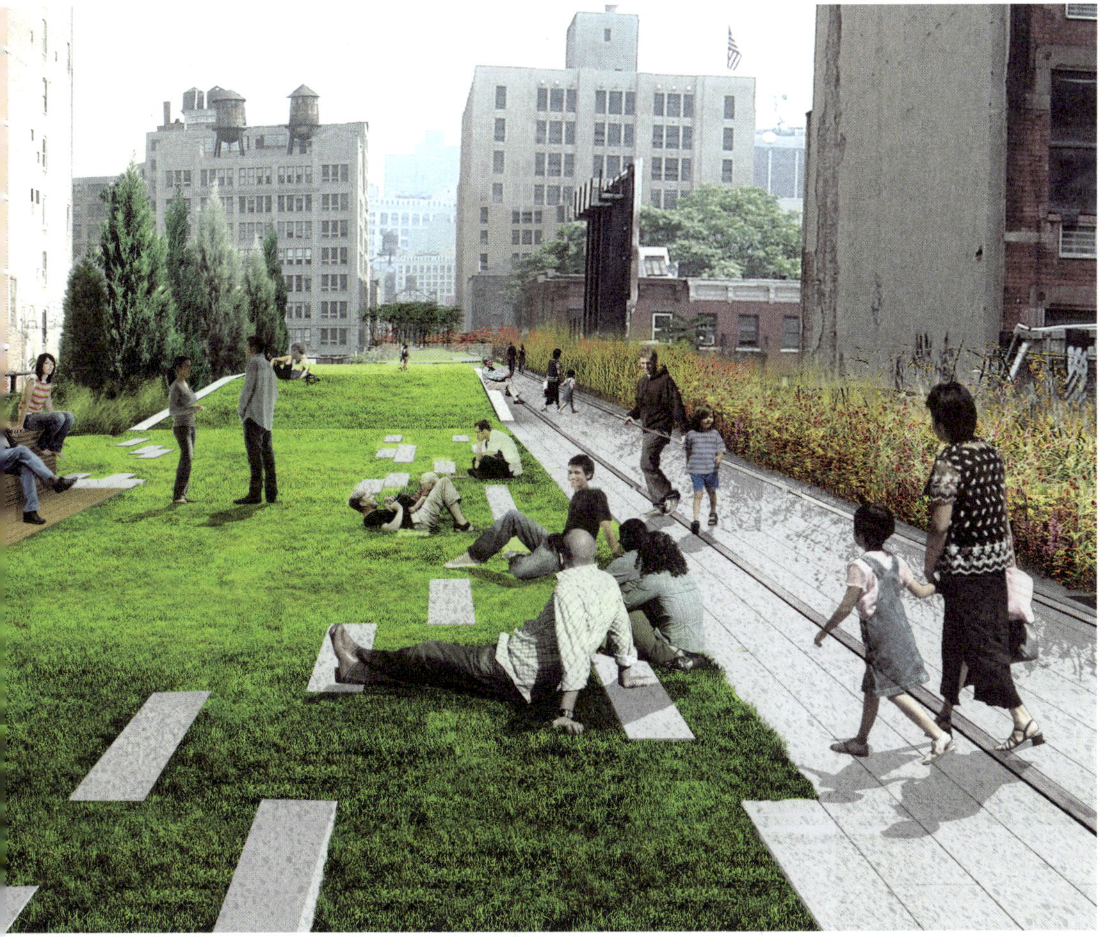

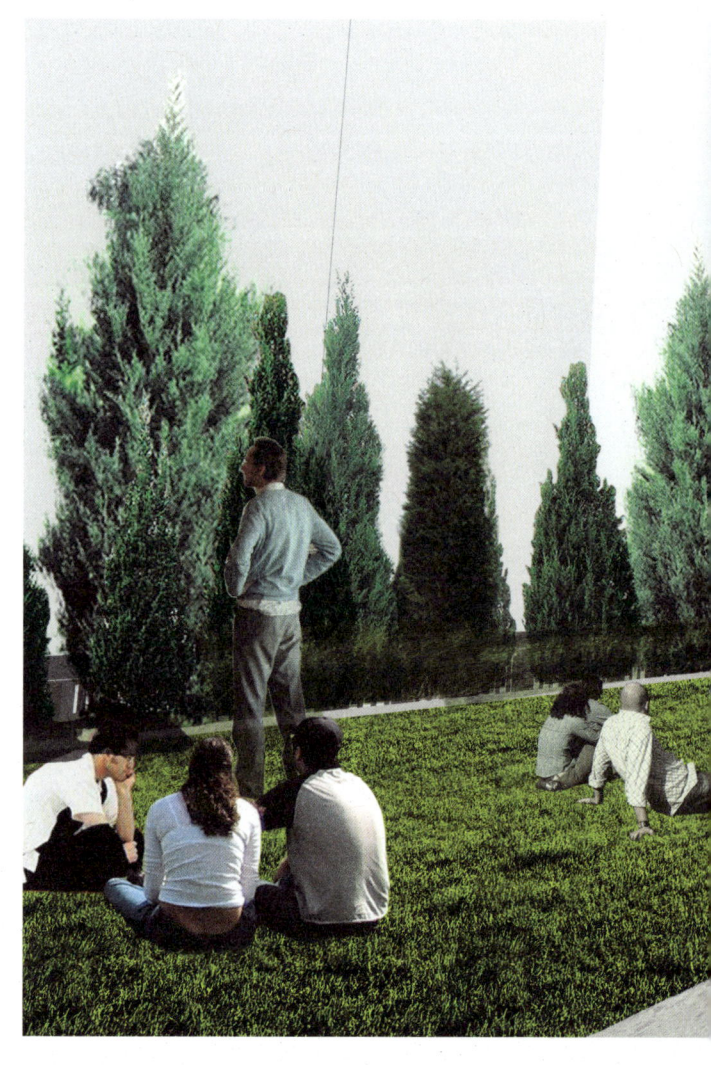

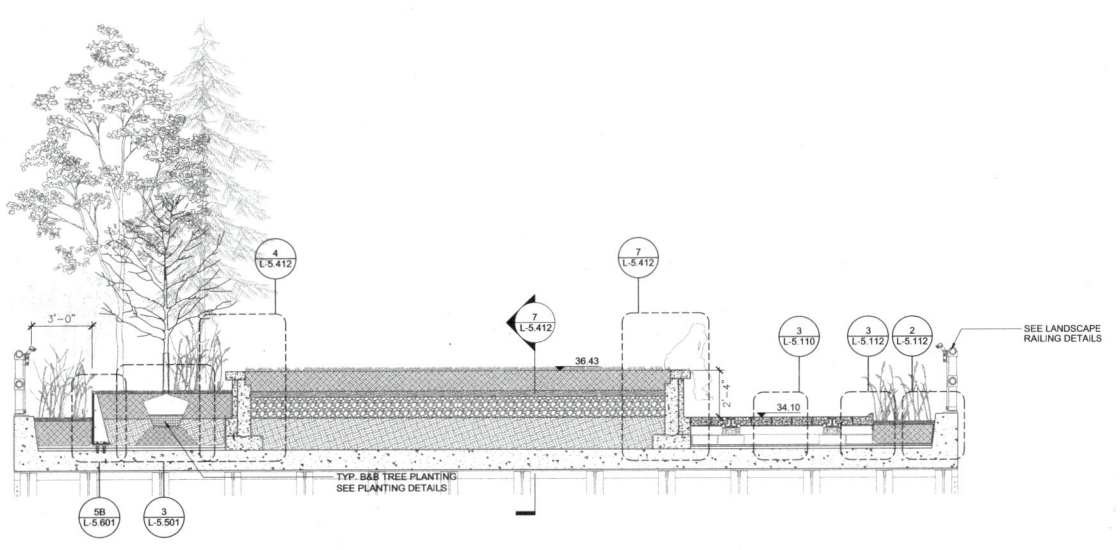

3'-0"

4
L-5.412

7
L-5.412

7
L-5.412

36.43

3
L-5.110

3
L-5.112

2
L-5.112

SEE LANDSCAPE
RAILING DETAILS

2'-4"

34.10

TYP. B&B TREE PLANTING
SEE PLANTING DETAILS

5B
L-5.601

3
L-5.501

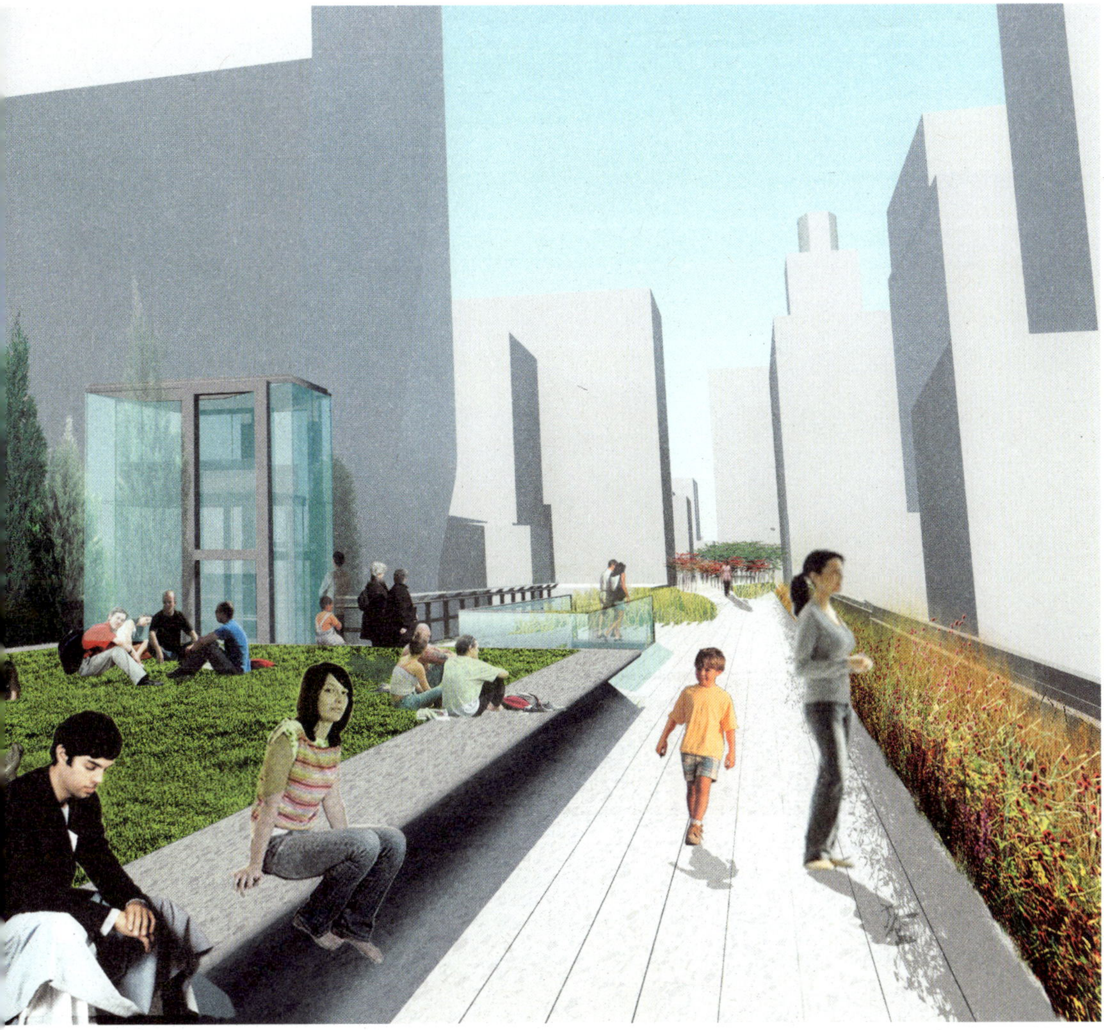

23rd Street Entry

Stairs rise up between High Line beams at 23rd Street, supplemented by a glass elevator.

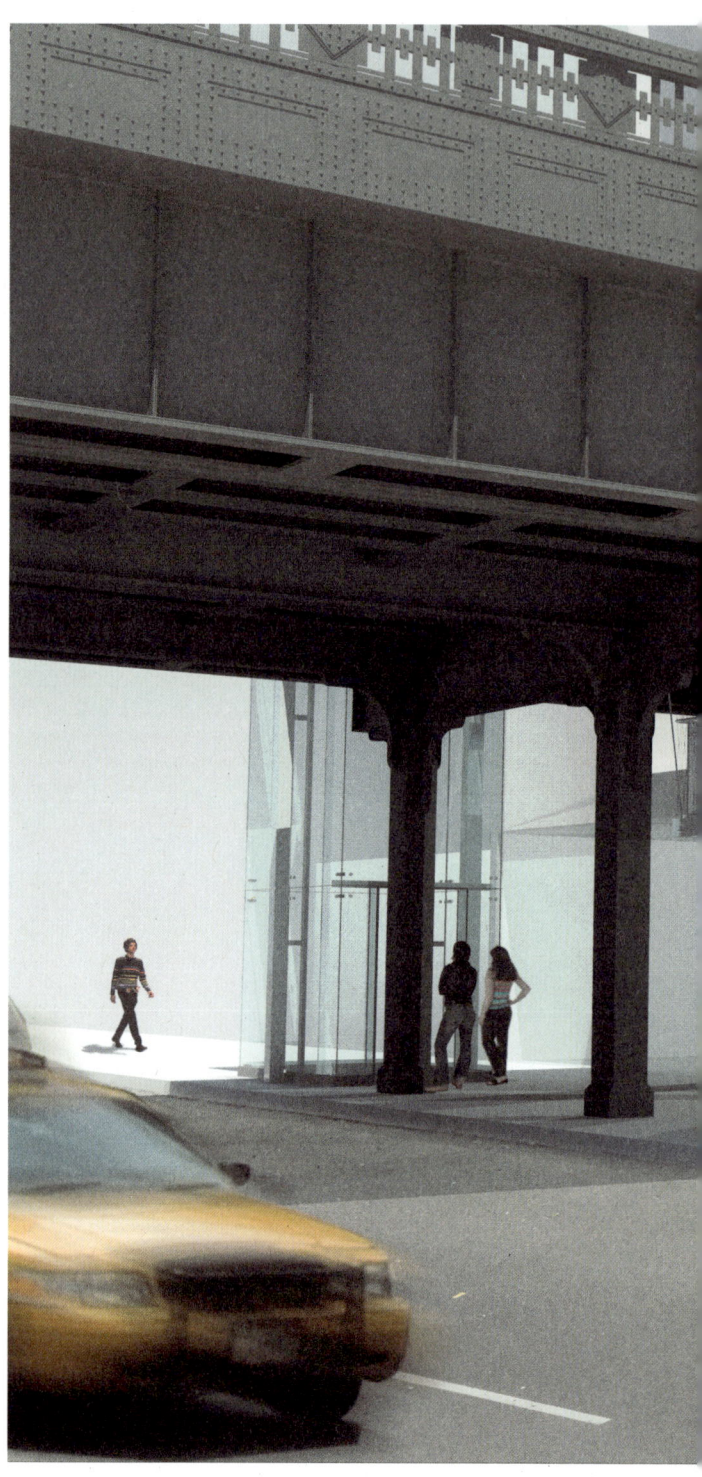

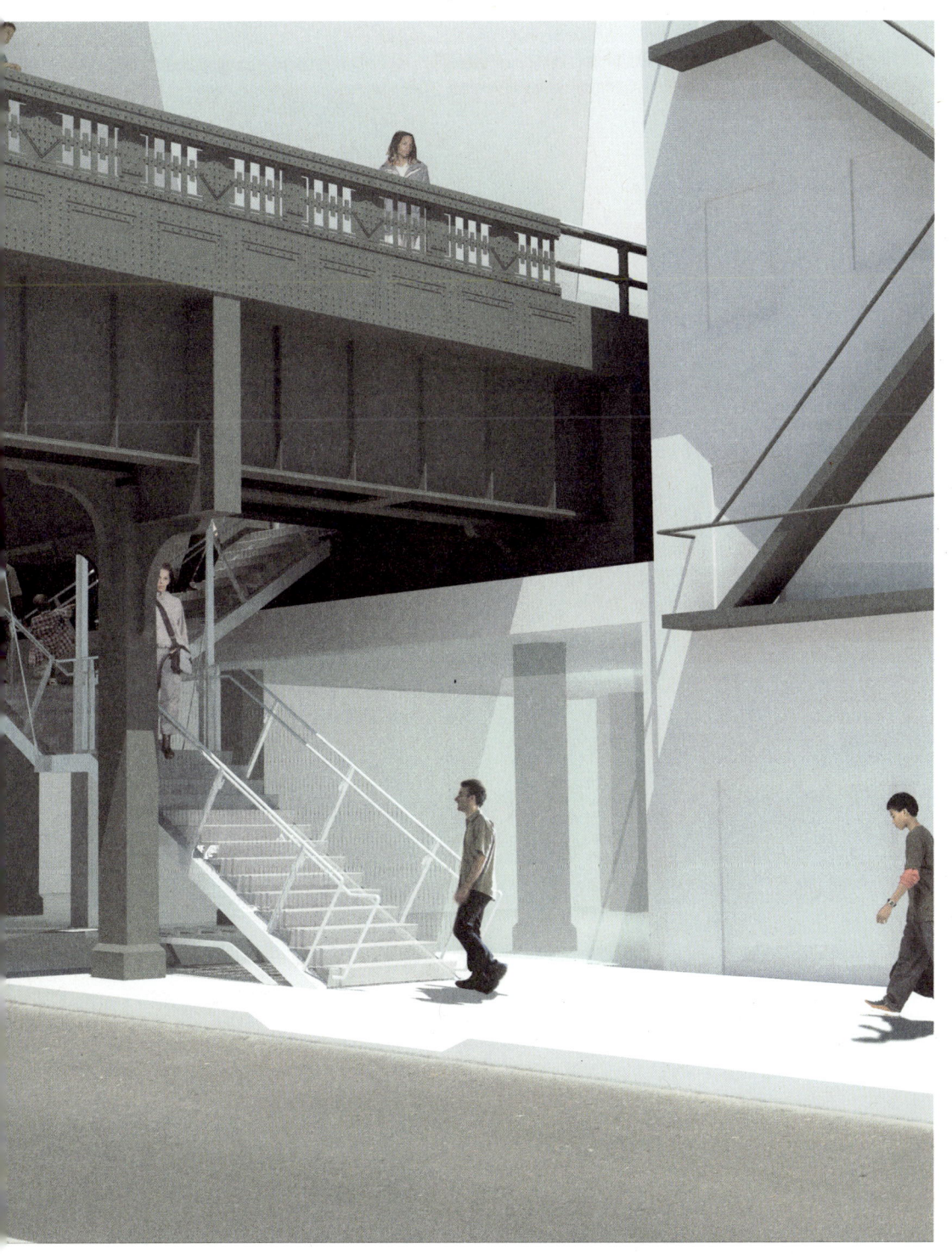

24th Street /
27th Street

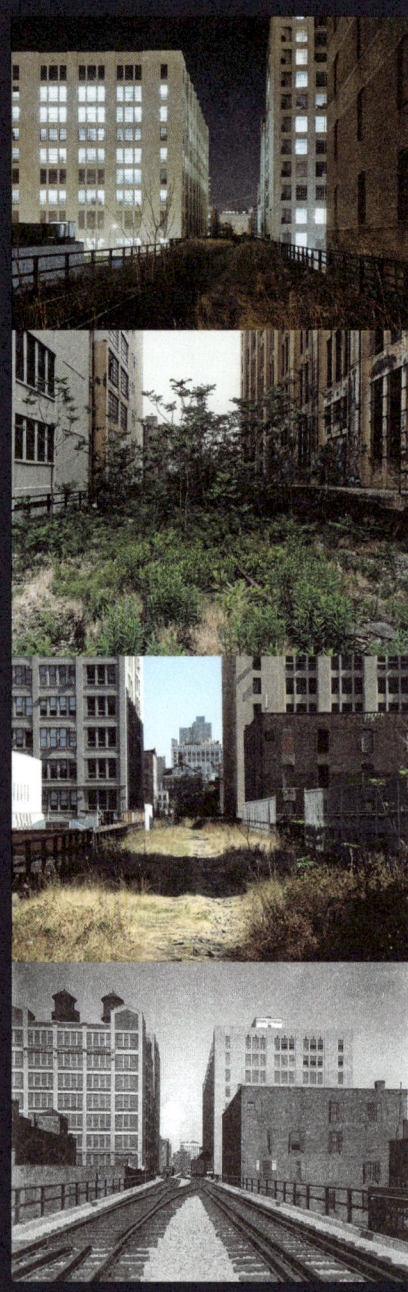

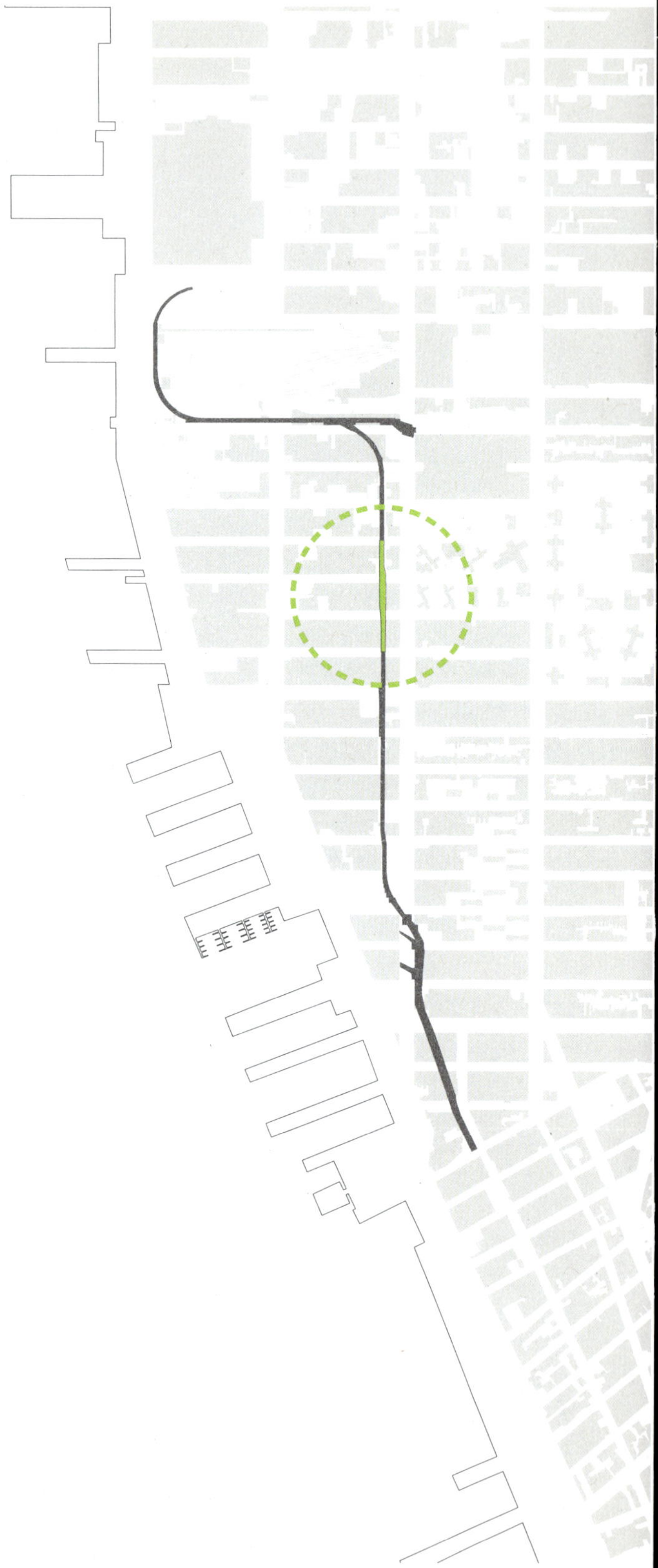

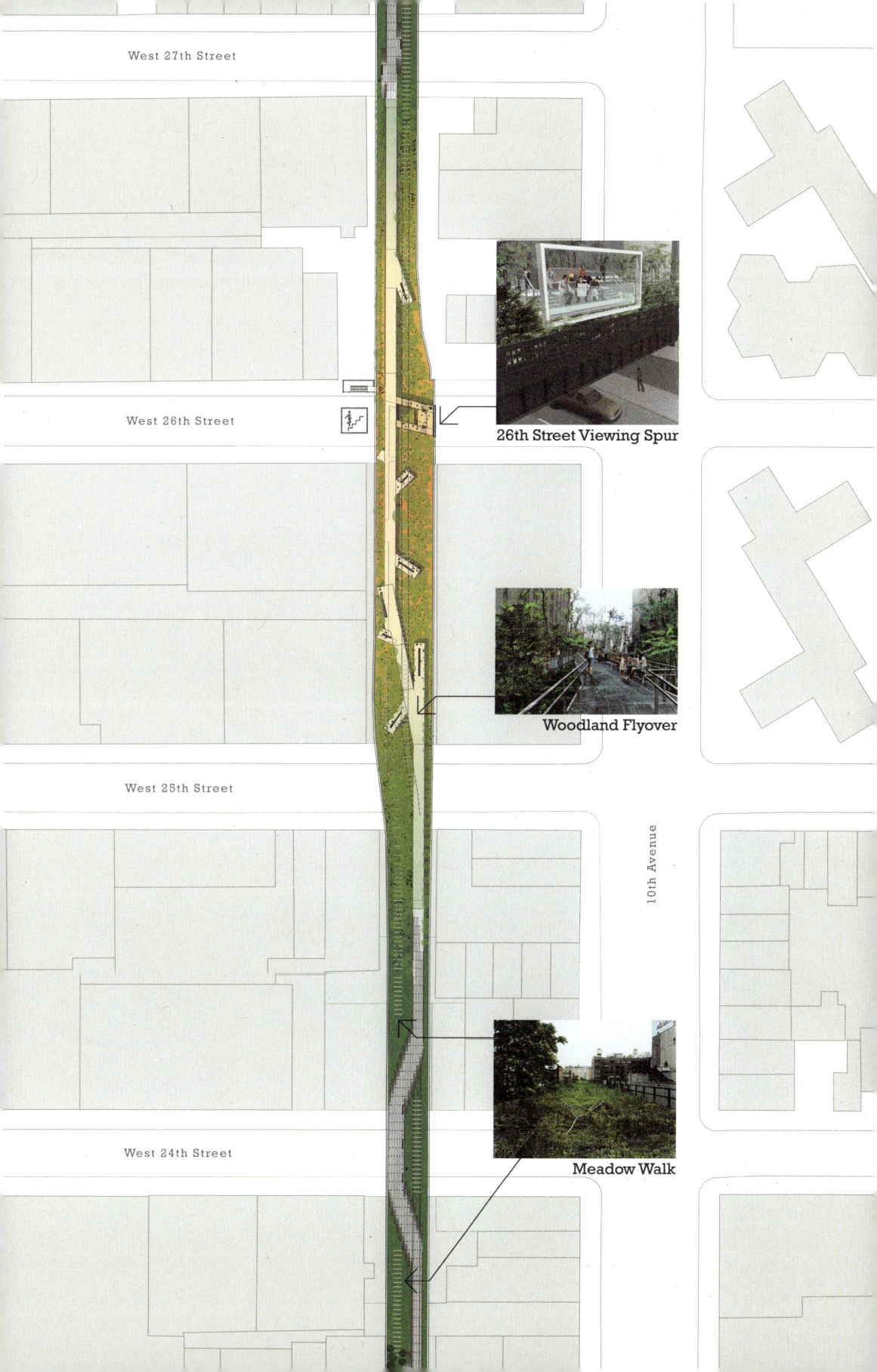

West 27th Street

West 26th Street

26th Street Viewing Spur

Woodland Flyover

West 25th Street

10th Avenue

West 24th Street

Meadow Walk

Woodland Flyover

In response to the microclimate created by adjacent buildings, which supports dense plant growth, a metal walkway lifts off from the High Line level and allows the landscape to fill in below. While an undulating terrain of moss and shade groundcover blankets the High Line bed, the Flyover carries visitors upward, into the shady canopy of a stand of sumac trees.

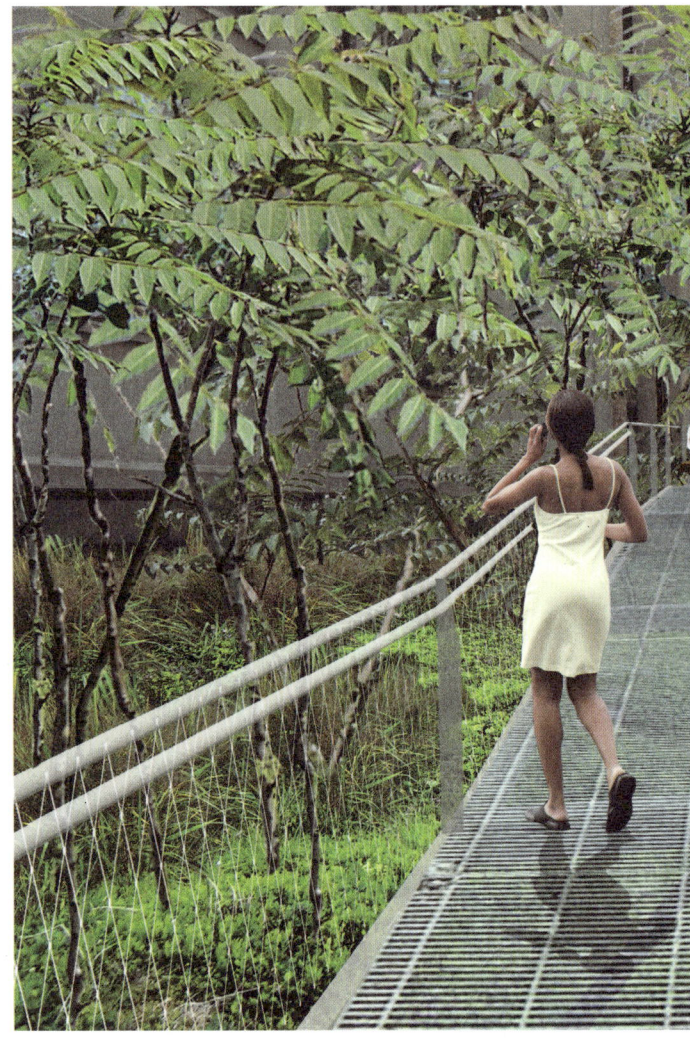

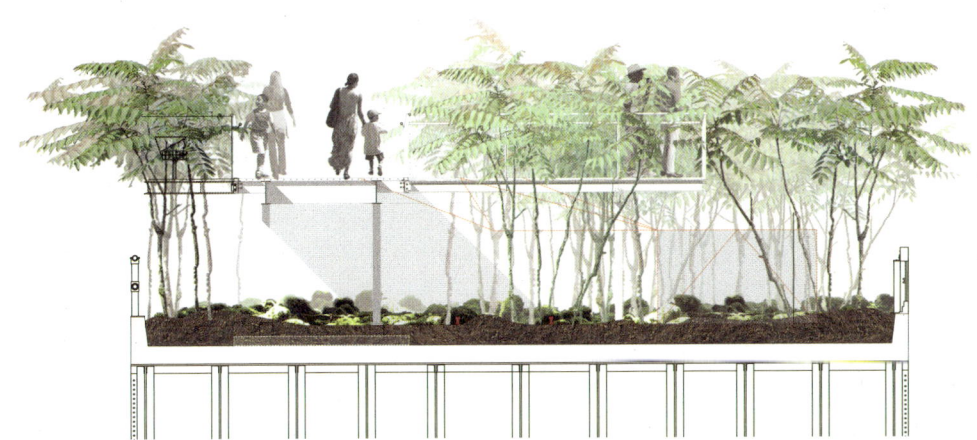

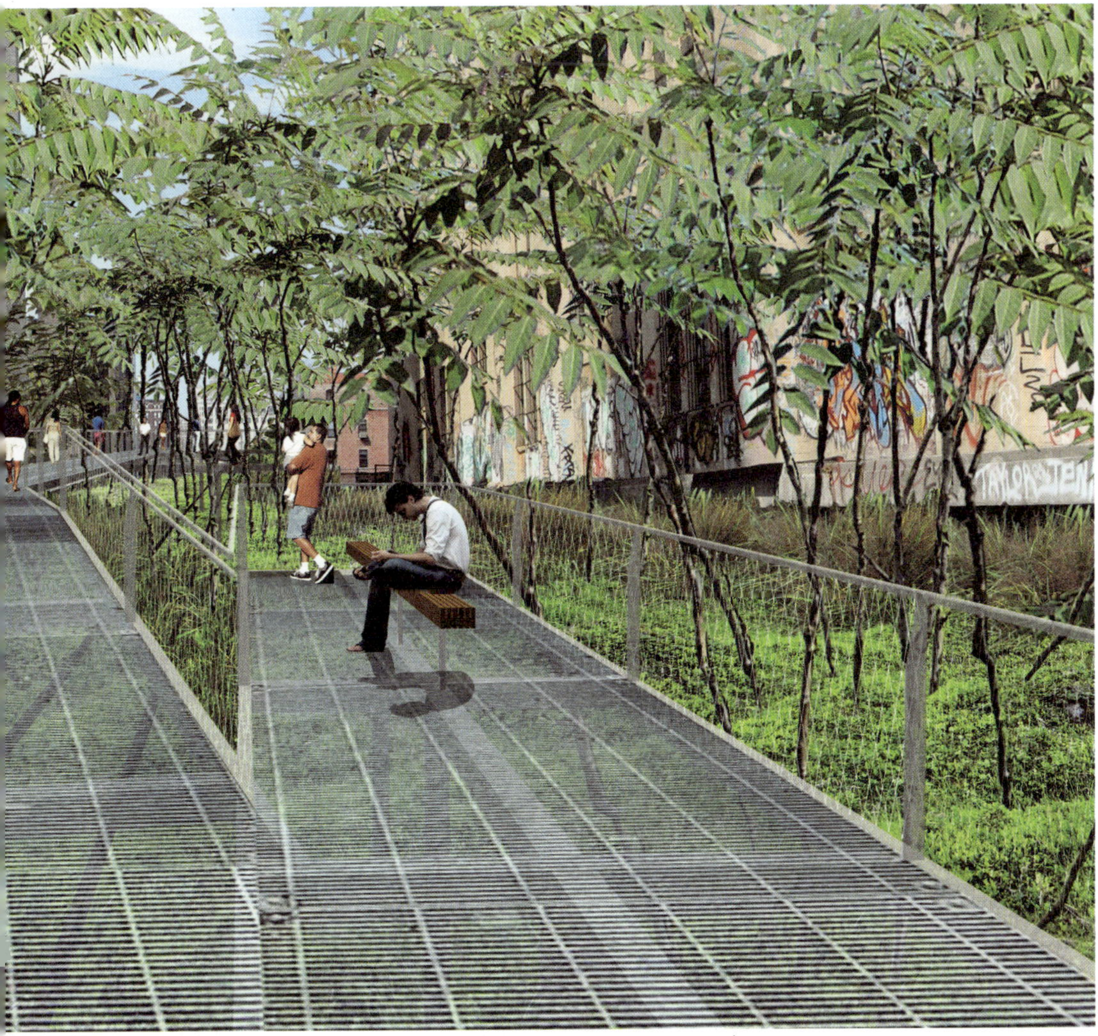

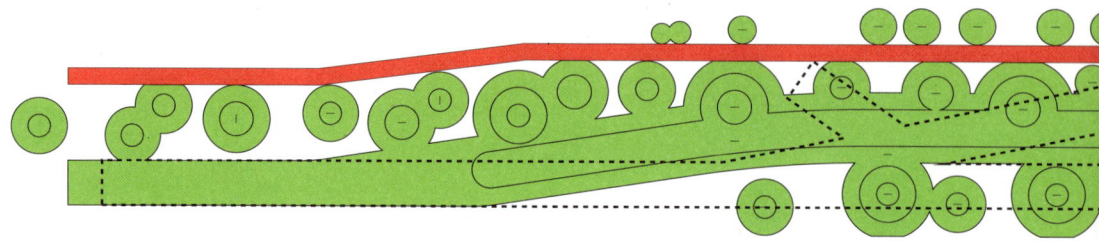

Topography / Maintenance Path

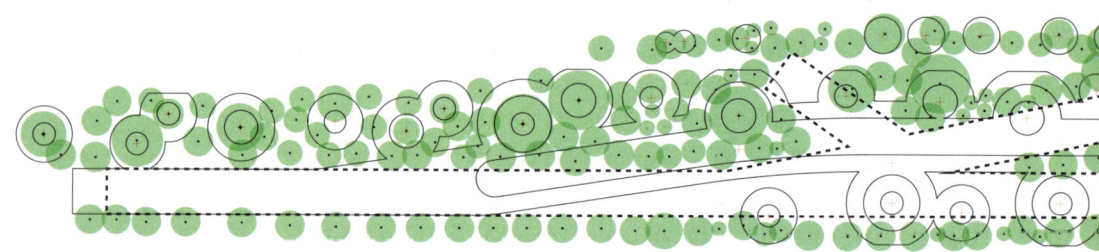

Trees and Shrubs

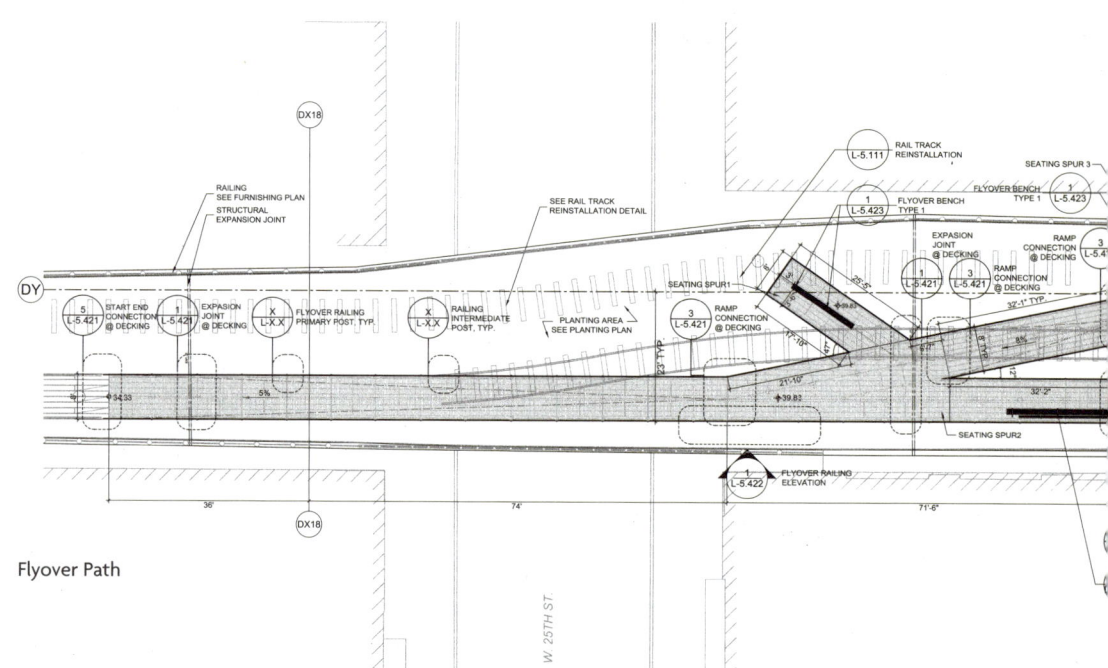

Flyover Path

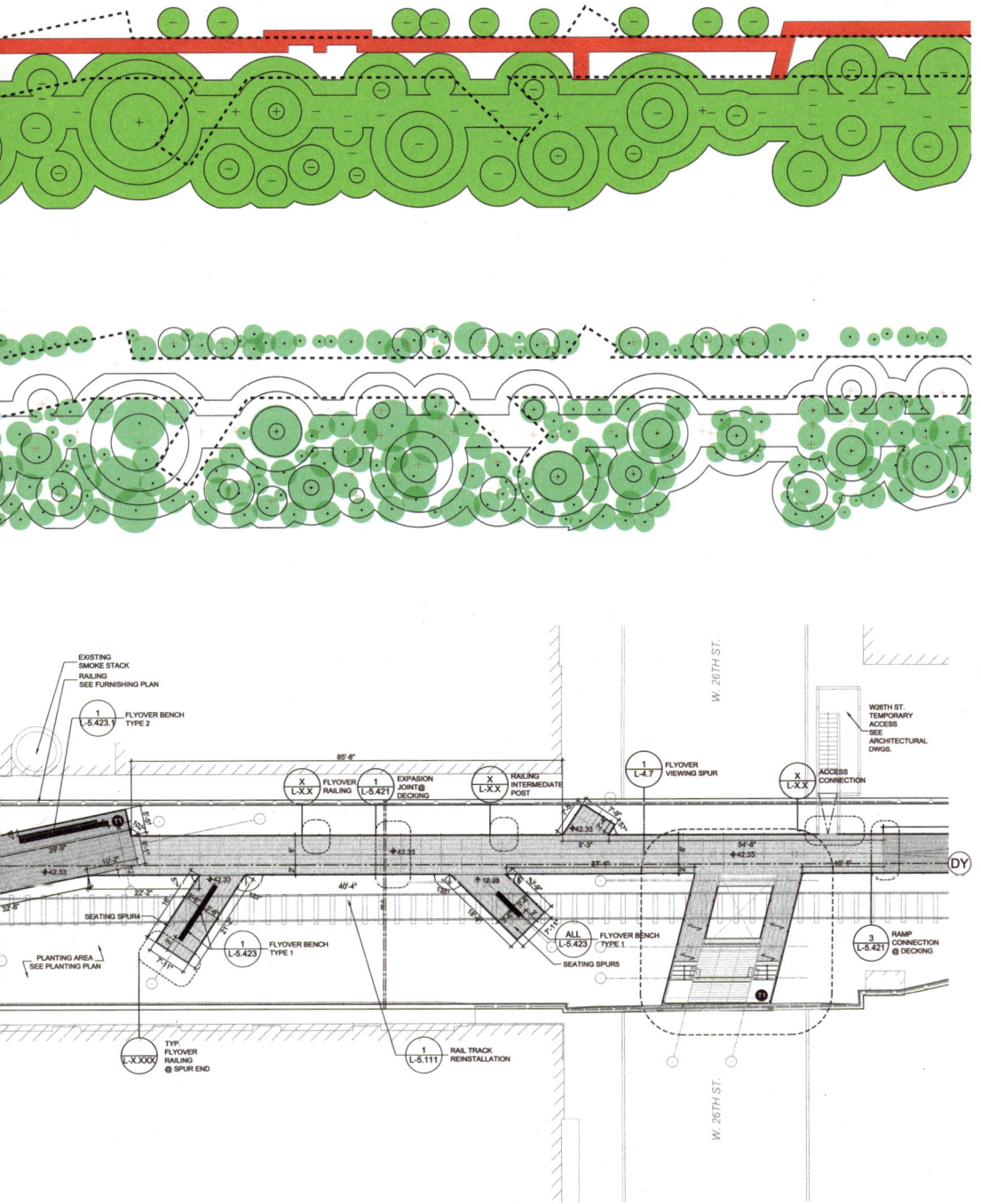

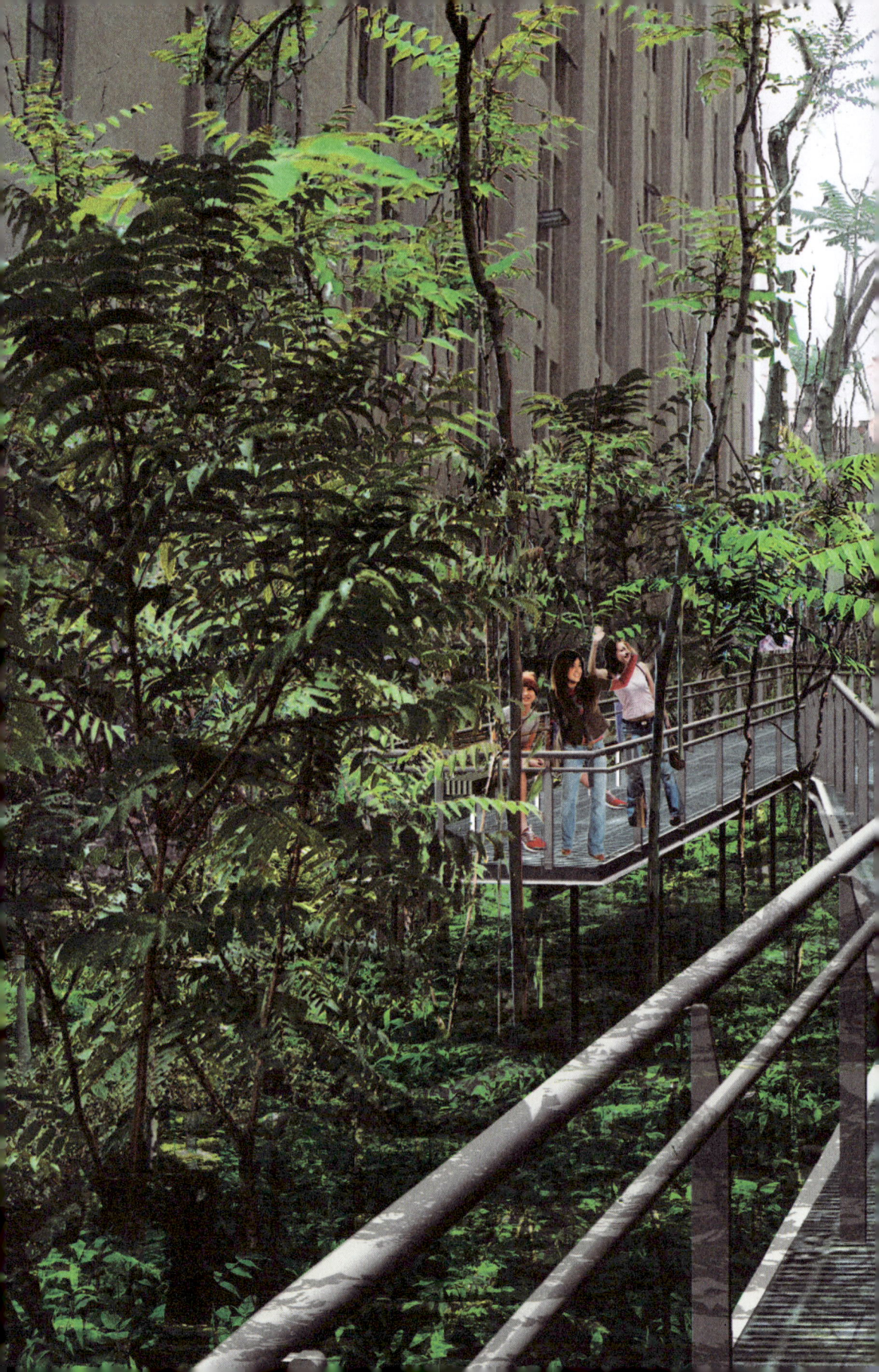

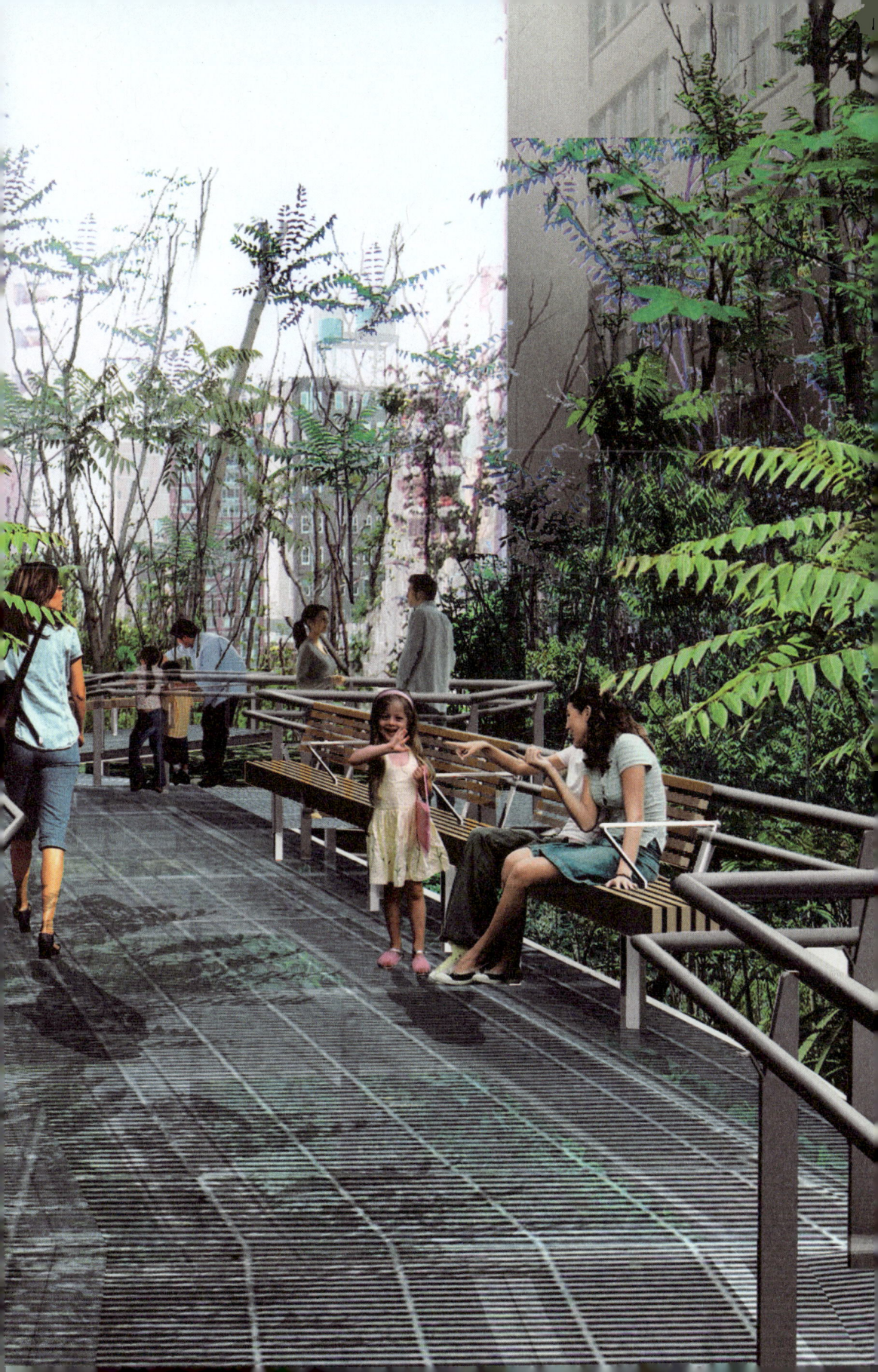

26th Street Viewing Spur

This viewing spur recalls the billboards that were once attached to the High Line. Now the frame enhances, rather than blocks, views of the city, showcasing High Line visitors instead of advertisements.

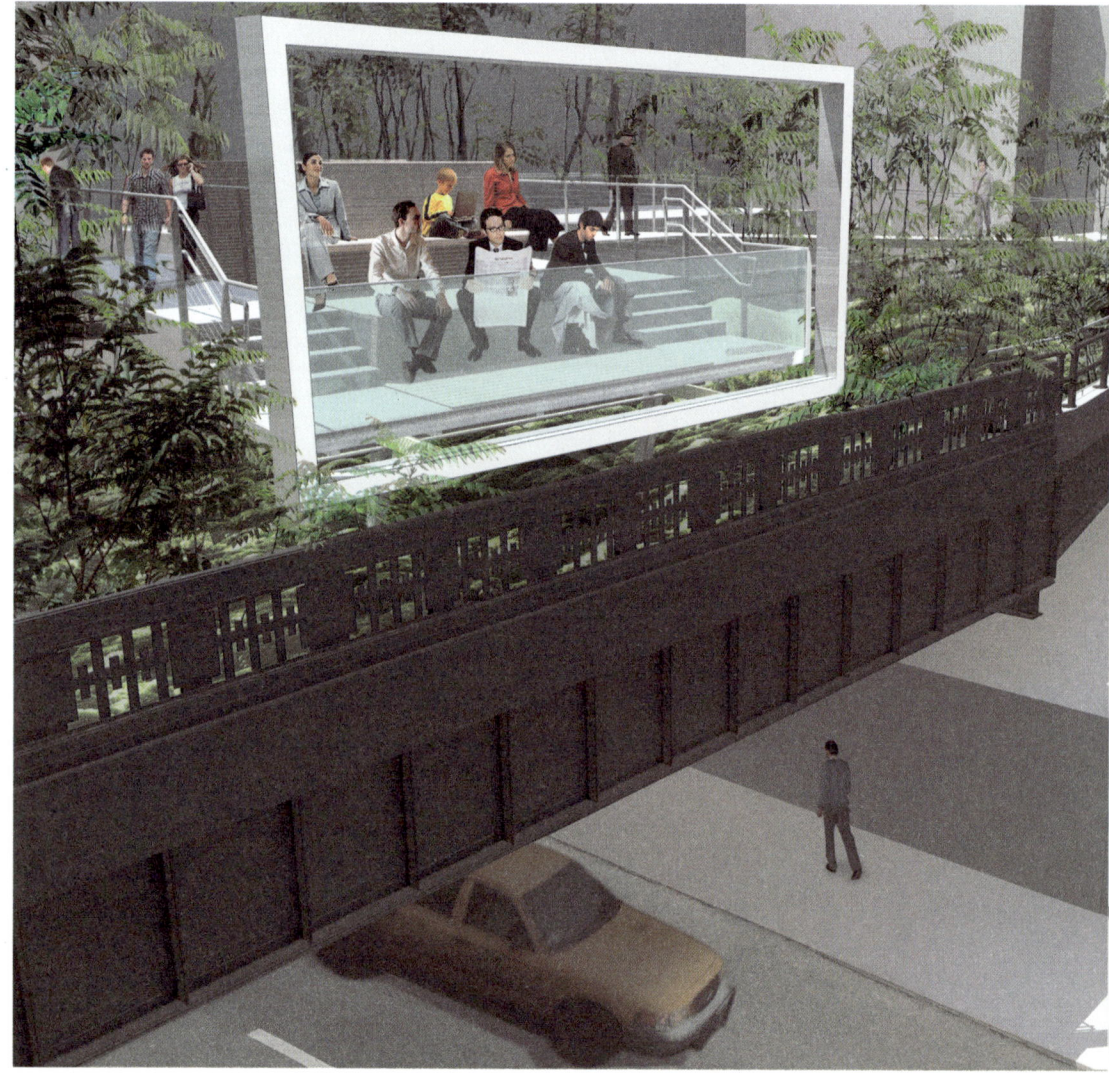

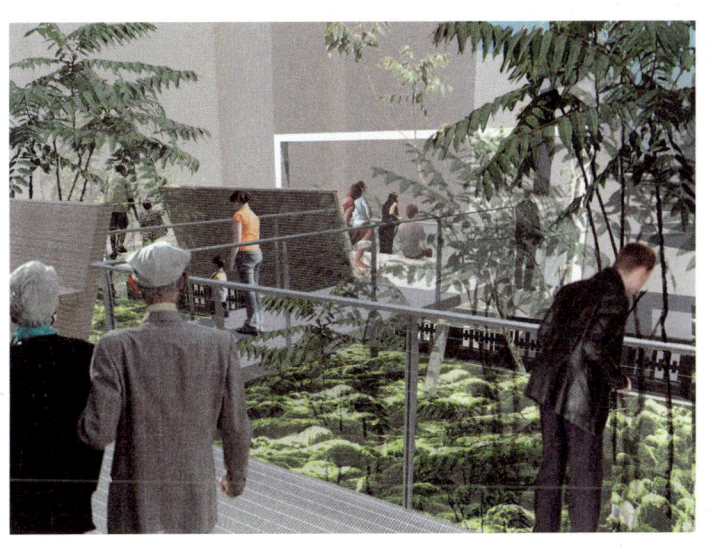

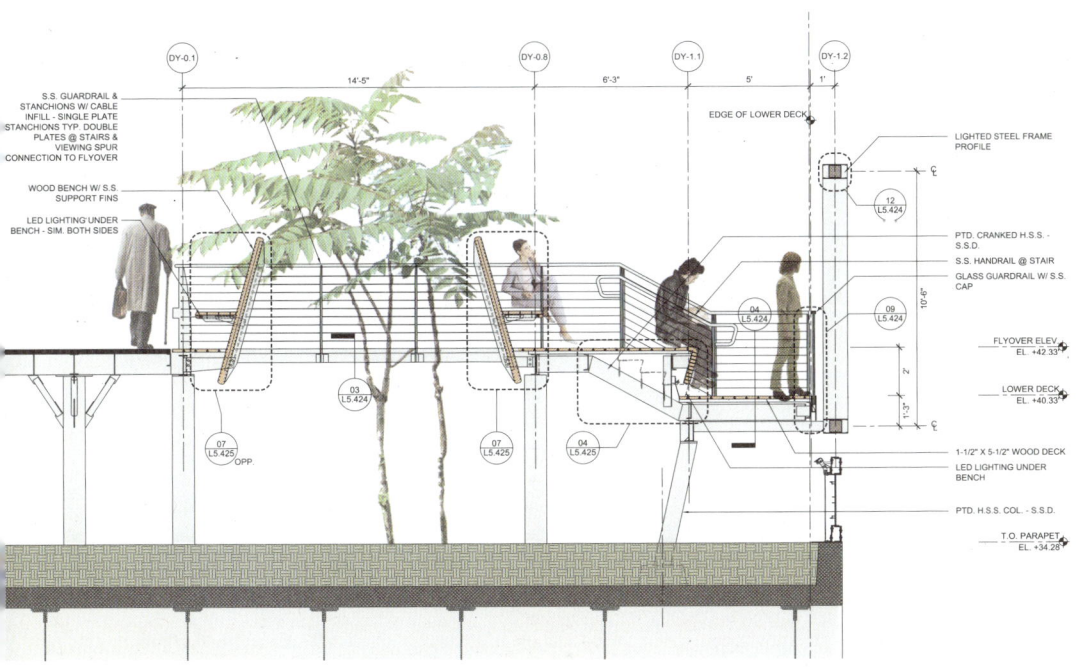

S.S. GUARDRAIL &
STANCHIONS W/ CABLE
INFILL - SINGLE PLATE
STANCHIONS TYP. DOUBLE
PLATES @ STAIRS &
VIEWING SPUR
CONNECTION TO FLYOVER

WOOD BENCH W/ S.S.
SUPPORT FINS

LED LIGHTING UNDER
BENCH - SIM. BOTH SIDES

EDGE OF LOWER DECK

LIGHTED STEEL FRAME
PROFILE

PTD. CRANKED H.S.S. -
S.S.D.

S.S. HANDRAIL @ STAIR

GLASS GUARDRAIL W/ S.S.
CAP

FLYOVER ELEV
EL. +42.33'

LOWER DECK
EL. +40.33'

1-1/2" X 5-1/2" WOOD DECK

LED LIGHTING UNDER
BENCH

PTD. H.S.S. COL. - S.S.D.

T.O. PARAPET
EL. +34.28'

14'-5"   6'-3"   5'   1'

DY-0.1   DY-0.8   DY-1.1   DY-1.2

03
L5.424

07
L5.425
OPP.

07
L5.425

04
L5.425

04
L5.424

09
L5.424

12
L5.424

27th Street /
30th Street

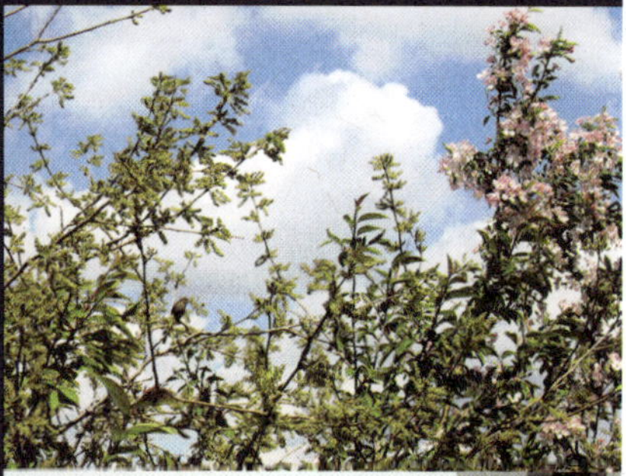

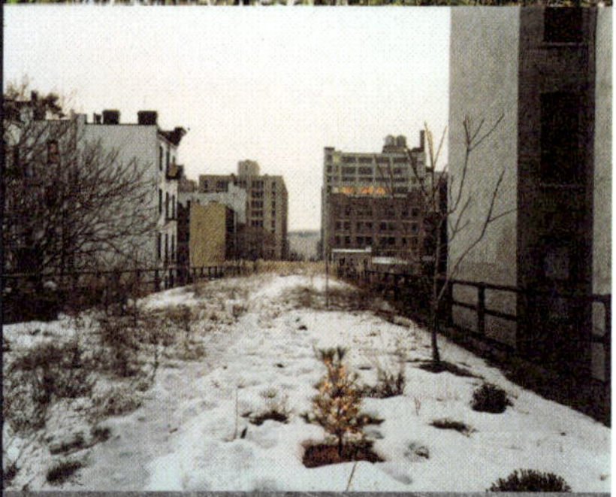

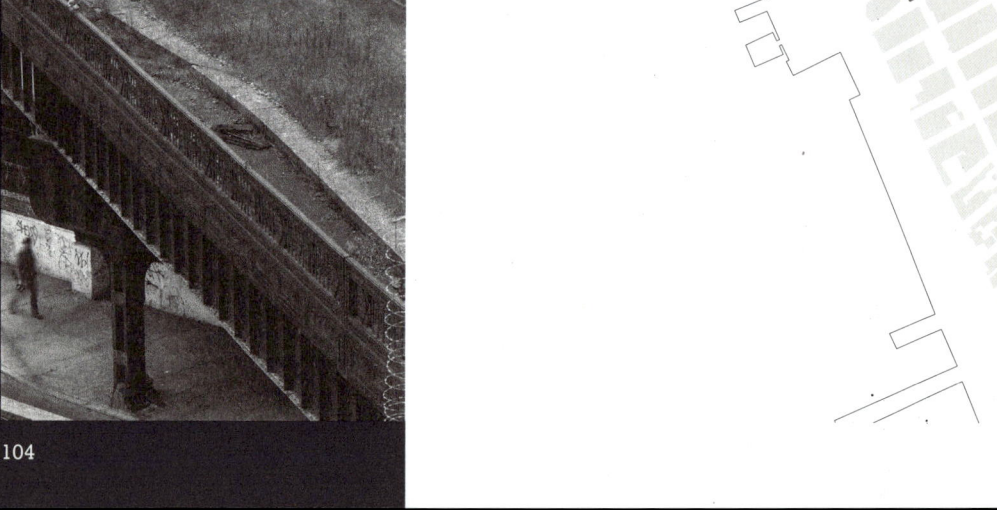

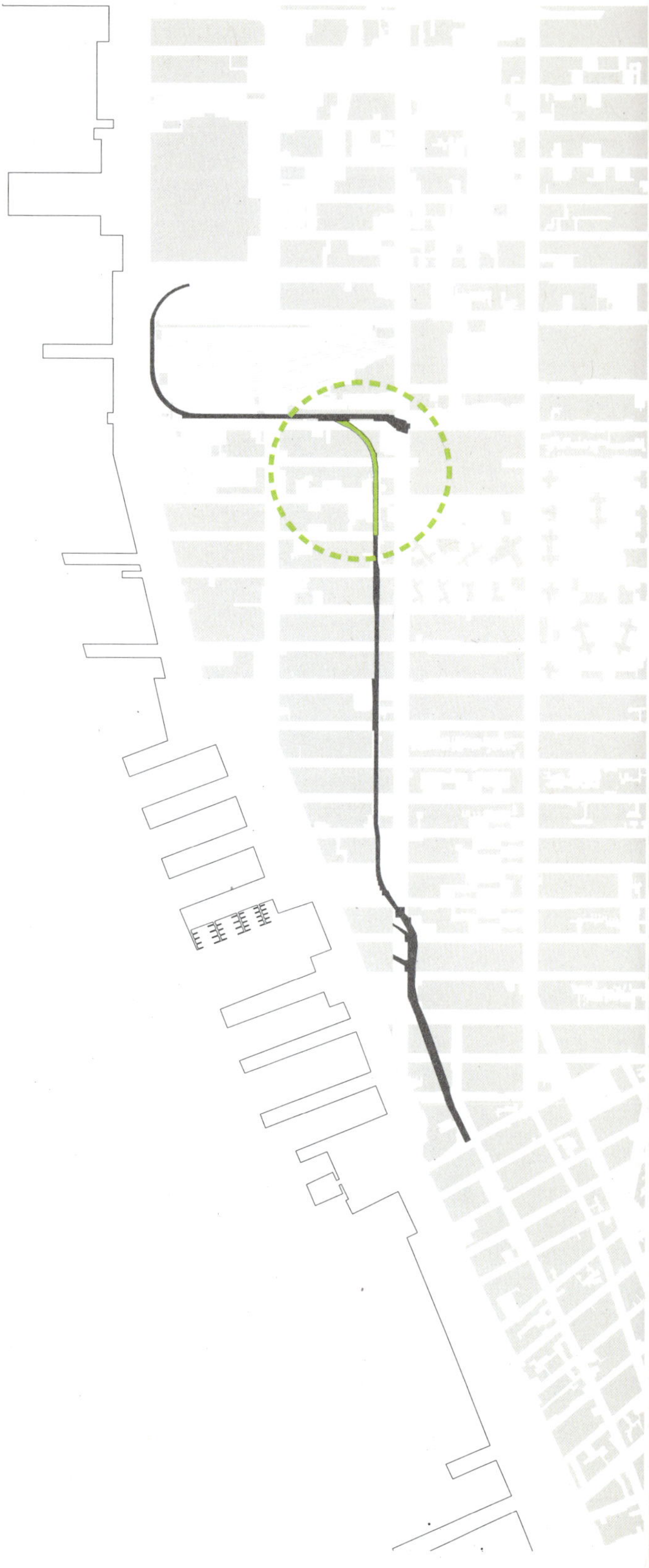

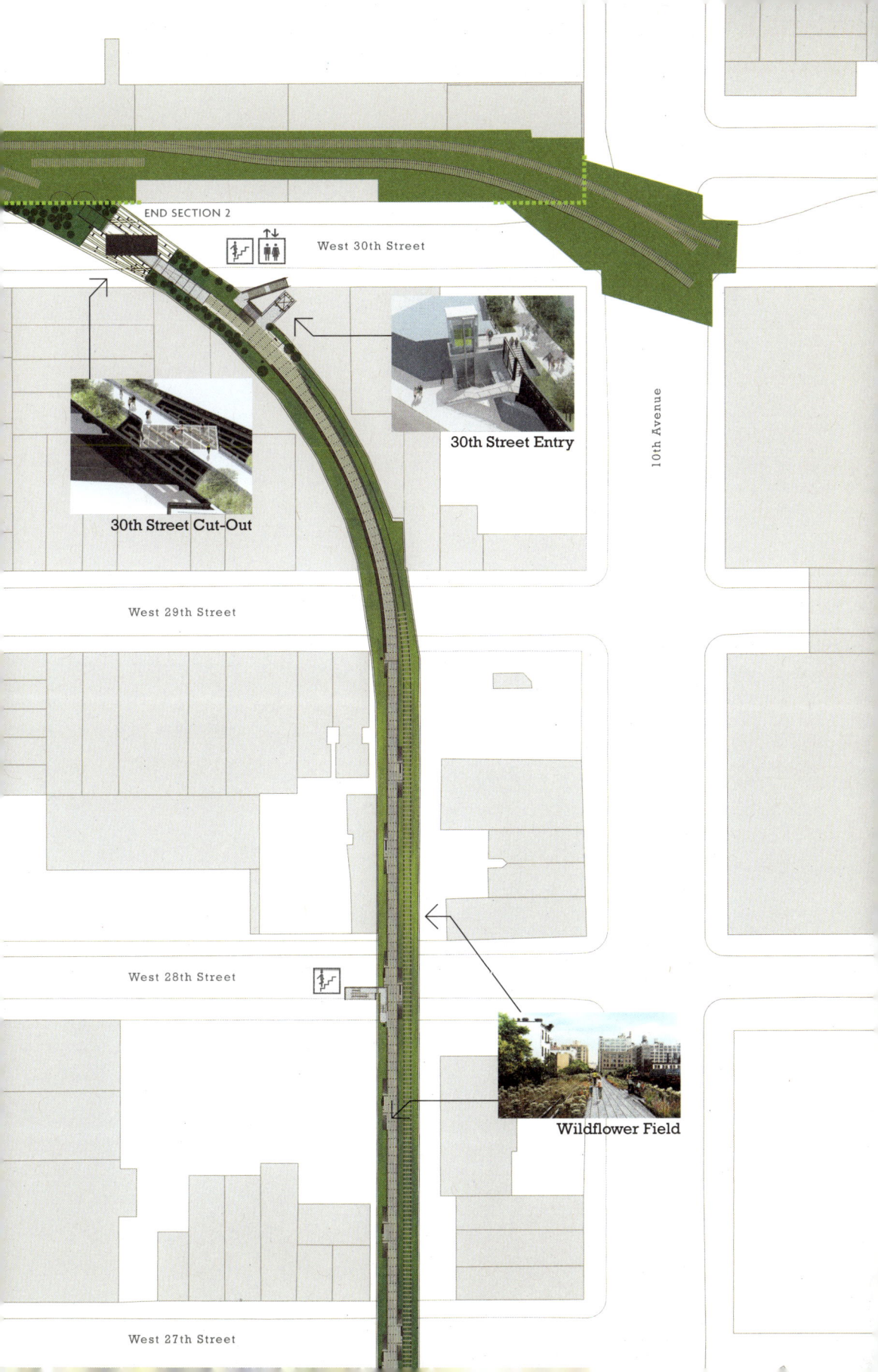

END SECTION 2

West 30th Street

30th Street Entry

30th Street Cut-Out

10th Avenue

West 29th Street

West 28th Street

Wildflower Field

West 27th Street

Wildflower Field

The simplicity of a straight walkway, running alongside the railroad tracks, allows the visitor to fully appreciate the green axis of the High Line as it moves through West Chelsea. The new planting design features a landscape of native species that once grew spontaneously on the High Line, interspersed with new species that ensure bloom throughout the growing seasons.

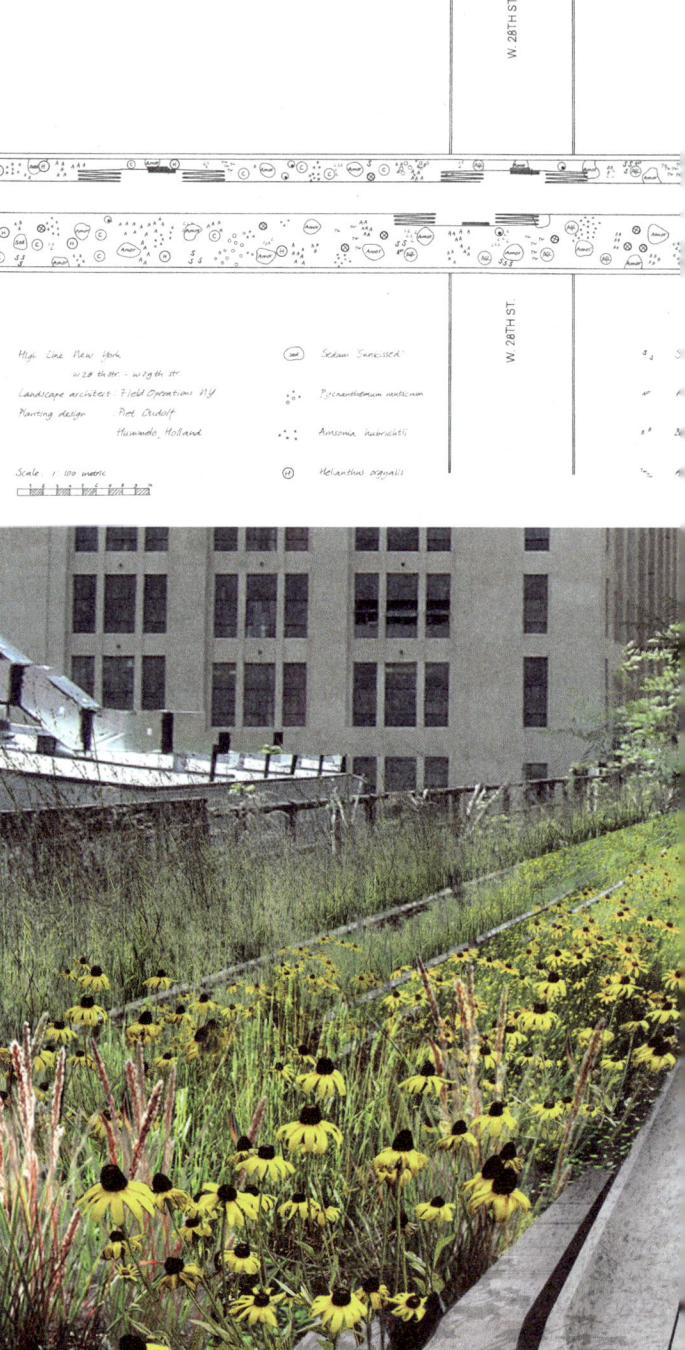

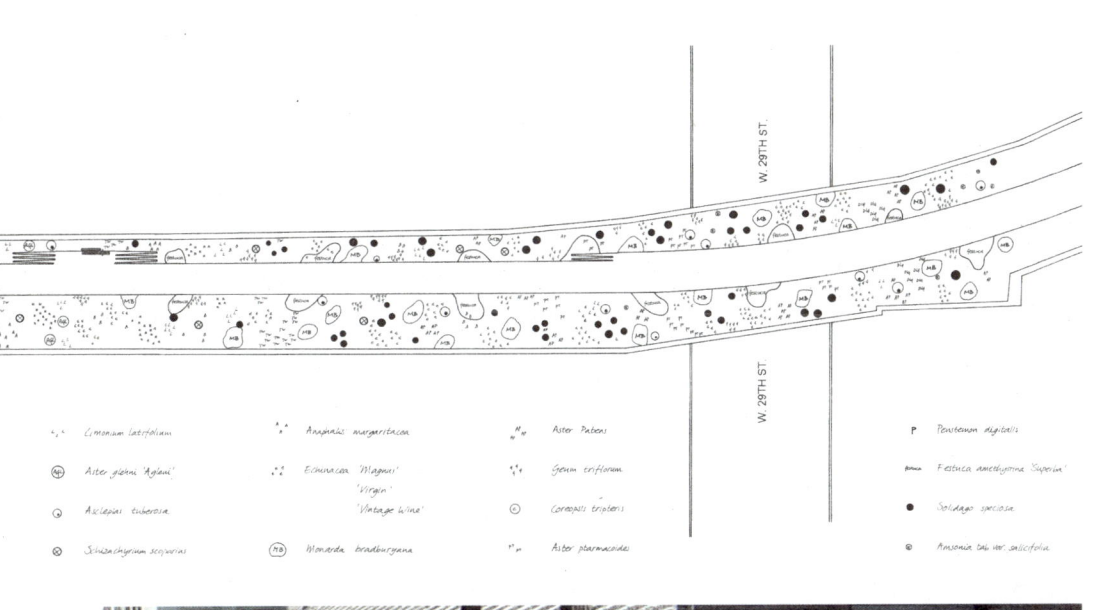

Cimonium latifolium	Anaphalis margaritacea	Aster Patens	P Penstemon digitalis
Aster gilassi 'Aglani'	Echinacea 'Magnus' 'Virgin' 'Vintage Wine'	Geum triflorum	Festuca amethystma 'Superba'
Asclepias tuberosa		Coreopsis tripteris	Solidago speciosa
Schizachyrium scoparius	Monarda bradburyana	Aster pharmacoides	Amsonia tab. var. salicifolia

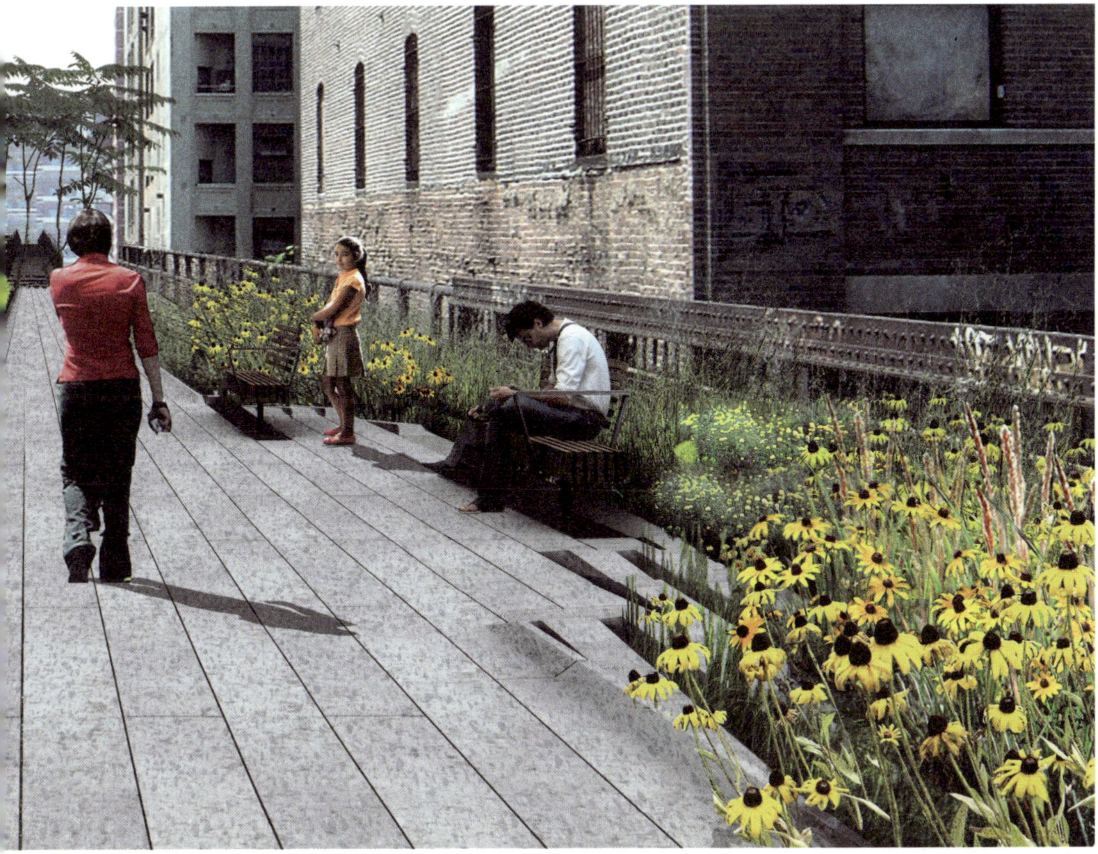

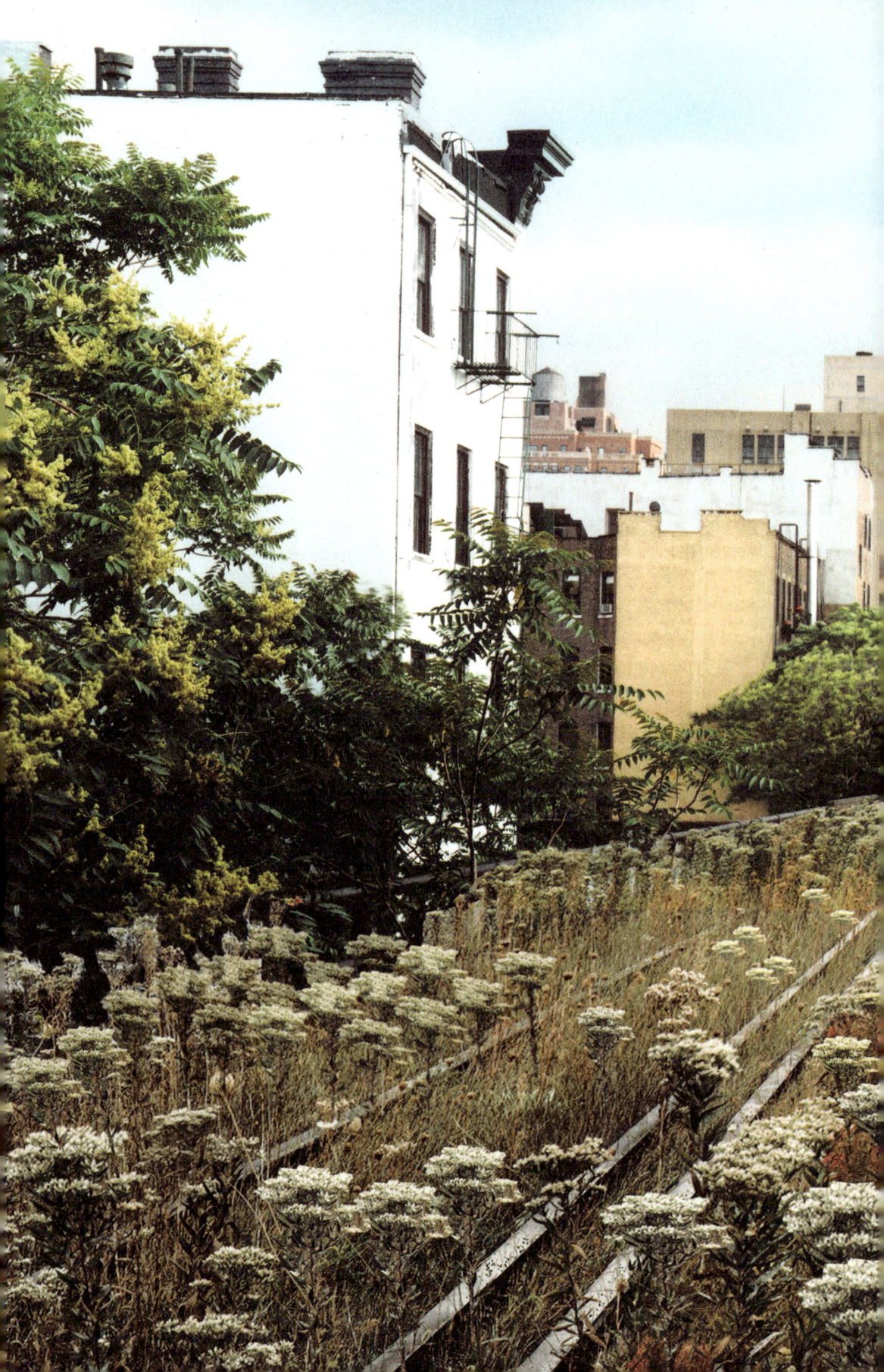

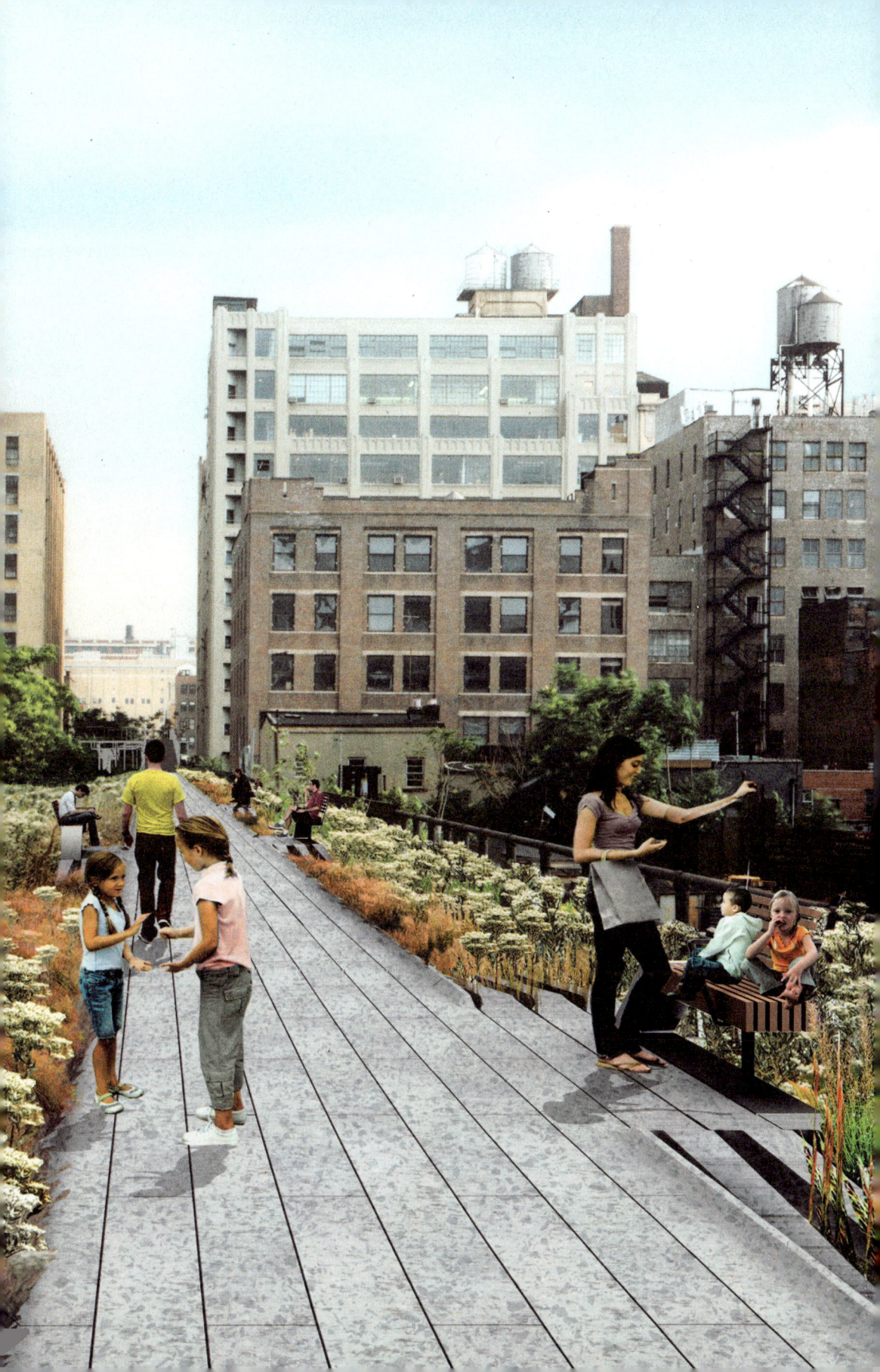

30th Street Entry

The High Line's curve, between 29th and 30th Streets, creates a unique opportunity for an access point, with the stair intersecting the edge of the High Line structure, and rising up through it.

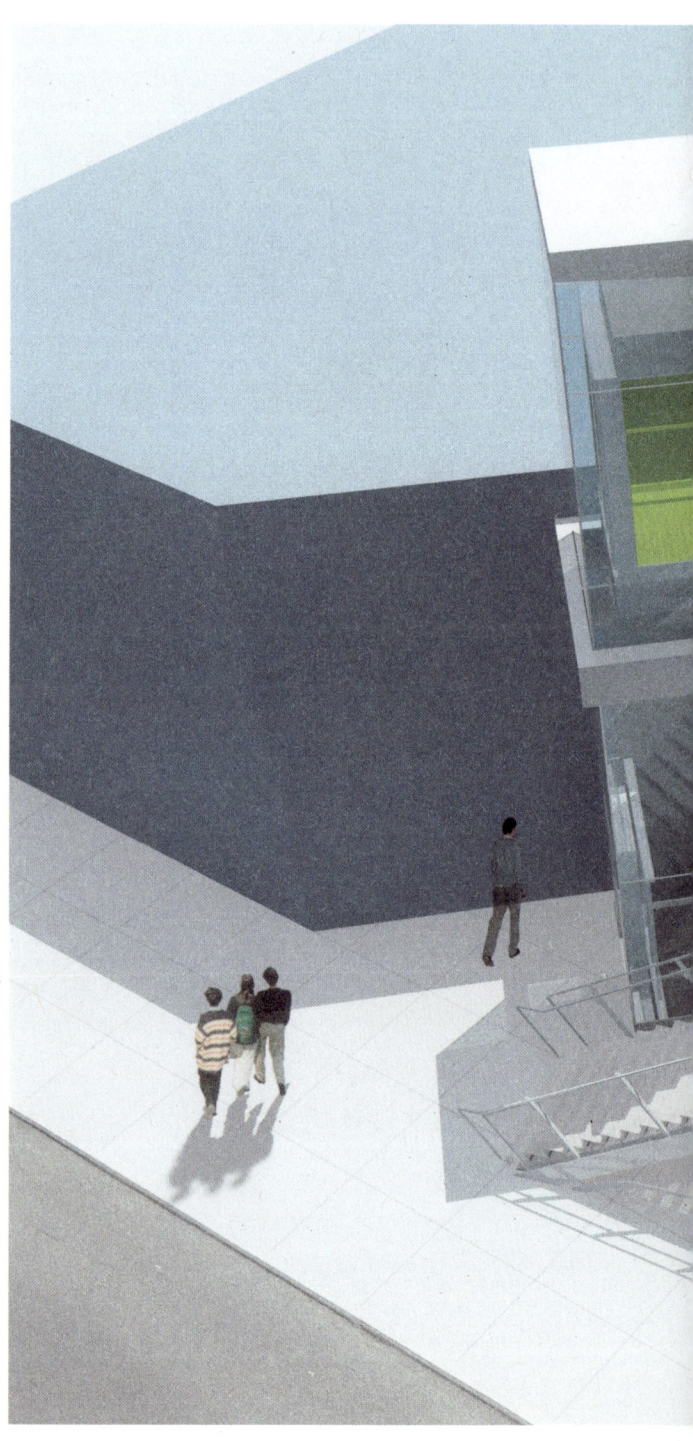

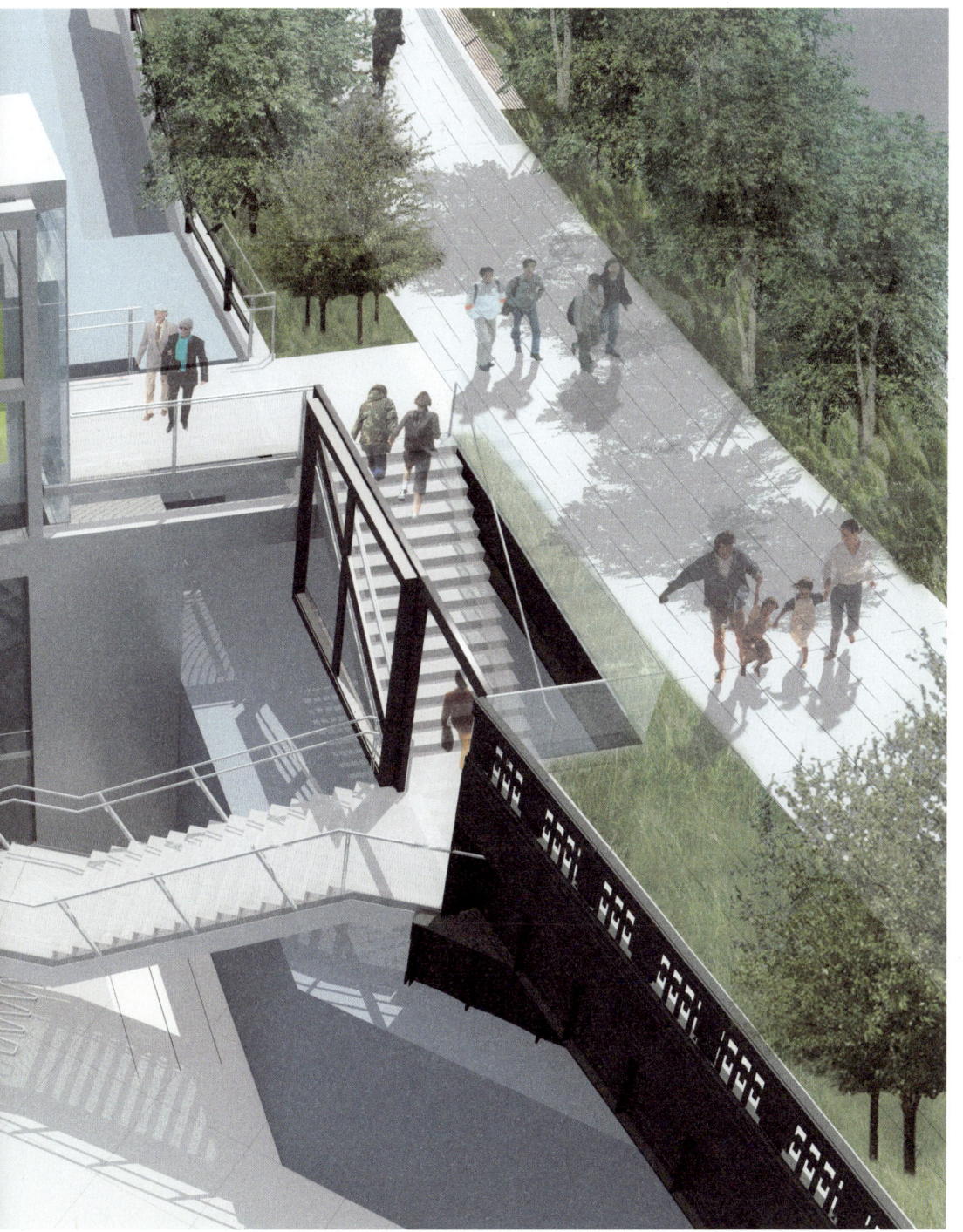

30th Street Cut-Out

By removing the High Line's concrete deck, the gridwork of the High Line's beams and girders is revealed. This exposure of the structural framework creates a dramatic transition to the rail yards section of the High Line to the north.

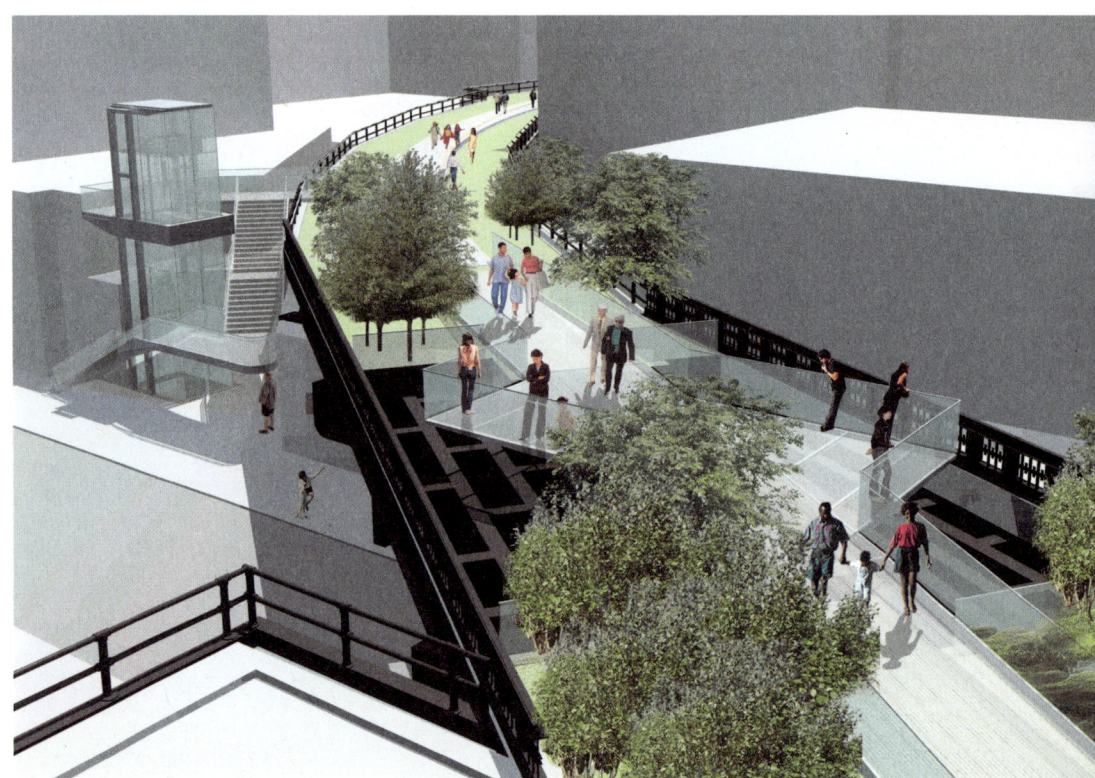

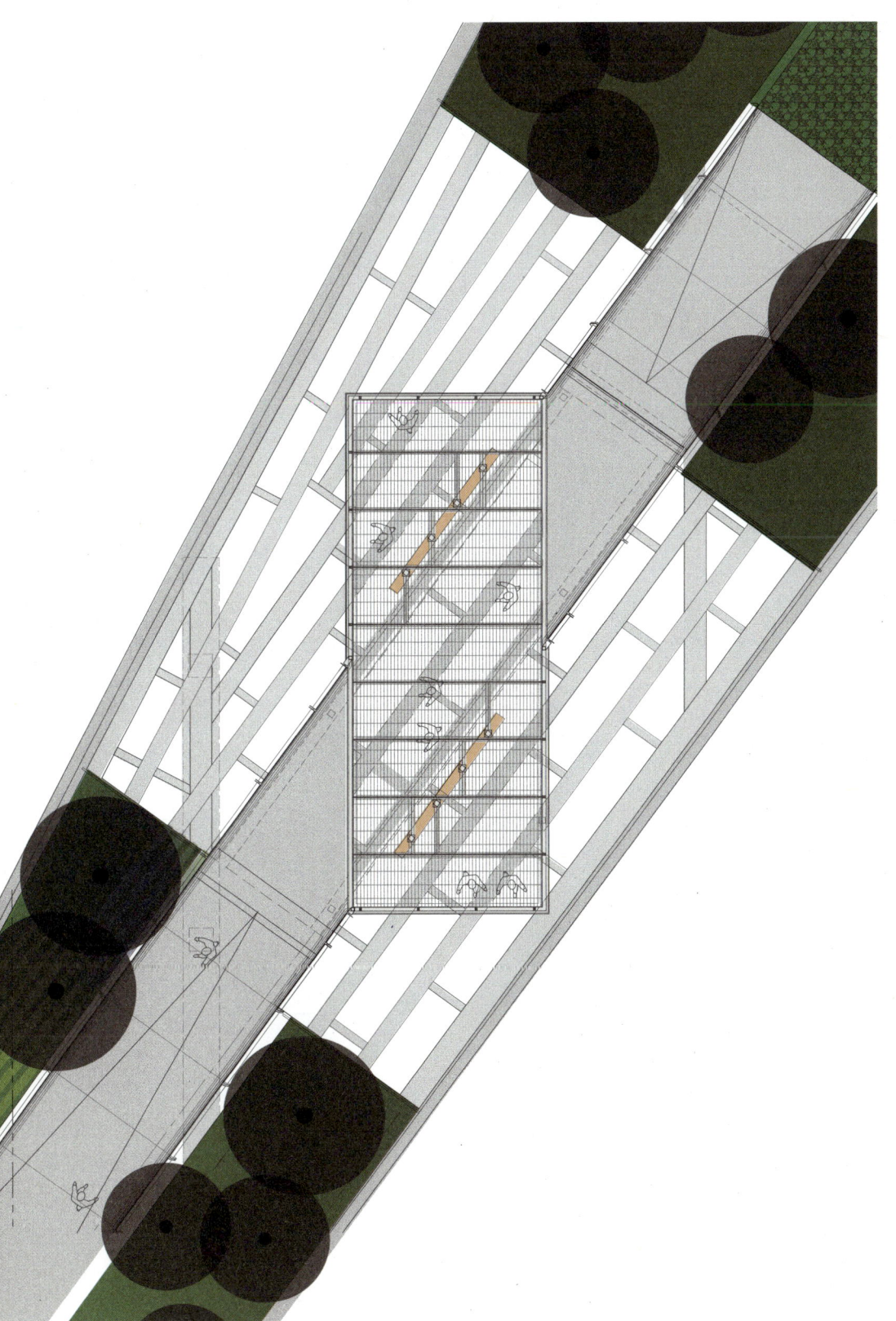

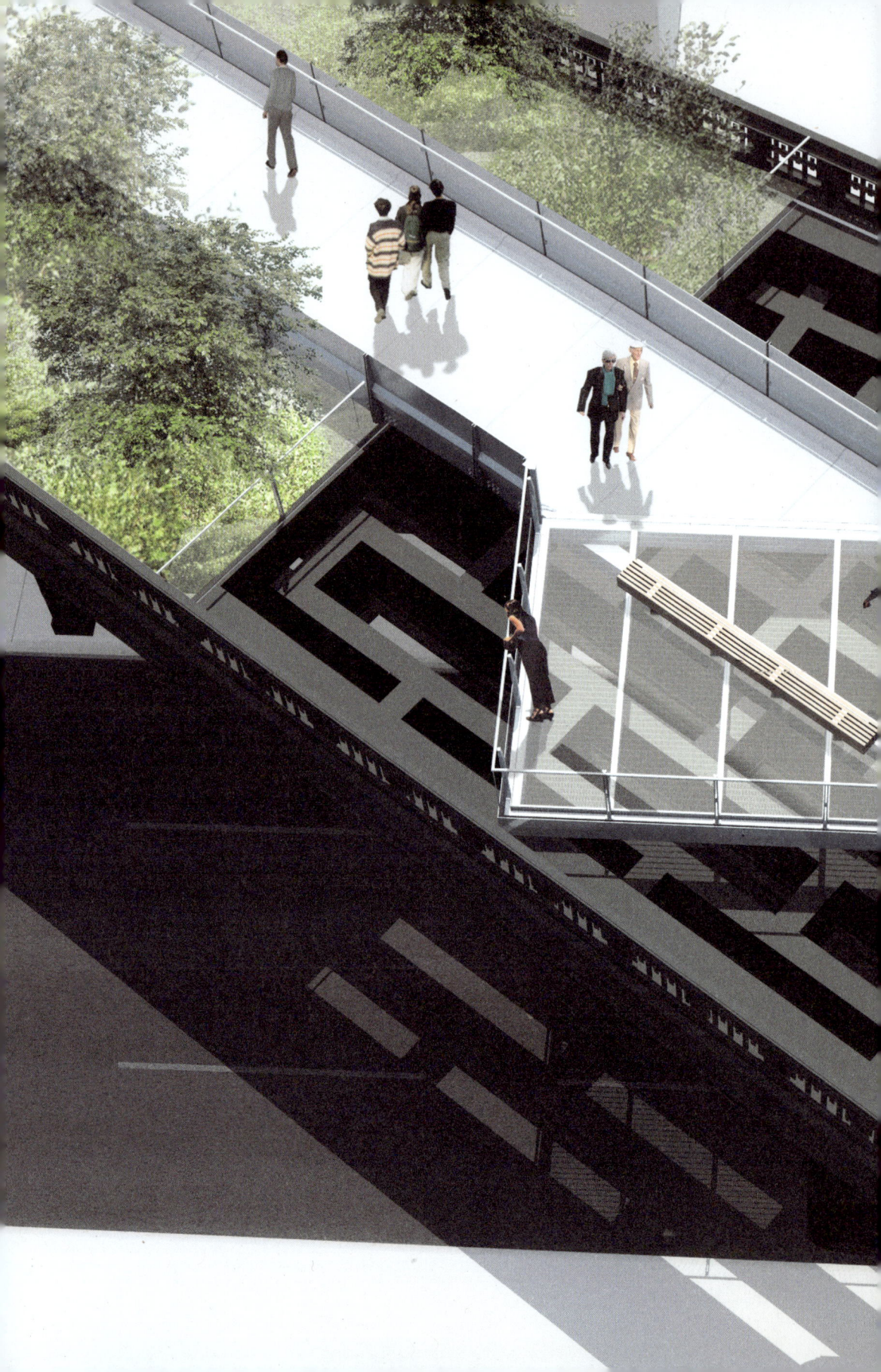

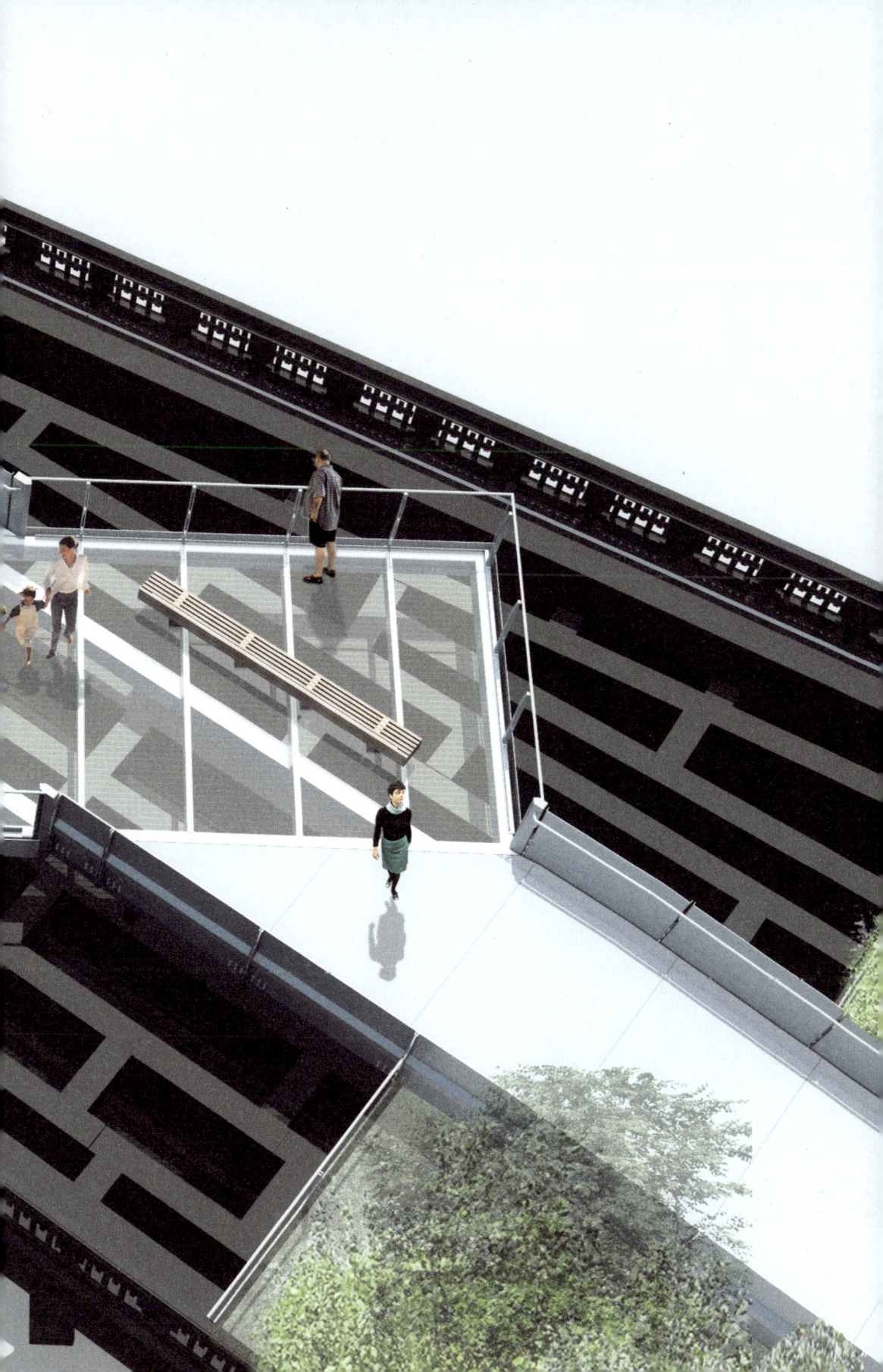

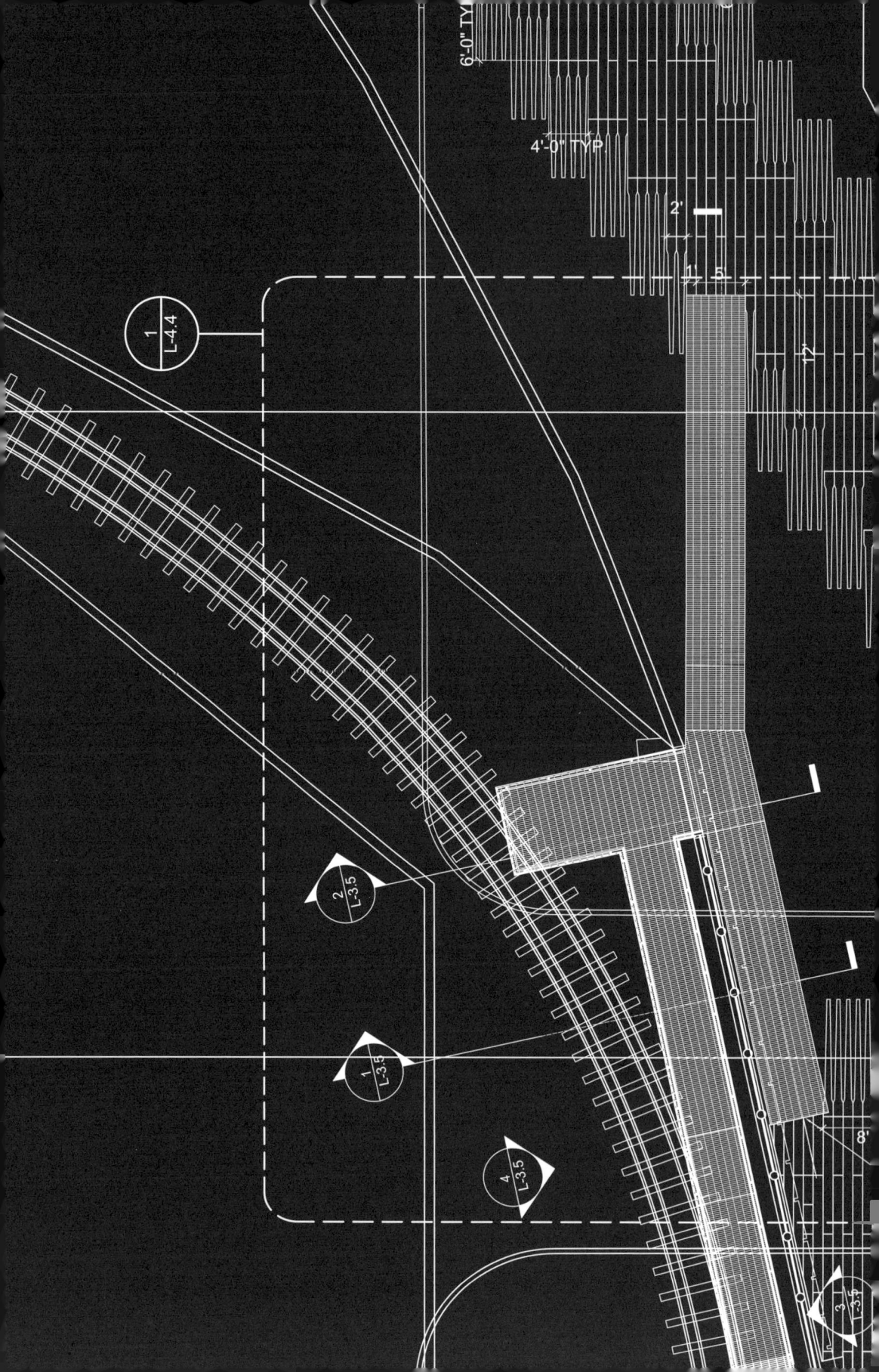

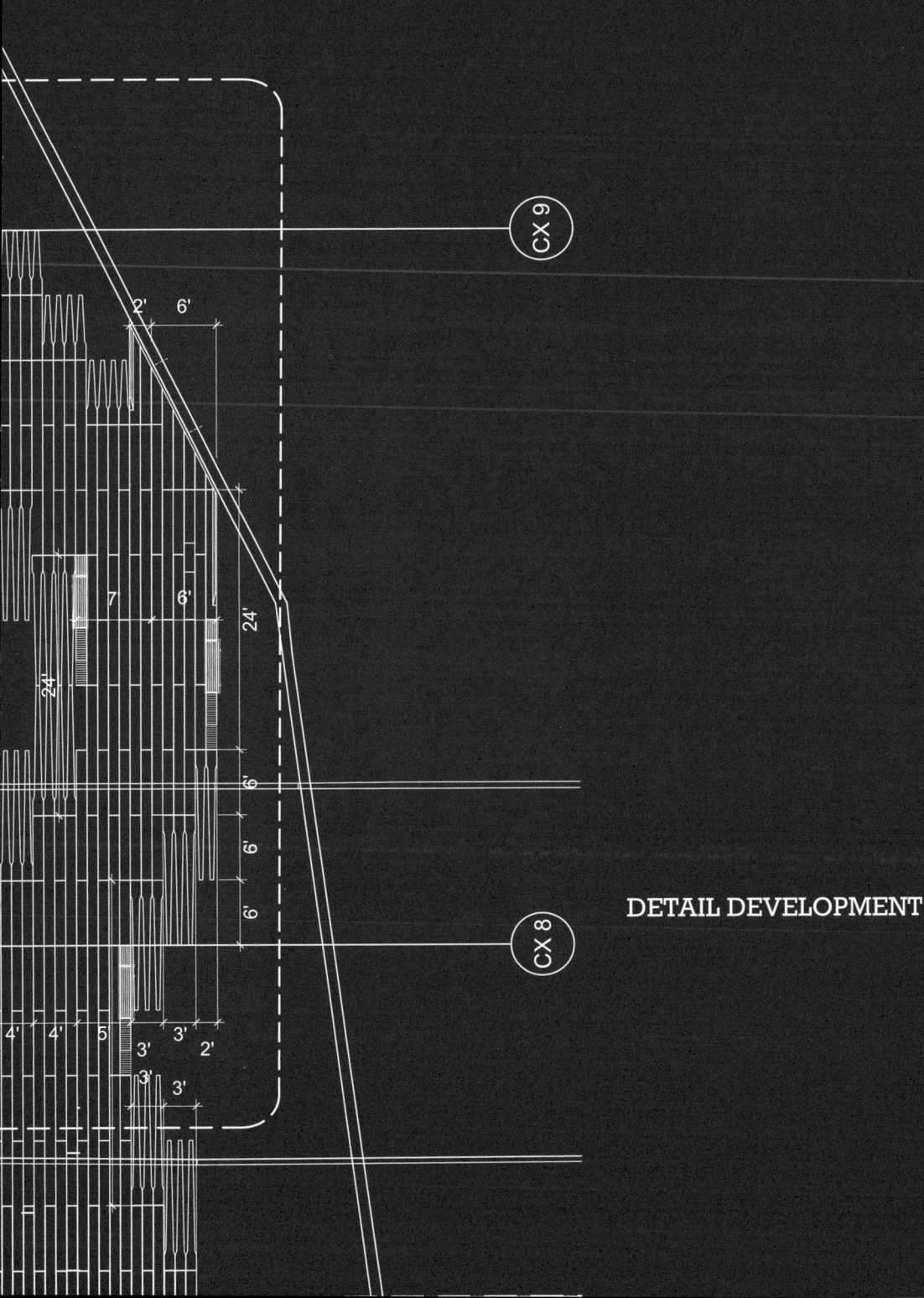

DETAIL DEVELOPMENT

Planking

A striated system of modular, pre-cast concrete planks allows for meandering, unscripted movement along the High Line. Long, gradual tapering of planks into planting beds forms a richly integrated and combed carpet rather than segregated pathways and planting areas. Four basic plank types are re-configured to construct a variety of surface layouts that are materially consistent and spatially variable.

STANDARD PLANK TYPES

STRAIGHT 12' UNIT
12'(L) x 1'(W) x 8"(D)

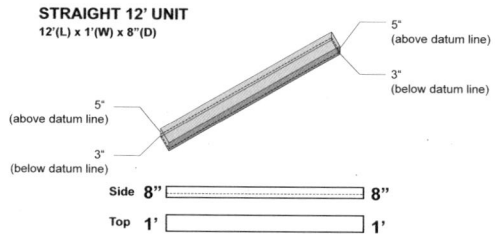

5"
(above datum line)

3"
(below datum line)

5"
(above datum line)

3"
(below datum line)

Side 8" 8"

Top 1' 1'

STRAIGHT 6' UNIT
6'(L) x 1'(W) x 8"(D)

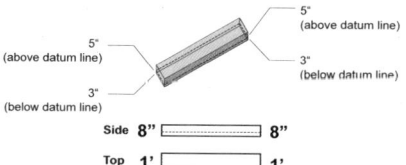

5"
(above datum line)

3"
(below datum line)

5"
(above datum line)

3"
(below datum line)

Side 8" 8"

Top 1' 1'

TRANSITION PLANK TYPES

TAPERED 12' UNIT
12'(L) x 1'(W) x 8"-4"(D)

1"
(above datum line)

3"
(below datum line)

5"
(above datum line)

3"
(below datum line)

Side 8" 4"

Top 1' 4"

TAPERED 24' UNIT
24 '(L) x 1'(W) x 8"-4"(D)

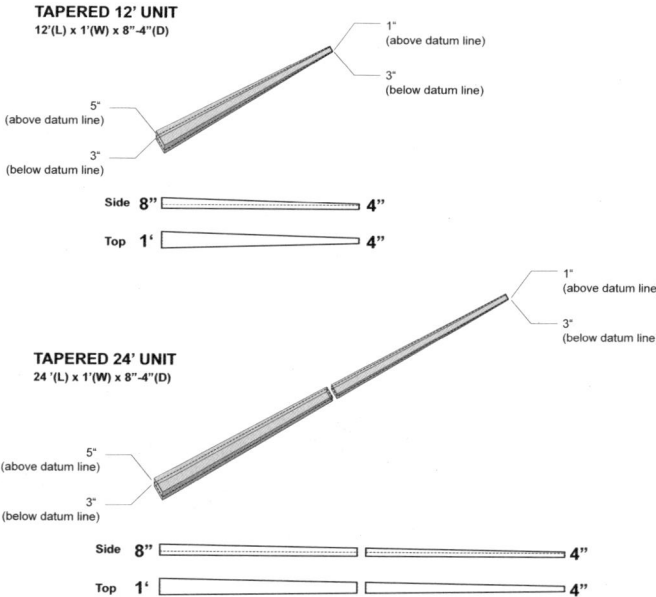

1"
(above datum line)

3"
(below datum line)

5"
(above datum line)

3"
(below datum line)

Side 8" 4"

Top 1' 4"

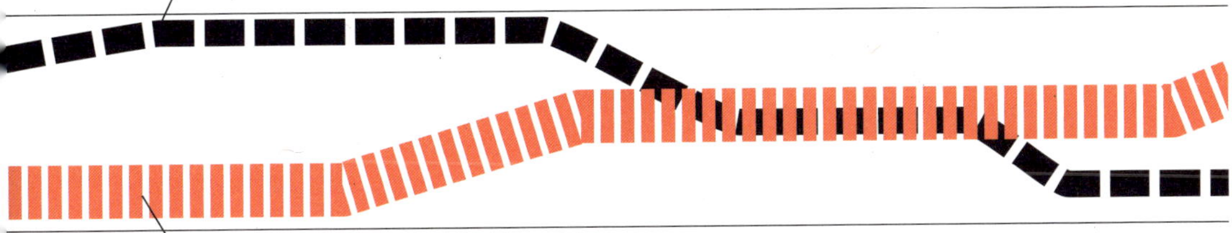

splinter path (width 3'-7') :
secondary circulation route w/ a minimum width of 3' (complying w/ the ADA recommended minimum clear path width for single wheelchair traffic)

CIRCULATION

primary path (width 8'-15'):
main path continues throughtout the project w/ a minimum width of 8' (complying w/ the width requirement for maintenance vehicles (5'),
and the ADA recommended minimum clear path width (6'))

void

planting bed area

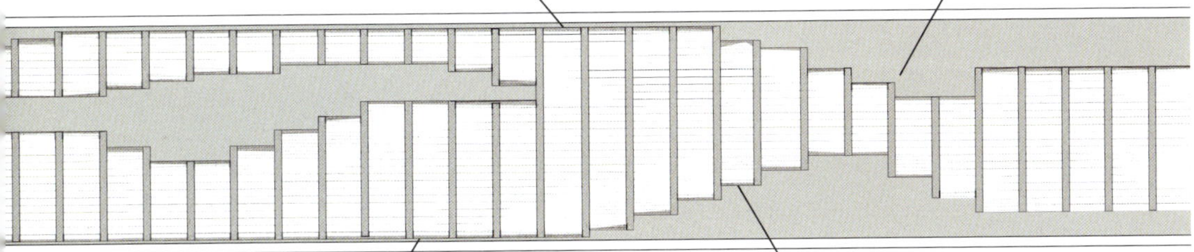

UNDERSTRUCTURE

infills
components: 12"(w)x 8"(d) x 16"(l) standard CMU
typical kneewall heights: 16" (8" x 2 layers of CMU)

structural kneewalls
components: 12"(w)x 8"(d) x 16"(l) standard CMUs
typical kneewall heights: 16" (8" x 2 layers of CMUs

typical street crossing
30'-0"

gathering space

overlook

seating

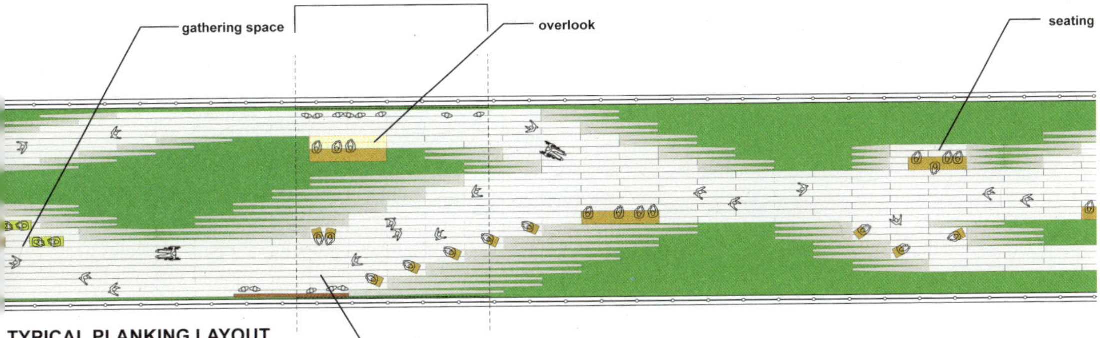

TYPICAL PLANKING LAYOUT

overlook

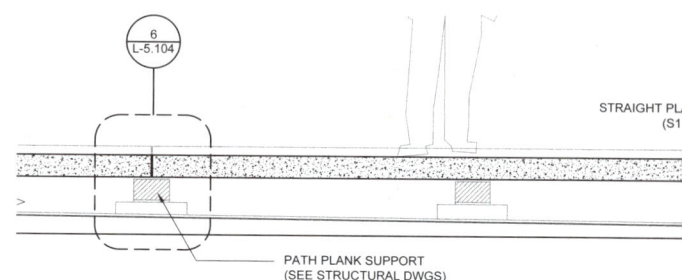

6
L-5.104

STRAIGHT PL
(S1

PATH PLANK SUPPORT
(SEE STRUCTURAL DWGS)

2 TYP. LONG SECTION

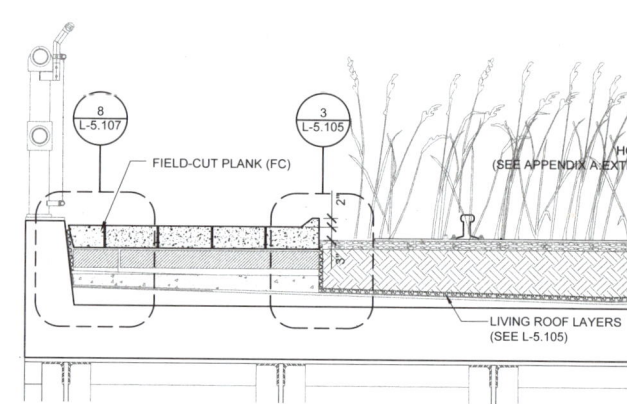

8
L-5.107

3
L-5.105

FIELD-CUT PLANK (FC)

HC
(SEE APPENDIX A:EXTE

LIVING ROOF LAYERS
(SEE L-5.105)

1 TYP. CROSS SECTION

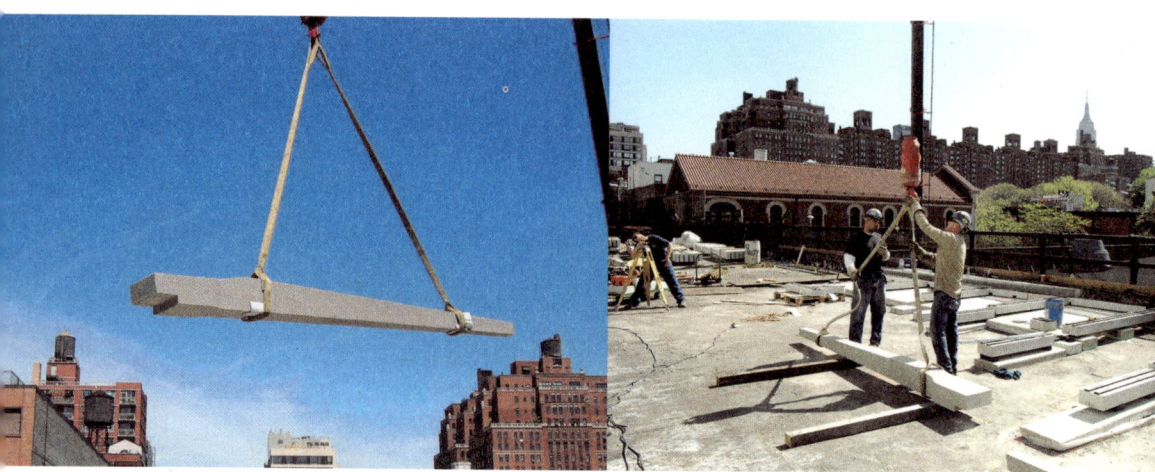

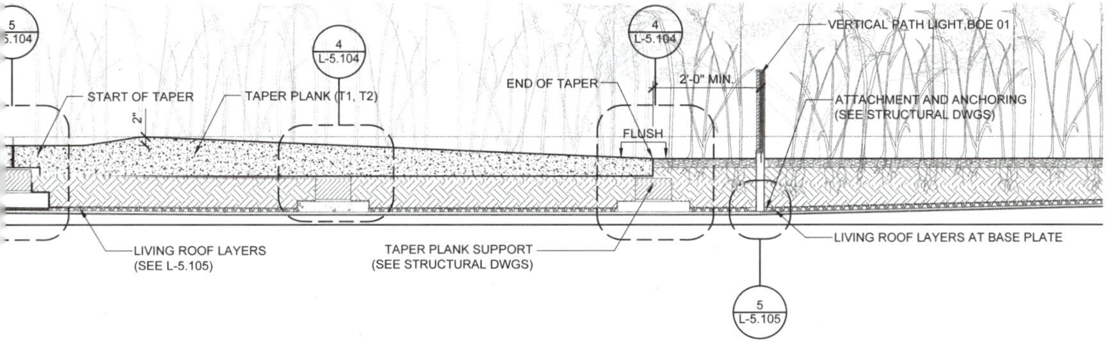

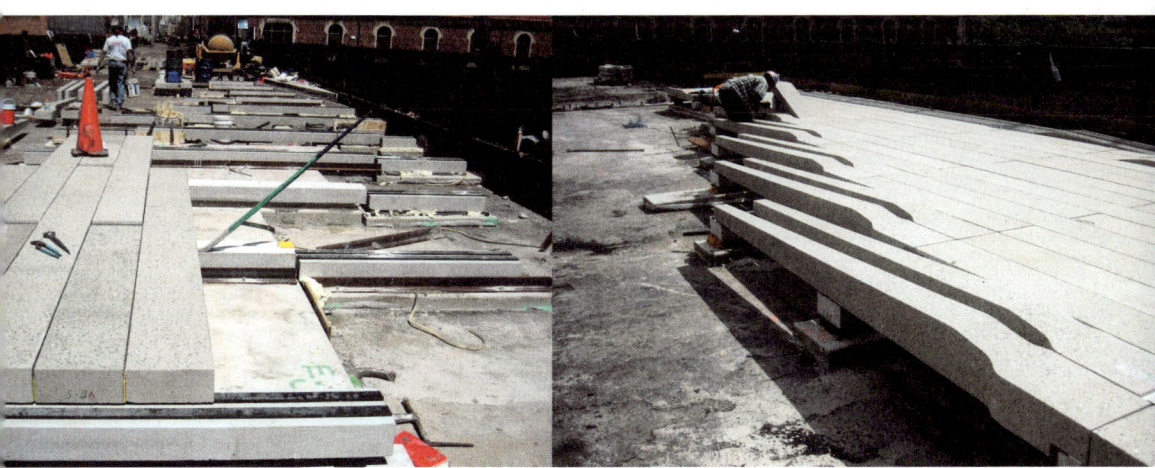

5
.104

START OF TAPER — TAPER PLANK (T1, T2)

4
L-5.104

END OF TAPER

4
L-5.104

2'-0" MIN.

VERTICAL PATH LIGHT, BOE 01

ATTACHMENT AND ANCHORING
(SEE STRUCTURAL DWGS)

2"

FLUSH

LIVING ROOF LAYERS
(SEE L-5.105)

TAPER PLANK SUPPORT
(SEE STRUCTURAL DWGS)

LIVING ROOF LAYERS AT BASE PLATE

5
L-5.105

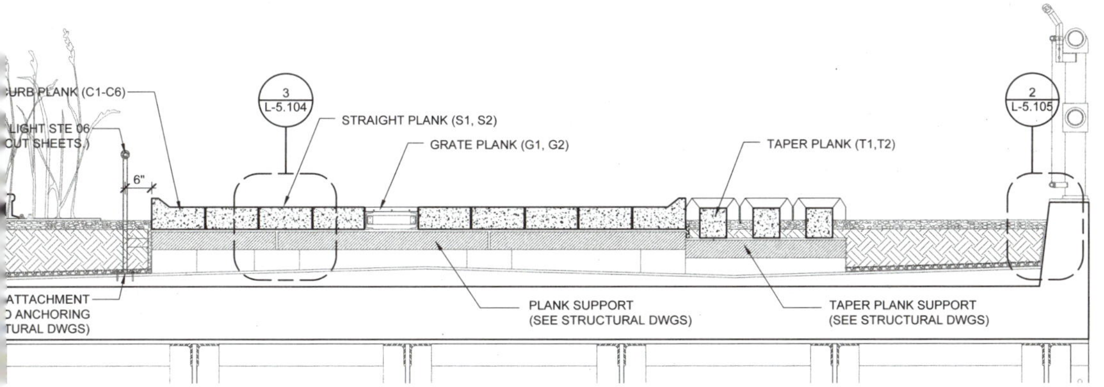

CURB PLANK (C1-C6)

LIGHT STE 06
UT SHEETS,)

3
L-5.104

STRAIGHT PLANK (S1, S2)

GRATE PLANK (G1, G2)

TAPER PLANK (T1,T2)

2
L-5.105

6"

ATTACHMENT
D ANCHORING
TURAL DWGS)

PLANK SUPPORT
(SEE STRUCTURAL DWGS)

TAPER PLANK SUPPORT
(SEE STRUCTURAL DWGS)

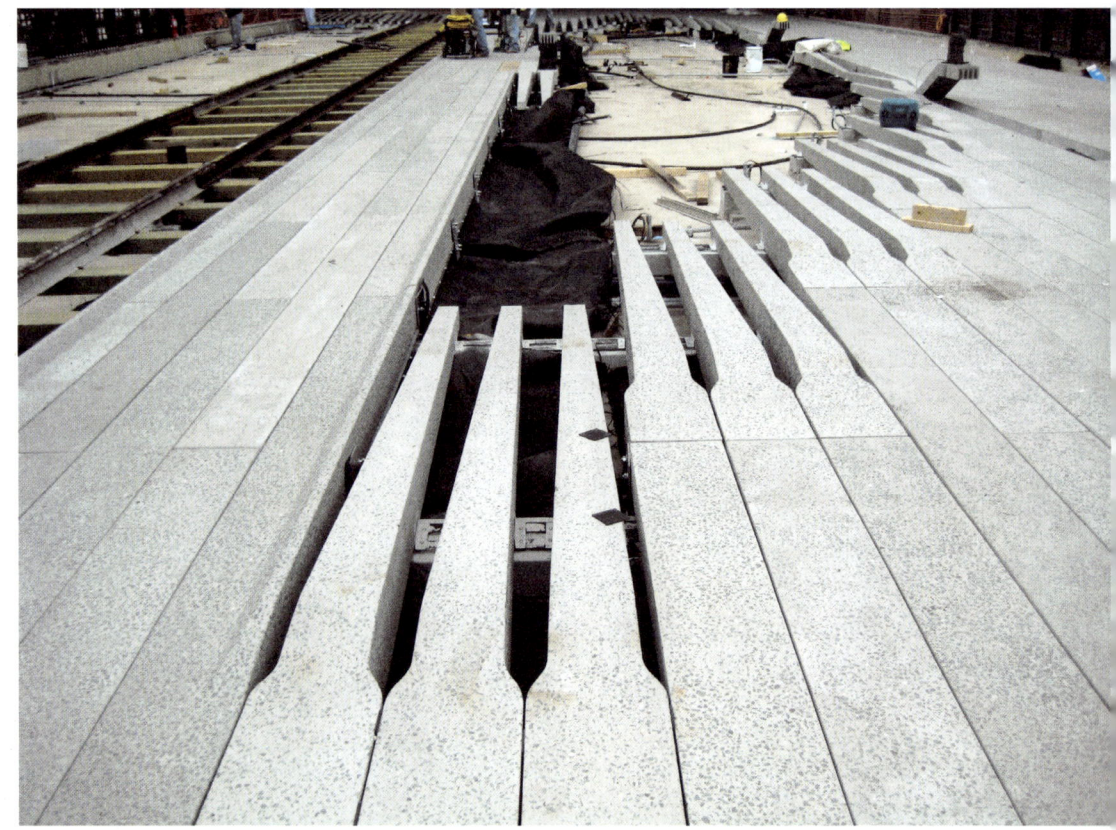

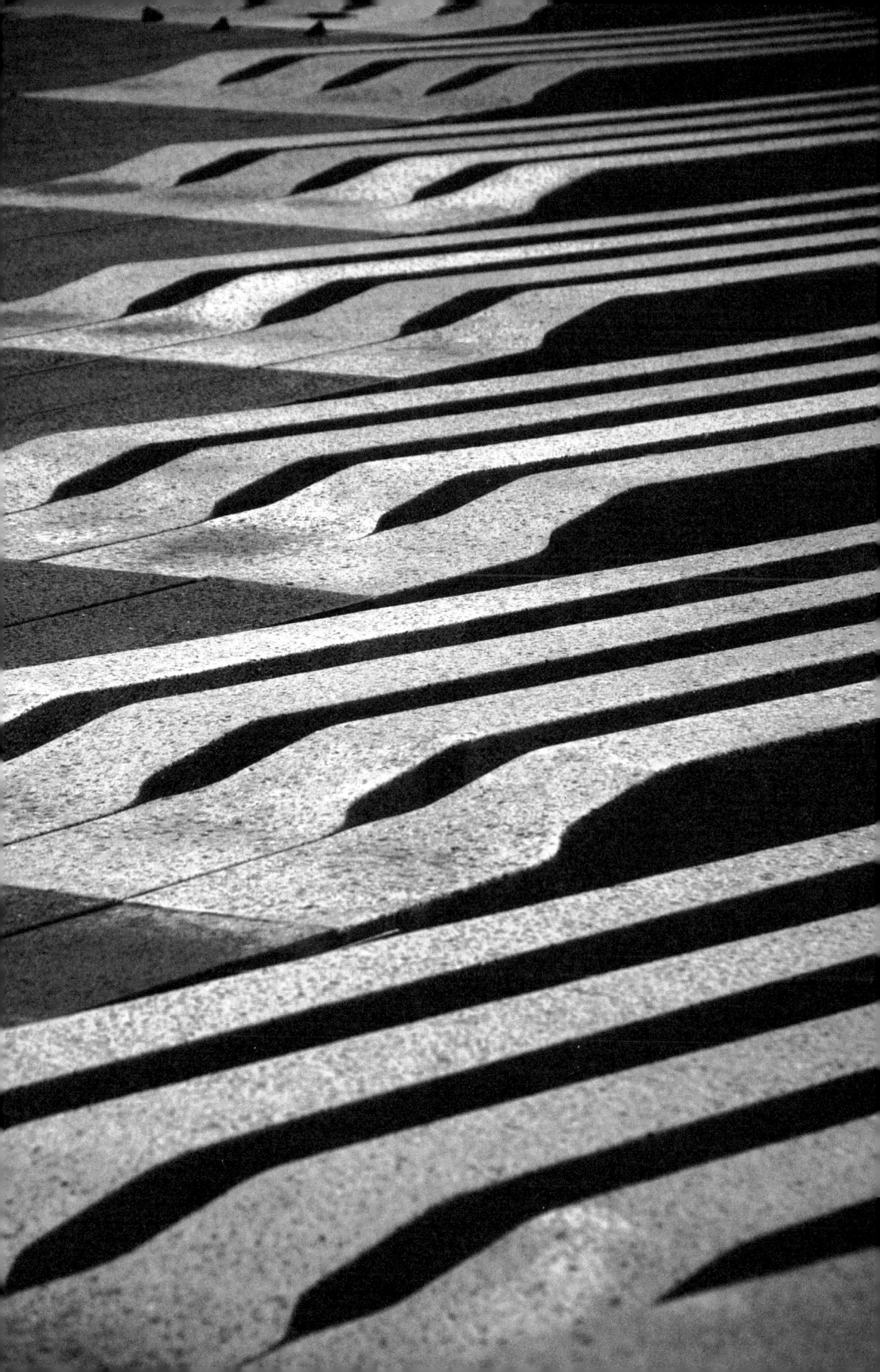

Peel-up Bench

The High Line's "Peel-up" benches rise organically from the planks of the walkway. Thus, an essential park amenity – seating – becomes an integral part of the High Line landscape.

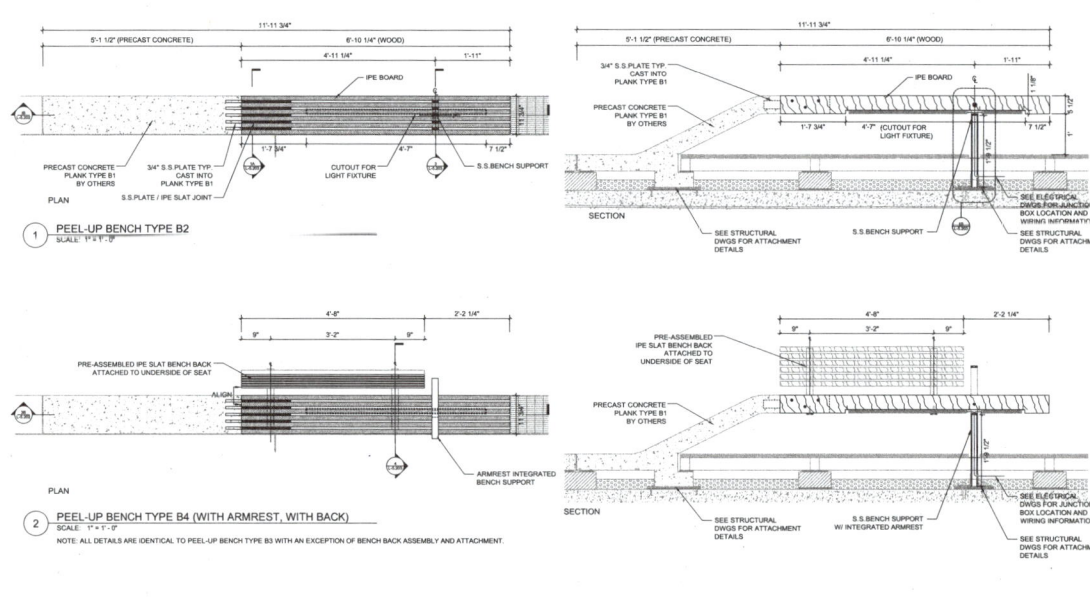

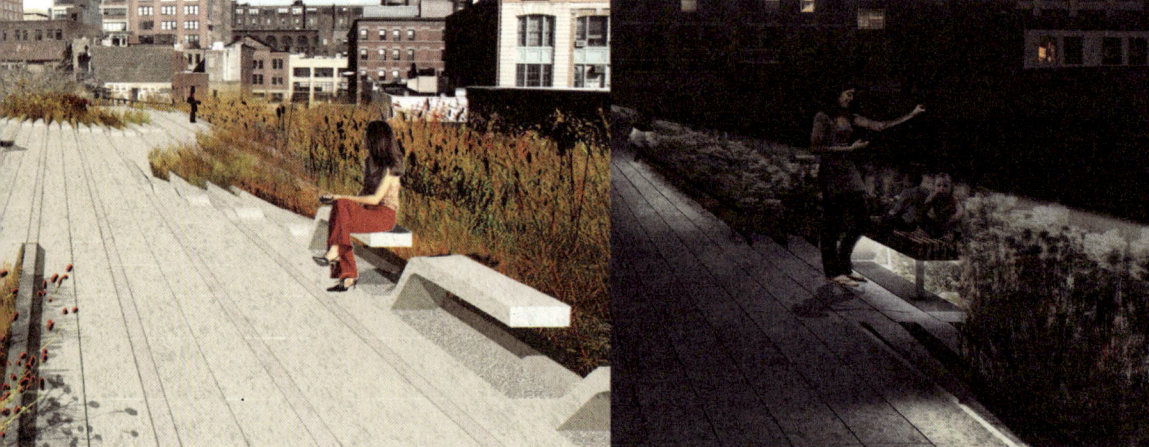

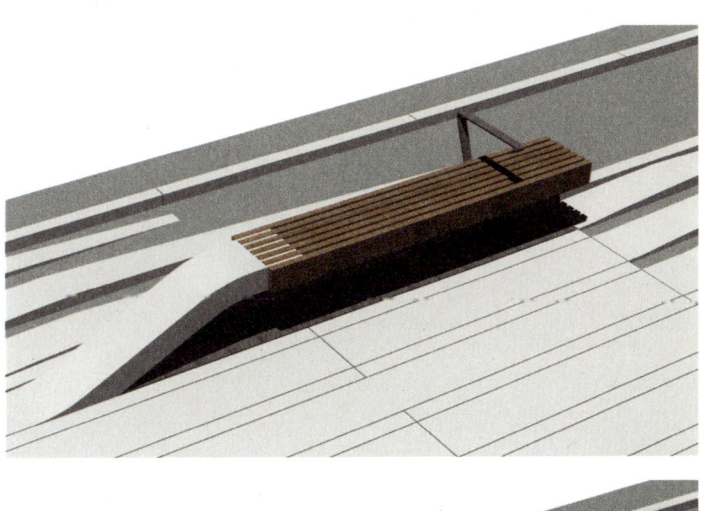

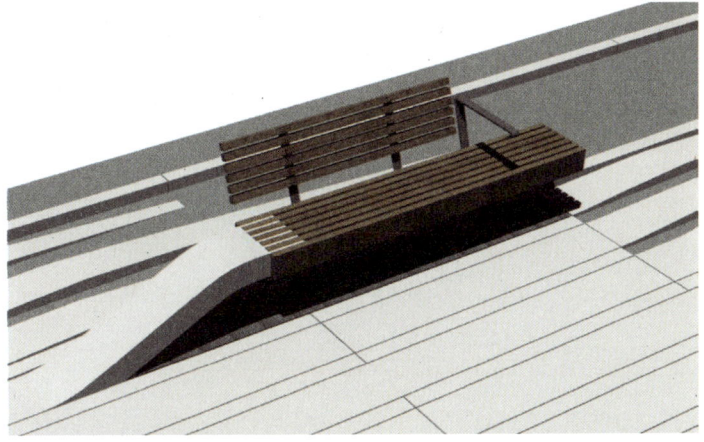

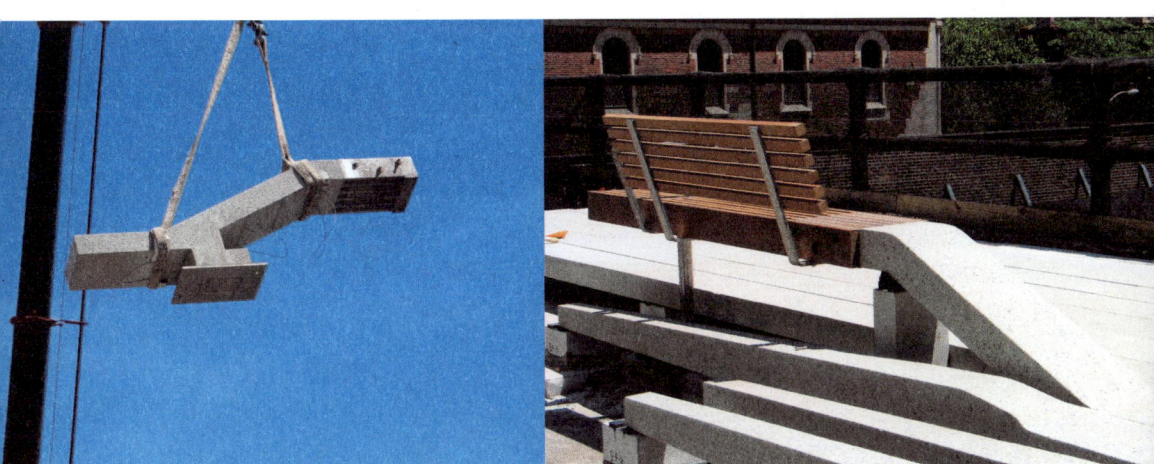

Planting

Plant communities build on existing species and conditions to produce a primarily wild, native, resilient, and low-maintenance landscape with great diversity, seasonal change, and height and color variation. Grassland mixes establish a new datum line one to three feet above the surface, reinforcing the unusual, intimate character of the High Line. Wetland and dry woodland species vary the spatial and horticultural mix.

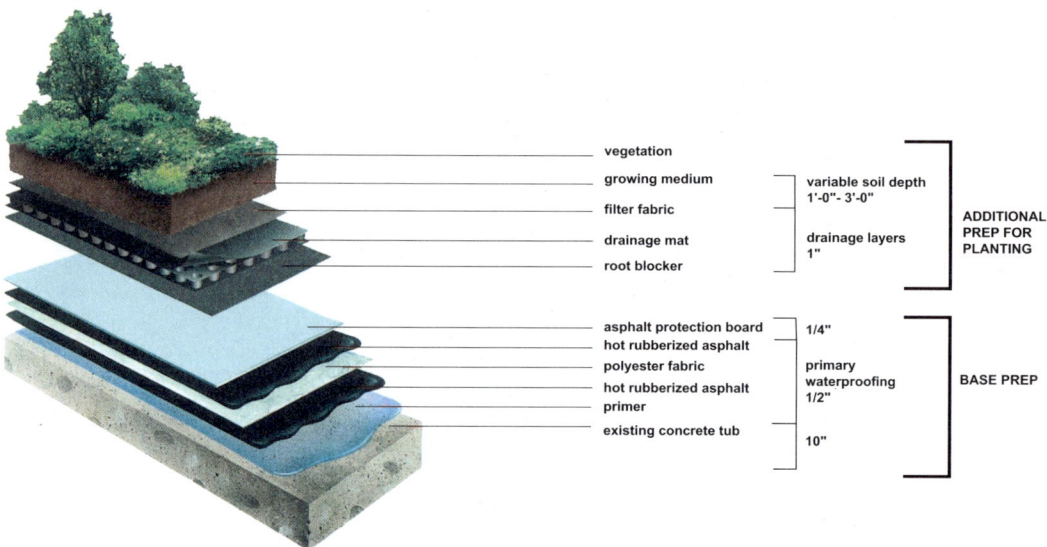

vegetation
growing medium
filter fabric   variable soil depth
                                       1'-0"- 3'-0"   ADDITIONAL
drainage mat   drainage layers   PREP FOR
root blocker   1"   PLANTING

asphalt protection board   1/4"
hot rubberized asphalt
polyester fabric   primary
hot rubberized asphalt   waterproofing   BASE PREP
                                       1/2"
primer
existing concrete tub
                                       10"

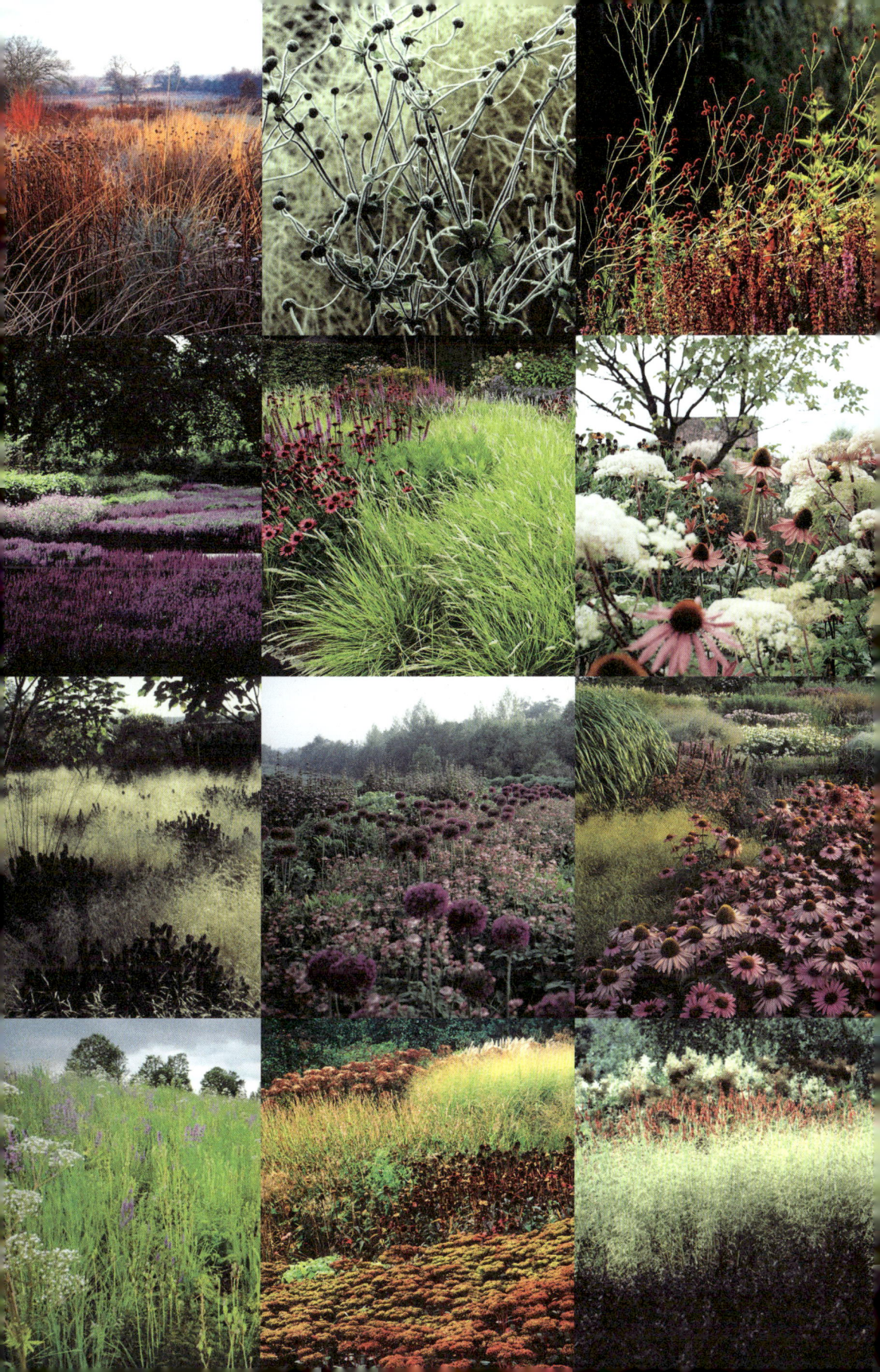

TREES + SHRUBS FOR BEDS 6-7

SYMBOL/ ABB.	BED 6 (3516 SF)	BED 7 (5953 SF)	TOTAL
AME1	0	0	0
AME2	4	0	4
AME3	11	11	22
BE1	0	0	0
BE2	8	3	11
BE3	10	17	27
BE4	7	0	7
CE1	3	1	4
CE2	0	1	1
CL	21	16	37
CLE	7	8	15
COTc	0	1	1
GA	7	11	18
Vlb	5	6	11

VINES FOR BED 6

SYMBOL/ ABB.	BED 6 (3516 SF)	TOTAL
CLj	5	5
CLm	5	5
CLo	5	5
CLt	8	8
CLv	2	2
PART	9	9
SCh	6	6
WI	8	8
VIT	1	1

PLANTING BED 6 - 3516 SF

SYMBOL / ABB.	SCIENTIFIC NAME	COMMON NAME	QTY (EA, 4" POT)
AMSt	Amsonia tabernaemontana v. salicifolia	Bluestar	33
ASTo	Aster oblongifolia 'Raydon's Favorite'	Aromatic Aster	38
BOc	Bouteloua curtipendula	Sideoats gamma	188
CAe	Carex eburnea	Bristle-leaf Sedge	628
CAl	Carex laxiculmis 'Hobb'	Spreading Sedge	288
CAp	Carex pennsylvanica	Pennsylvanica Sedge	790
SALn	Salvia nemorosa 'Rhapsody in Blue'	Meadow Sage	109
SEa	Sesleria autumnalis	Autumn Moor Grass	775
SOLI	Solidaster lemore	Yellow Solidaster	31
SP	Sporobolus heterolepis	Prairie Dropseed	40
STh	Stachys officinalis 'Hummelo'	Common Hedgenettle 'Hummelo'	140
		TOTAL	3060

PLANTING BED 7 - 5953 SF

SYMBOL / ABB.	SCIENTIFIC NAME	COMMON NAME	QTY (EA, 4" POT)
Af	Agastache foeniculum	Anise Hyssop	6
AMc	Amorpha canescens	Leadplant	21
AMSh	Amsonia hubrichtii	Thread-leaf Bluestar	9
AMSt	Amsonia tabernaemontana v. salicifolia	Bluestar	39
ASt	Asclepias tuberosa	Butterfly Milkweed	6
ASTo	Aster oblongifolia 'Raydon's Favorite'	Aromatic Aster	55
Bl	Baptisia leucantha	White False Indigo	36
BOc	Bouteloua curtipendula	Sideoats gamma	878
CALA	Calamintha nepeta subsp. nepeta	Calamint	47
CAe	Carex eburnea	Bristle-leaf Sedge	699
CAl	Carex laxiculmis 'Hobb'	Spreading Sedge	421
CAp	Carex pennsylvanica	Pennsylvanica Sedge	817
DA	Dalea purpurea	Violet Prairie Clover	76
DES	Desmodium canadense	Showy Tick Trefoil	4
ECj	Echinacea purpurea 'Vintage Wine'	Vintage Wine Coneflower	59
ERY	Eryngium yuccifolium	Button Snakeroot	31
EUPHc	Euphorbia corollata	Flowering Spurge	27
LIAs	Liatris spicata	Blazing Star	25
MOm	Molinia caerulea 'Moorhexe'	Moor Grass	160
PA	Panicum virgatum 'Shenandoah'	Shenandoah Switchgrass	19
RU	Ruellia humilis	Wild Petunia	35
SALn	Salvia nemorosa 'Rhapsody in Blue'	Meadow Sage	64
SCs	Schizachyrium scoparius 'The Blues'	Little Bluestem	256
SEDr	Sedum 'Red Cauli'	Red Cauli Stonecrop	27
SEa	Sesleria autumnalis	Autumn Moor Grass	964
SILI	Silphium laciniatum	Compass Plant	5
SOLI	Solidaster lemore	Yellow Solidaster	27
SP	Sporobolus heterolepis	Prairie Dropseed	566
STh	Stachys officinalis 'Hummelo'	Common Hedgenettle 'Hummelo'	124
		TOTAL	5,503

Trees, shrubs, and perennials for planting beds 6 and 7, along Washington Street near Gansevoort Street.

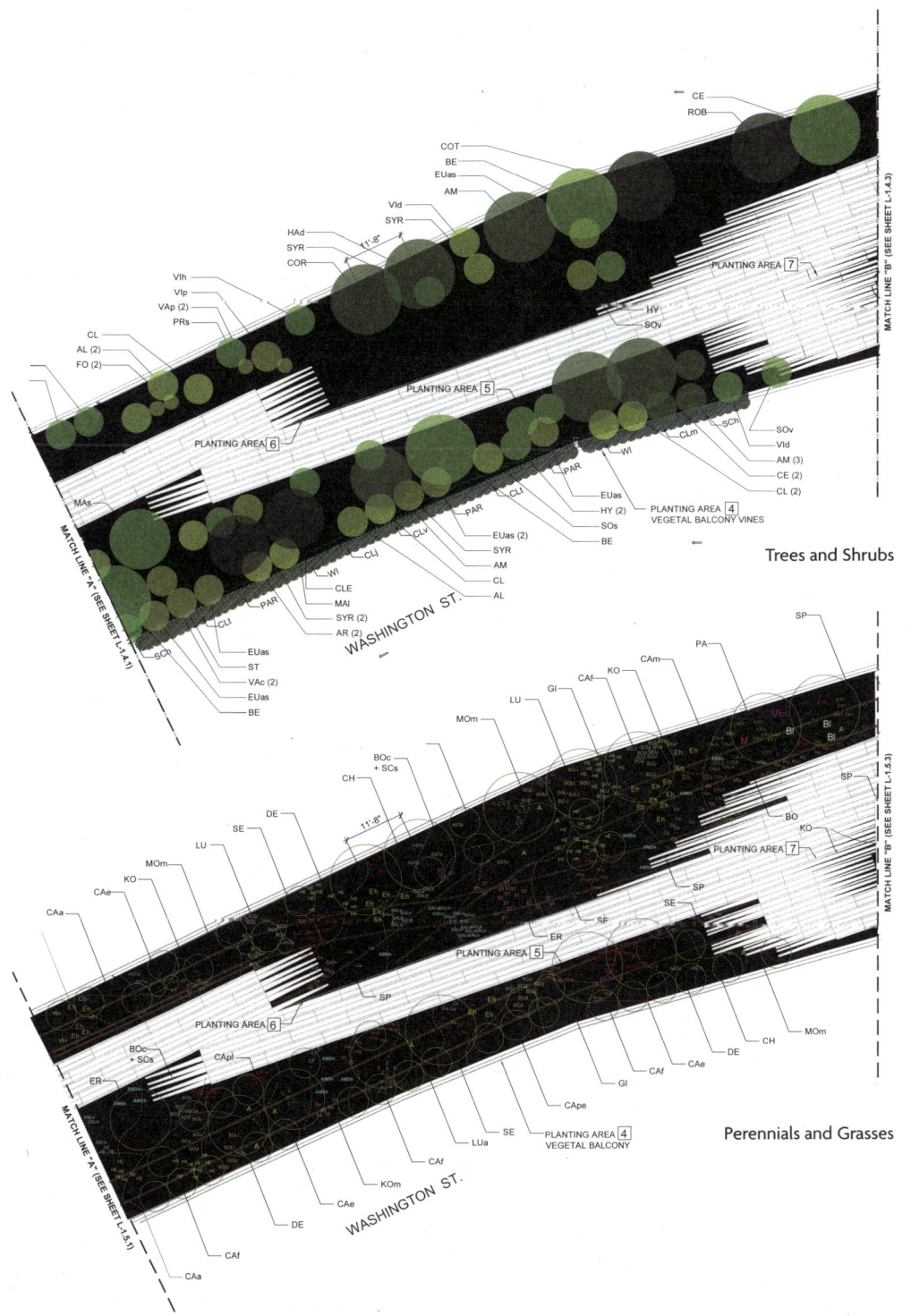

Trees and Shrubs

Perennials and Grasses

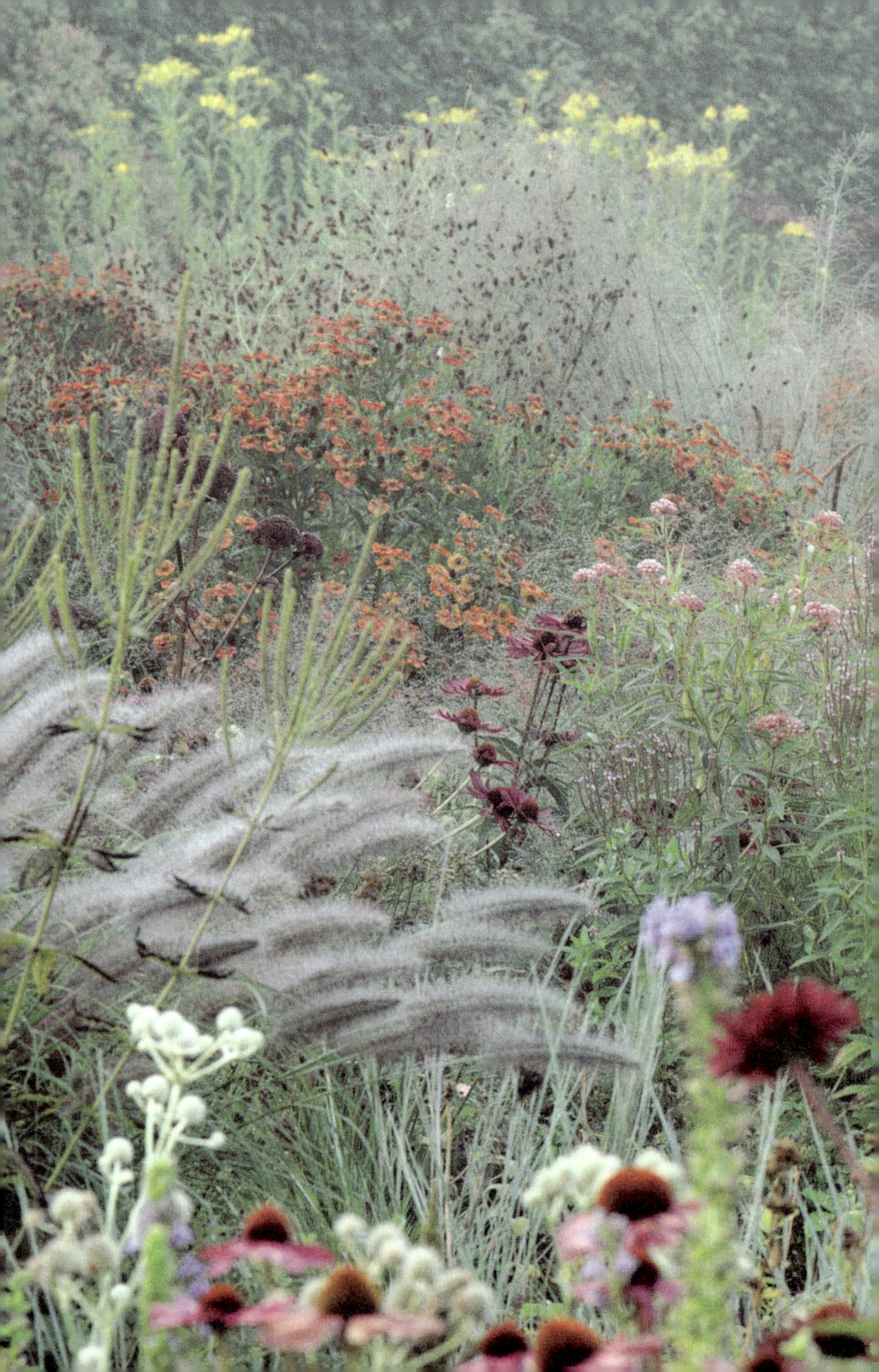

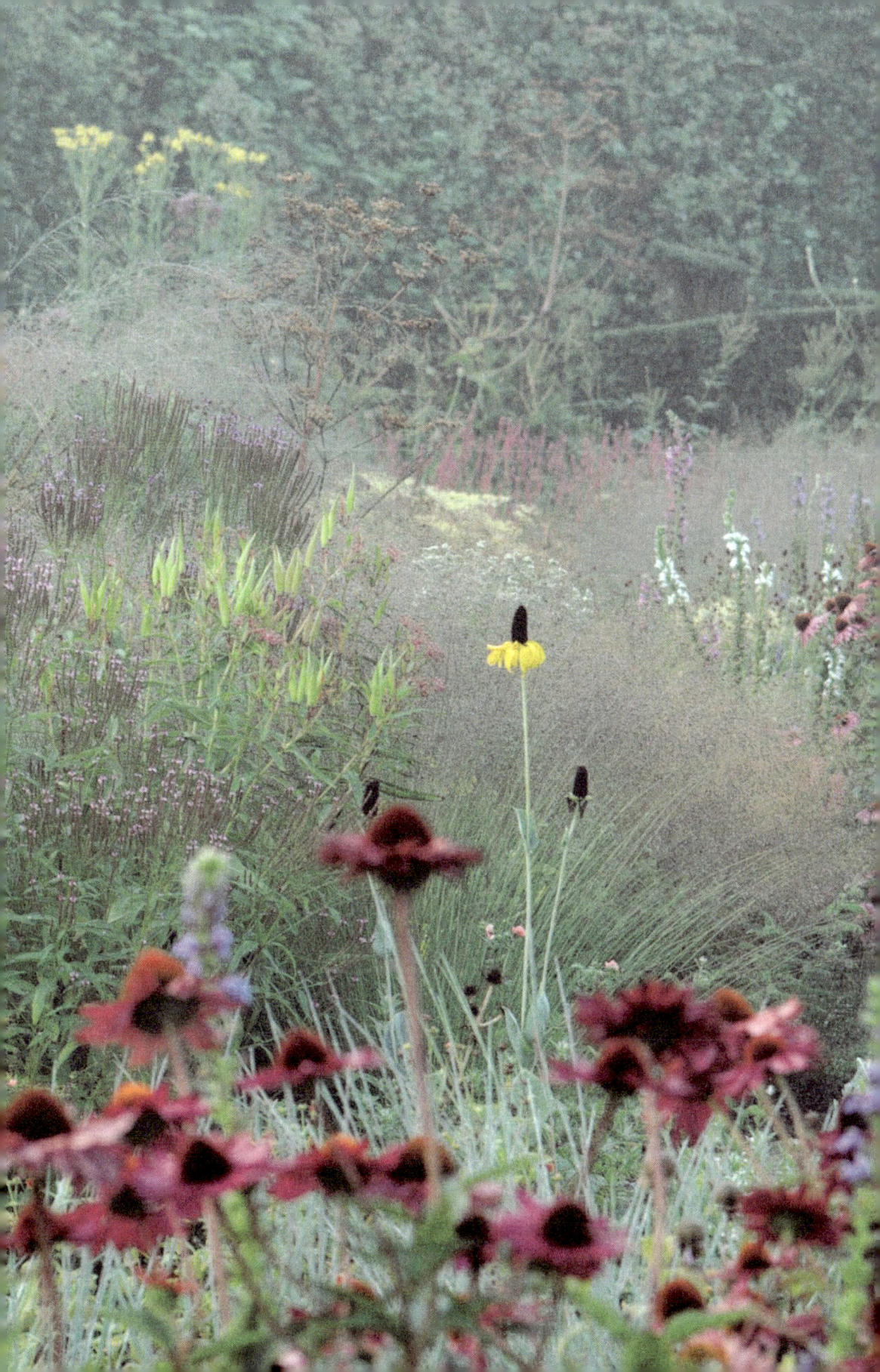

Bloom Chart

		SPRING			SUMMER
JANUARY	FEBRUARY	MARCH	APRIL	MAY	JUNE

BULBS

JANUARY	FEBRUARY	MARCH	APRIL	MAY	JUNE
	Crocus thomassinianus	Anemone blanda Crocus tomassinianus Eranthis hyemalis	Anemone blanda Eranthis hyemalis Erythronium 'Pagoda' Narcissus 'Hawera' Ornithogalum nutans Puschkinia scilloides Scilla litardierei Trillium luteum Tulipa clusiana	Allium christophii Eremurus 'Romford' Muscari armeniacum Narcissus 'Hawera' Nectaroscordum siculum Ornithogalum nutans Trillium luteum Tulipa clusiana	Eremurus 'Romford' Nectaroscordum siculum
		Puschkinia scilloides			

PERENNIALS

JANUARY	FEBRUARY	MARCH	APRIL	MAY	JUNE
			Asclepias purpurascens Corydalis solida Geranium maculatum	Achillea filipendulina Amsonia hubrichtii Asclepias purpurascens Baptisia leucantha Corydalis solida Euphorbia amygdaloides Geum triflorum Geranium maculatum Iris fulva	Aruncus 'Horatio' Baptisia leucantha Campanula glomerata Dalea purpurea Dianthus carthusianorum Echinacea pallida Eryngium yuccifolium Euphorbia amygdaloides Geum triflorum Iris fulva
	Lysichiton americanum	Lysichiton americanum	Lysichiton americanum Penstemon digitalis	Lythrum alatam Nepeta siberica Penstemon digitalis Phlomis russeliana Sanguisorba officinalis Sisyrinchium angustifolium Tiarella cordifolia	Lythrum alatam Nepeta siberica Papaver orientalis Persicaria amplexicaule Phlomis russeliana Pontederia cordata Sanguisorba officinalis Sisyrinchium angustifolium

TREES AND SHRUBS

JANUARY	FEBRUARY	MARCH	APRIL	MAY	JUNE
	Hamamelis x intermedia	Corylopsis willmottiae Hamamelis x intermedia	Amelanchier laevis Cercis canadensis Chaenomeles speciosa Cornus florida Malus floribunda Pyrus communis	Amorpha fruticosa Cercis canadensis Cornus florida Cotinus coggygria Malus floribunda Prunus virginiana Pyrus communis Robinia hispida Sorbus sargentiana Syringa laciniata Viburnum nudum	Amorpha fruticosa Cotinus coggygria Indigofera heterantha Philadelphus coronarius Rosa virginiana Viburnum nudum

VINES

JANUARY	FEBRUARY	MARCH	APRIL	MAY	JUNE
				Clematis montana Clematis occidentalis Wisteria frutescens	Clematis montana Clematis occidentalis Clematis tangutica Wisteria frutescens

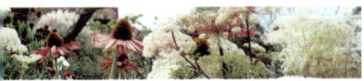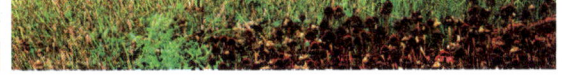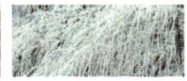

| | | FALL | | | WINTER |
JULY	AUGUST	SEPTEMBER	OCTOBER	NOVEMBER	DECEMBER
Achillea filipendulina	Achillea filipendulina				
Agastache foeniculum	Agastache foeniculum	Agastache foeniculum			
Aruncus 'Horatio'					
		Aster azureus	Aster azureus		
Dalea purpurea	Dalea purpurea				
Desmodium canadense	Desmodium canadense				
Dianthus carthusianorum	Dianthus carthusianorum				
Echinacea pallida					
Eryngium yuccifolium	Eryngium yuccifolium	Eryngium yuccifolium			
Eupatorium rugosum	Eupatorium rugosum	Eupatorium rugosum	Eupatorium rugosum		
	Gentiana crinita	Gentiana crinita	Gentiana crinita		
Geum triflorum					
Helenium 'Rubinzwerg'	Helenium 'Rubinzwerg'	Helenium 'Rubinzwerg'			
Knautia macedonica	Knautia macedonica	Knautia macedonica			
	Liatris aspera	Liatris aspera	Liatris aspera		
Lythrum alatam	Lythrum alatam	Lythrum alatam			
Monarda fistulosa	Monarda fistulosa	Monarda fistulosa			
Nepeta siberica					
Papaver orientalis					
Persicaria amplexicaule	Persicaria amplexicaule	Persicaria amplexicaule	Persicaria amplexicaule		
Pontederia cordata	Pontederia cordata	Pontederia cordata			
Rudbeckia subtomentosa	Rudbeckia subtomentosa	Rudbeckia subtomentosa			
Salvia azurea	Salvia azurea	Salvia azurea			
Silphium laciniatum	Silphium laciniatum	Silphium laciniatum			
	Solidago caesia	Solidago caesia			
	Solidaster luteus	Solidaster luteus			
Stachys officinalis	Stachys officinalis	Stachys officinalis			
		Tricyrtis 'Sinonome'	Tricyrtis 'Sinonome'		
	Verbascum thapsus	Verbascum thapsus			
Aesculus parviflora	Aesculus parviflora				
Amorpha fruticosa					
Clethra alnifolia	Clethra alnifolia				
Cotinus coggygria					
Hydrangea quercifolia	Hydrangea quercifolia				
Indigofera heterantha					
Koelreuteria paniculata					
Vitex agnus-castus	Vitex agnus-castus				
	Clematis jouiniana	Clematis jouiniana	Clematis jouiniana		
Clematis occidentalis					
		Clematis tangutica			
Clematis viticella rubra					

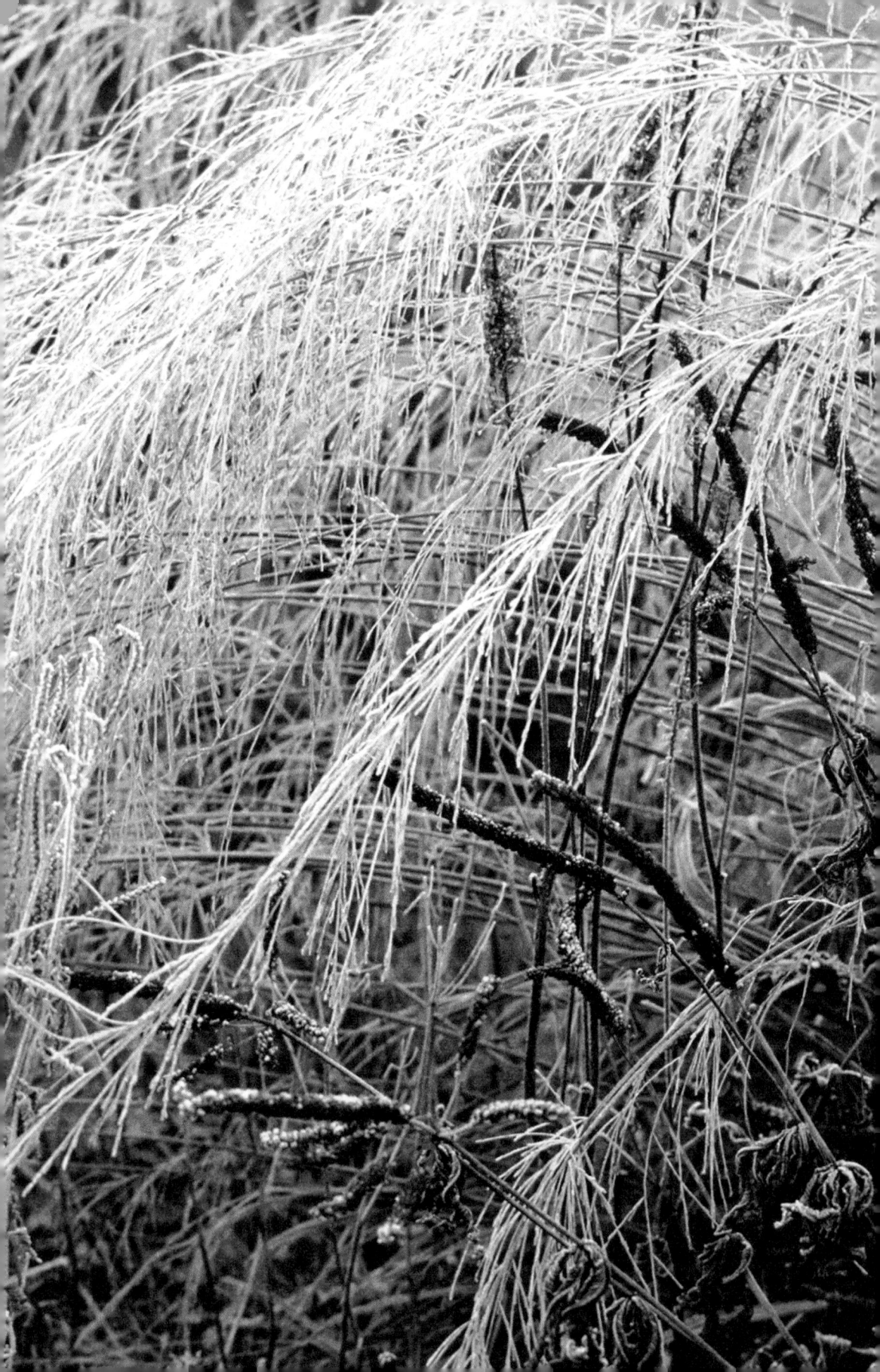

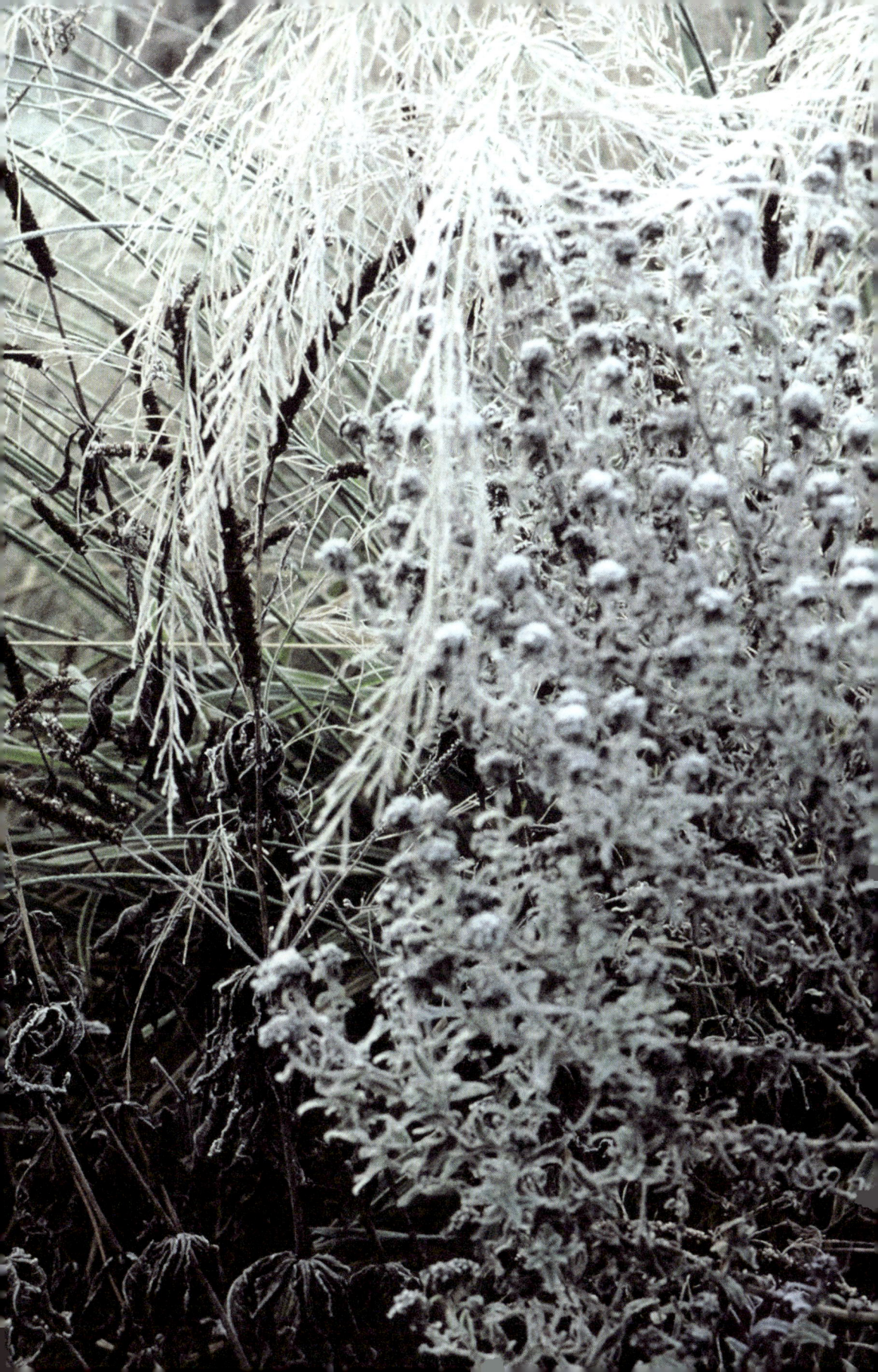

Lighting

Energy-efficient LED lighting, designed by Hervé Descottes, of the lighting design firm L'Observatoire International, is installed at waist-level and below, illuminating the pathway for safety, while allowing the eye to appreciate the city beyond and nighttime sky. Light fixtures are also installed under the High Line, between the girders, to cast pools of light on the sidewalks below.

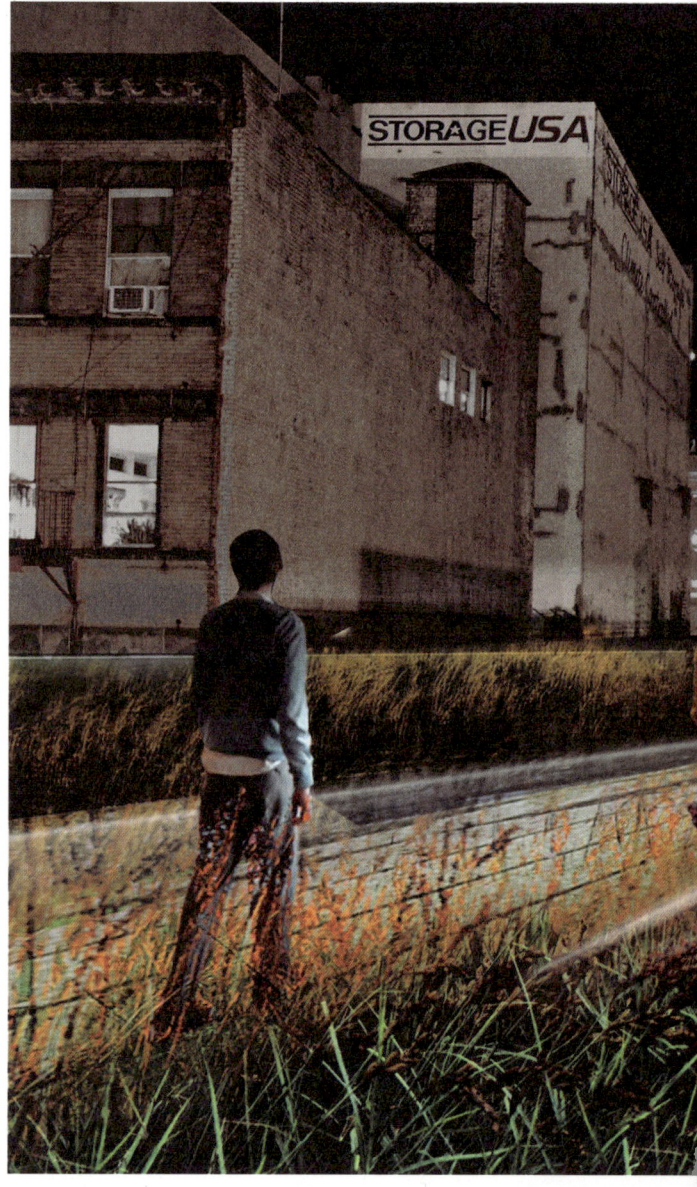

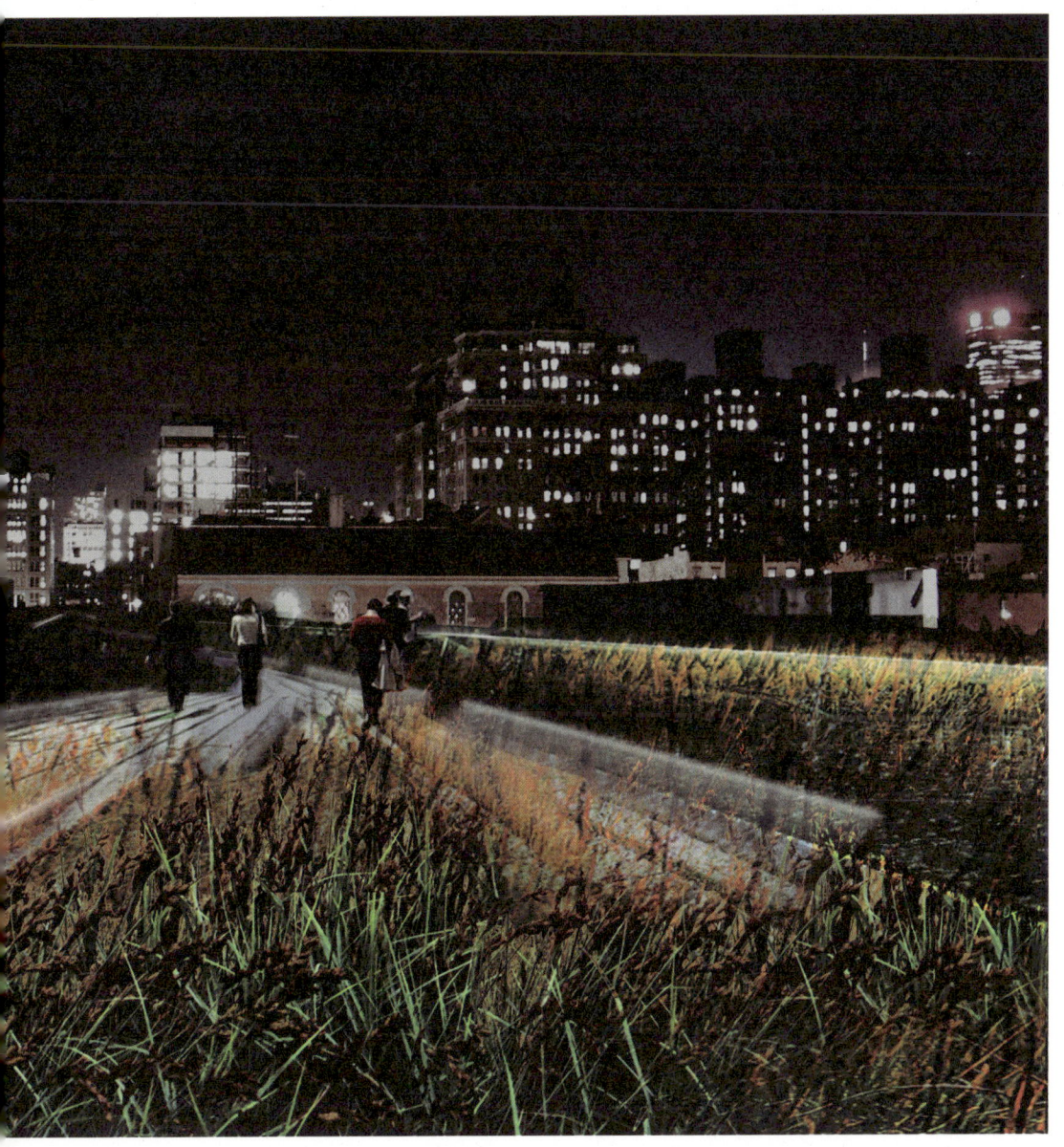

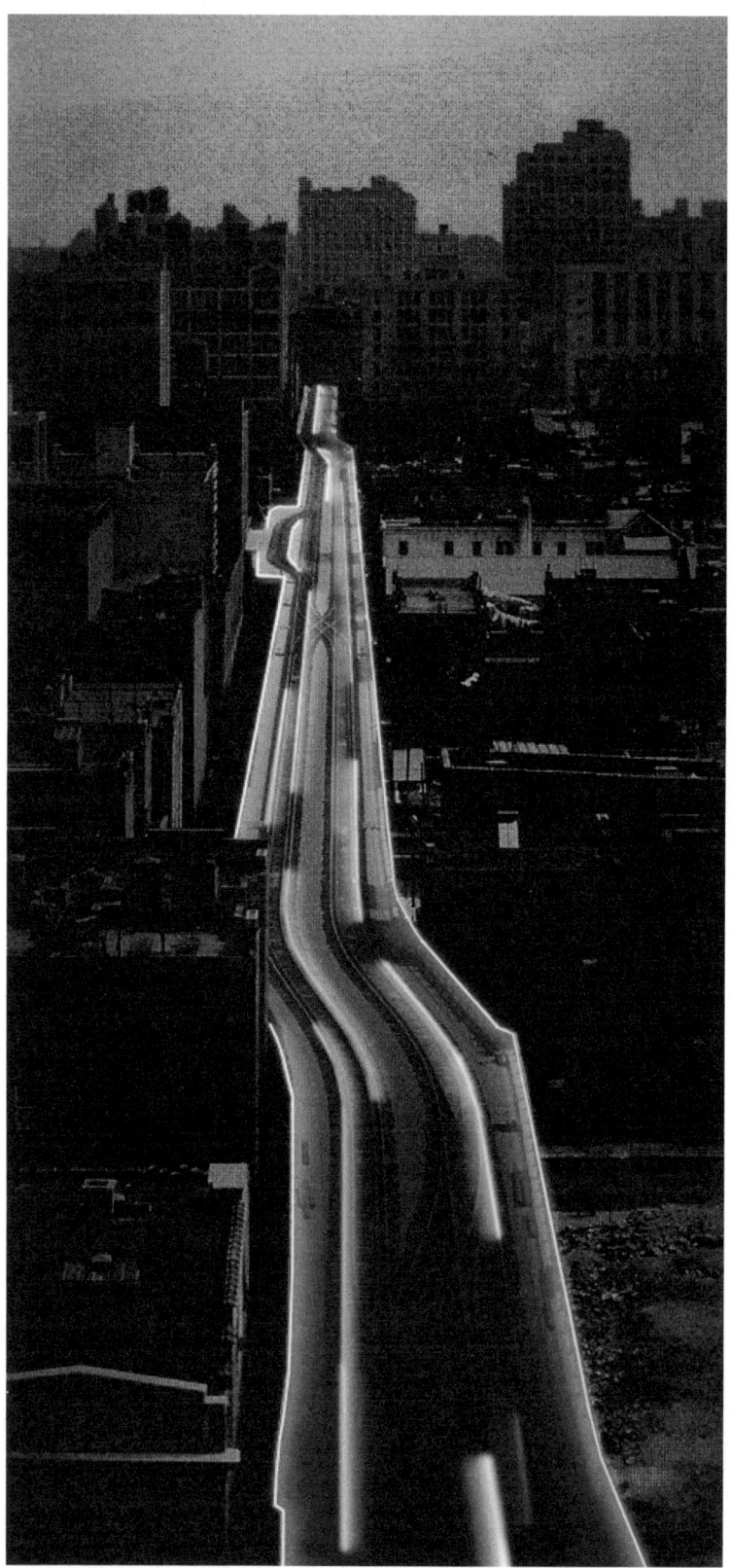

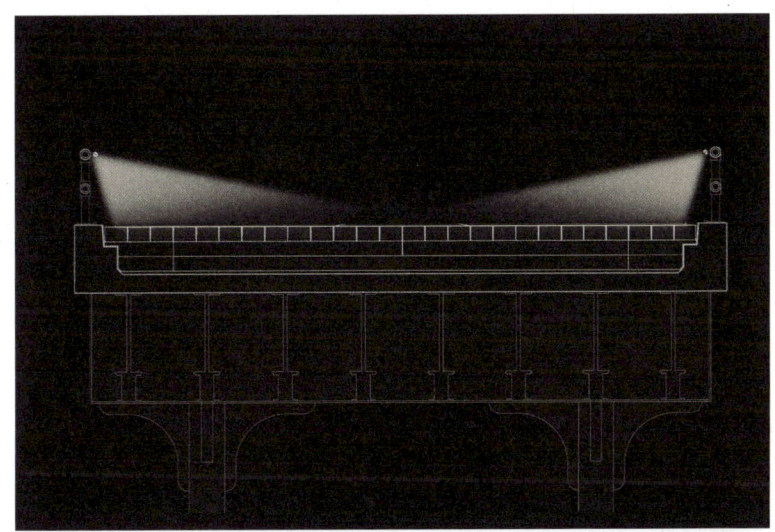

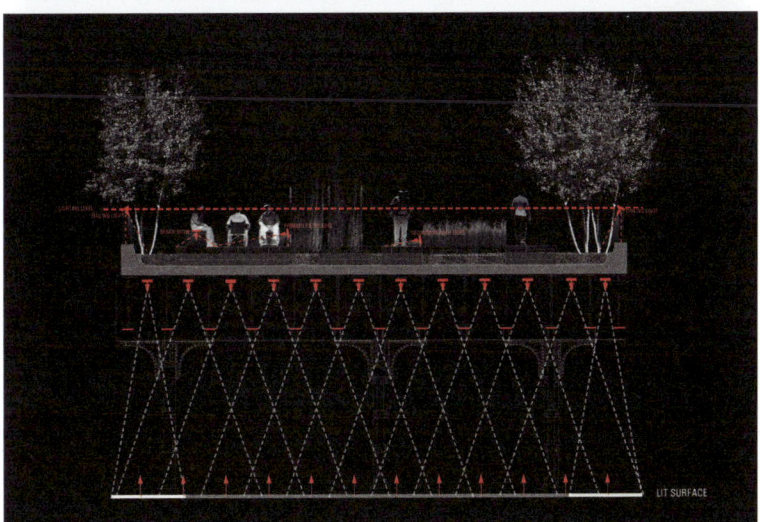

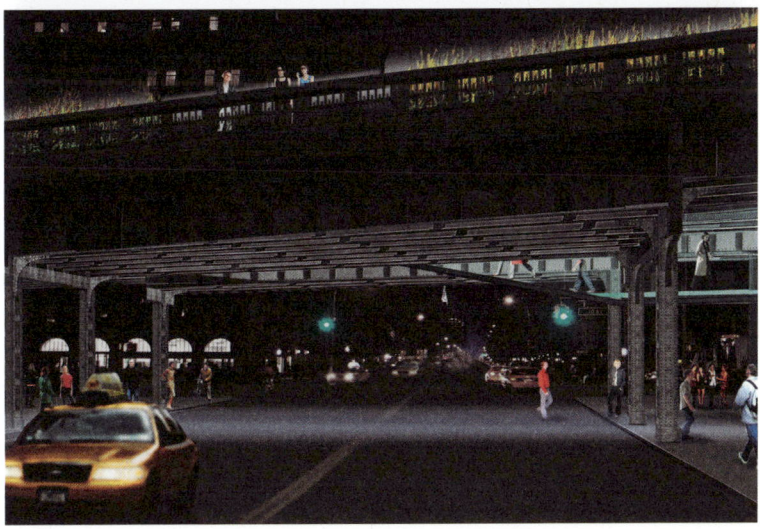

Rail Track Reinstallation

Many of the original railroad tracks, removed to allow repairs to the structure, are reinstalled in the planting beds, providing historical context. Prior to removal, all tracks were surveyed and tagged in place, allowing them to be returned to their original positions.

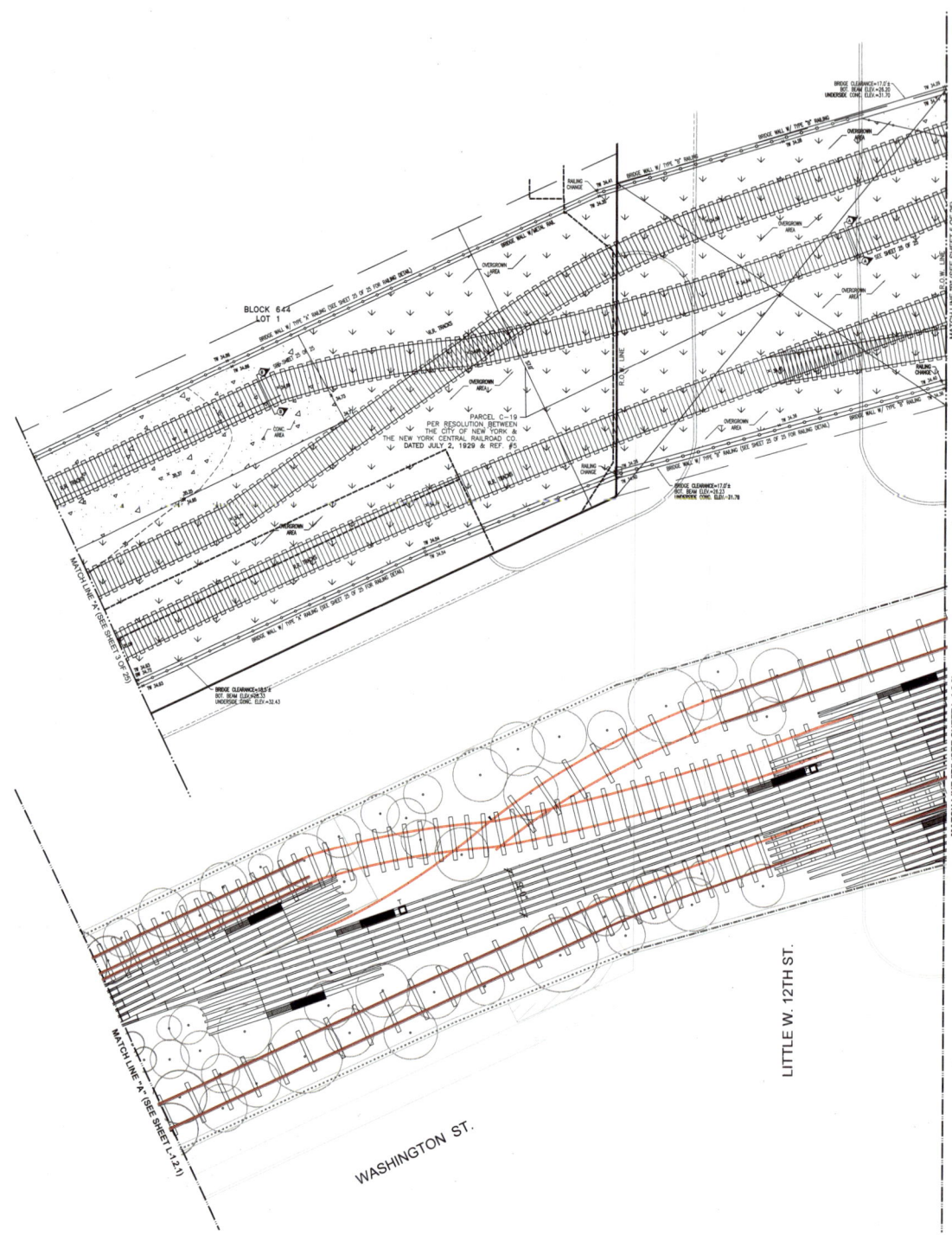

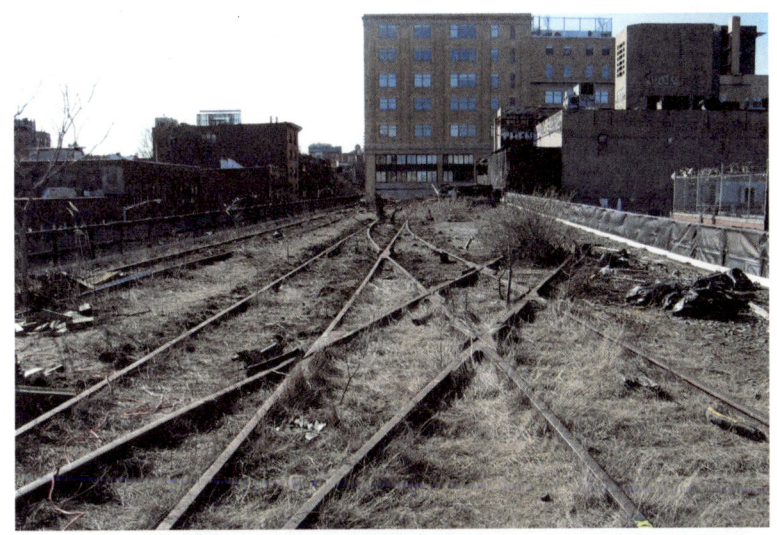

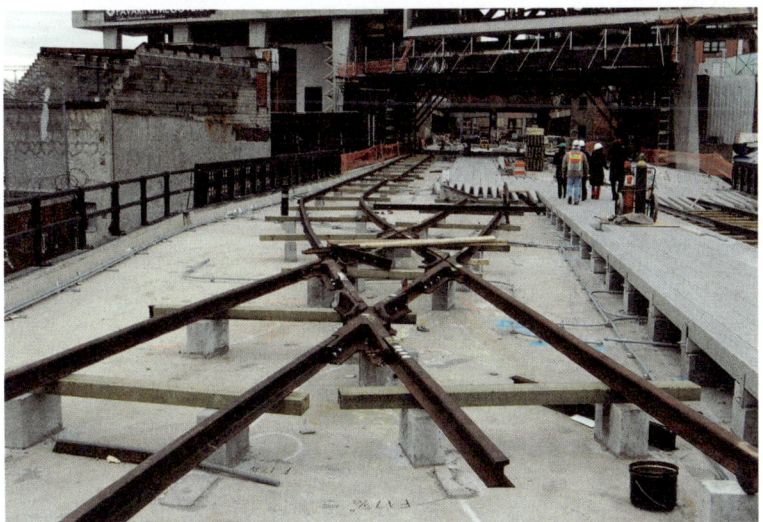

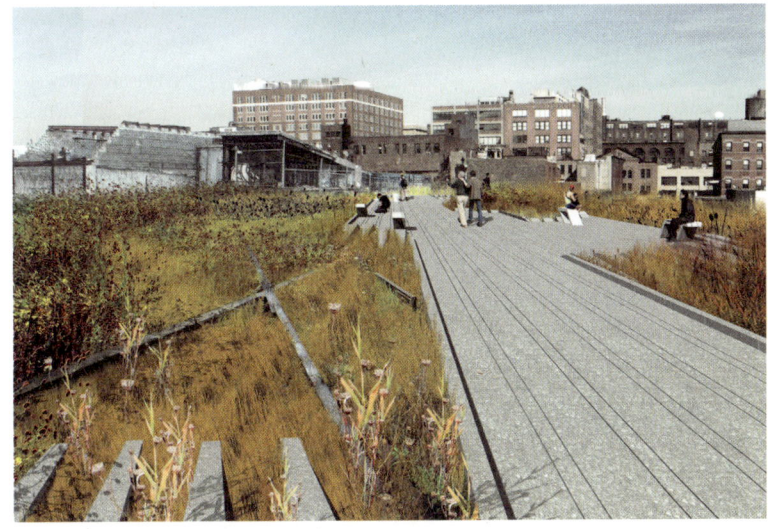

Historic Railing Restoration

The High Line's iconic Art Deco steel railings are located at every street crossing. All the railings are restored, damaged pieces are repaired, and all surfaces are sandblasted in a containment system prior to priming and repainting. At the Sundeck, restoration of the historic steel railings is made possible by Adam and Brittany Levinson.

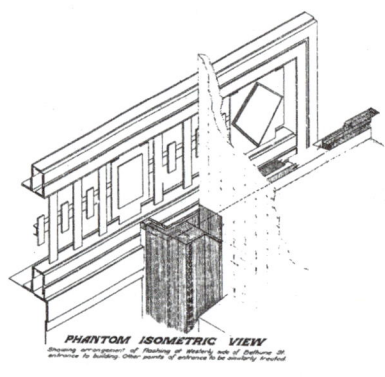

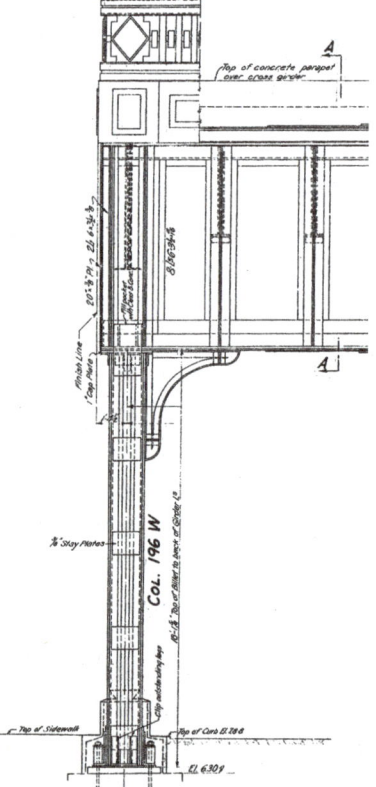

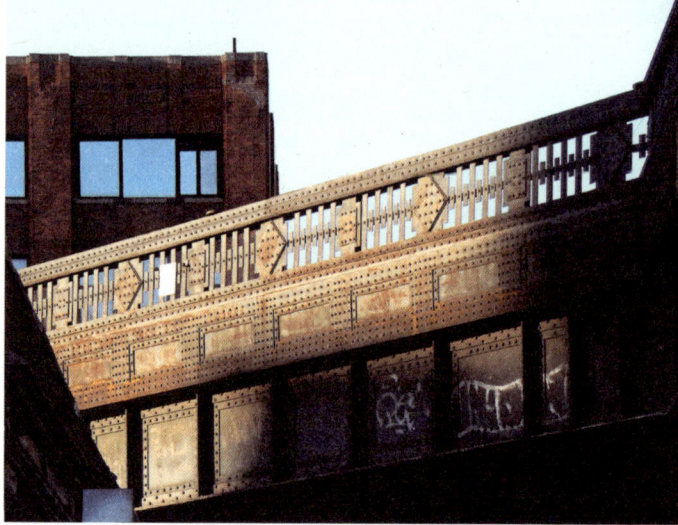

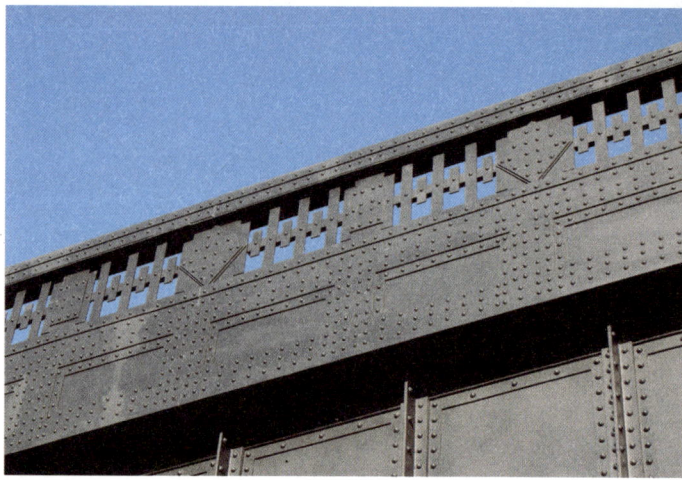

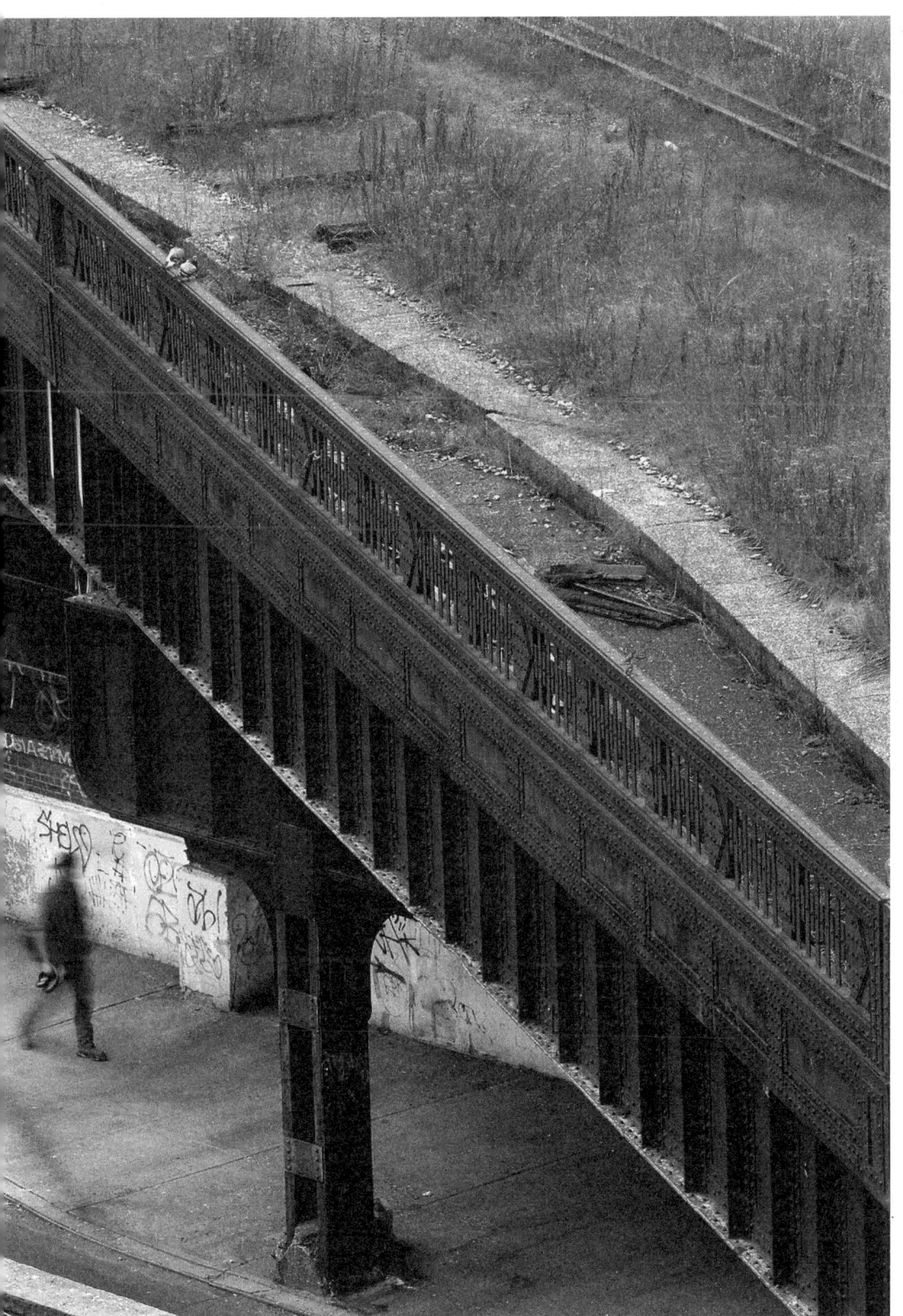

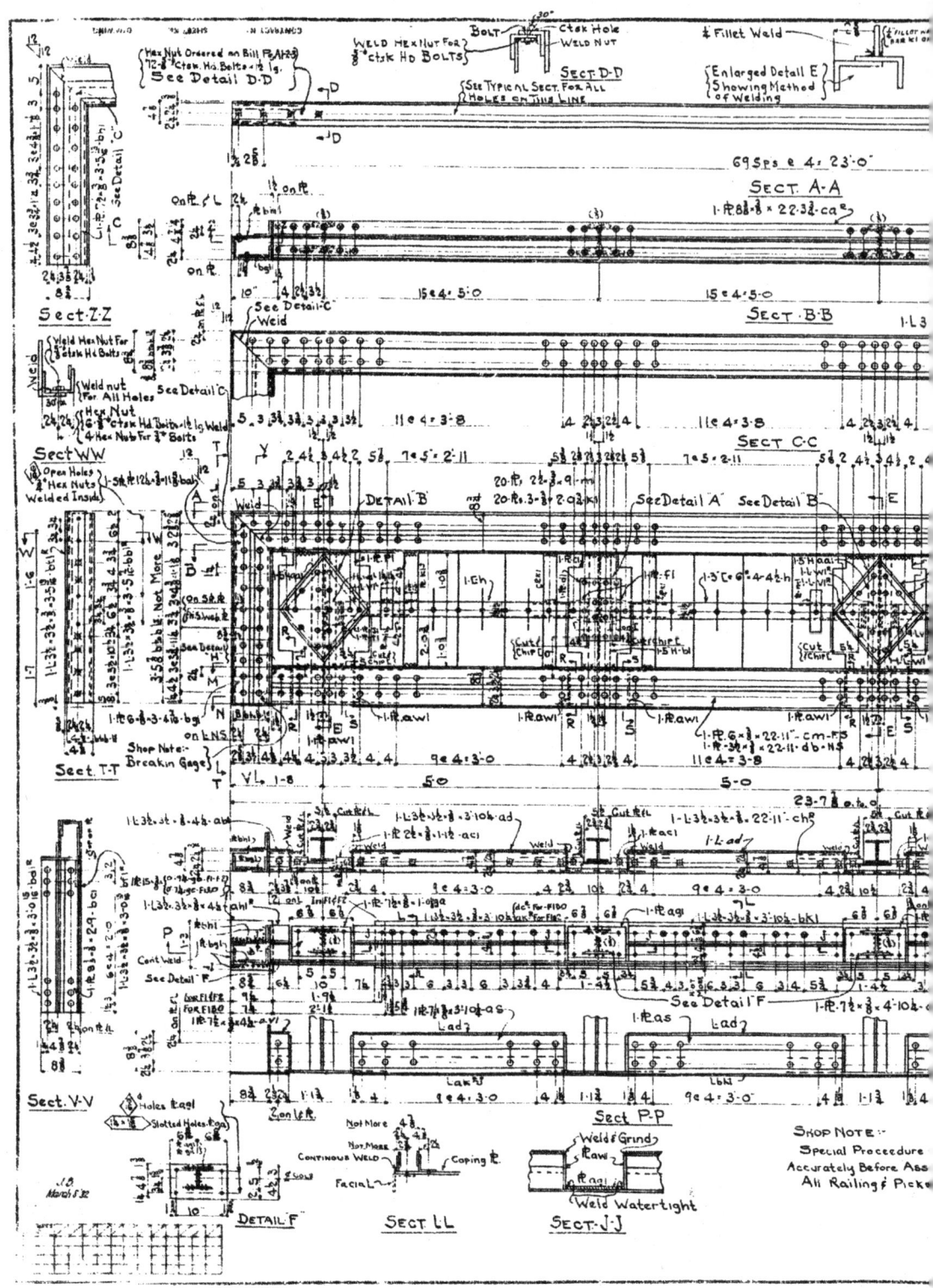

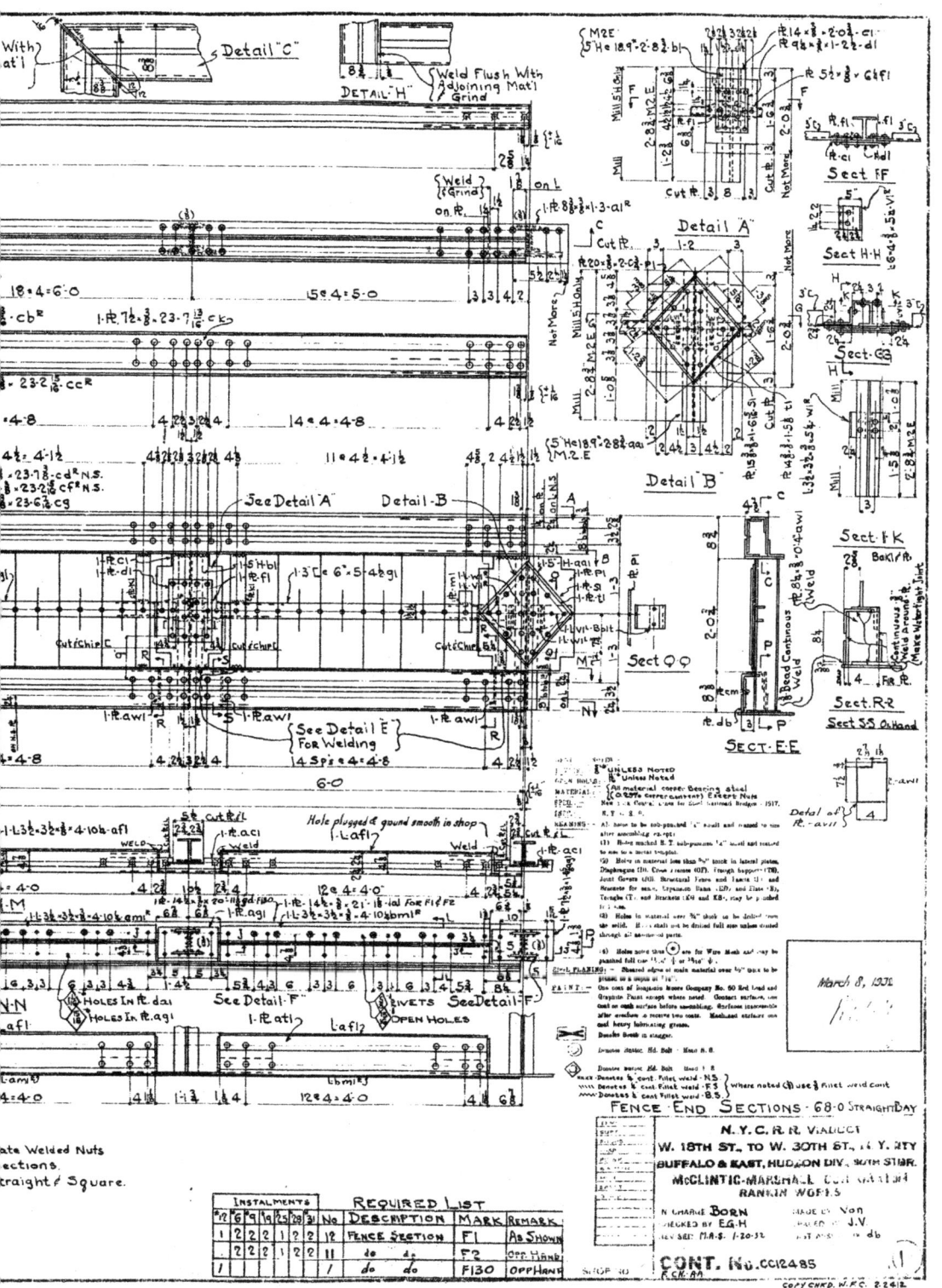

Construction

Construction on Section 1 began in the spring of 2006. Section 2 construction started in the spring of 2007. Retaining the existing, self-sown landscape was considered, but after much investigation, the design team, the City of New York, and Friends of the High Line concluded that it had to be removed – to properly assess the High Line's structural and maintenance needs, and to responsibly prepare the underlying structure for the creation of a park that will last decades into the future. First, rails, ties, and gravel ballast were removed. Next, steel was restored, sandblasted, primed, and repainted; drainage systems were upgraded; and the concrete deck was repaired as necessary. Finally, construction of the park landscape, including pathways, access points, reinstalled rail tracks, and all other park features, began on Section 1 in the fall of 2007.

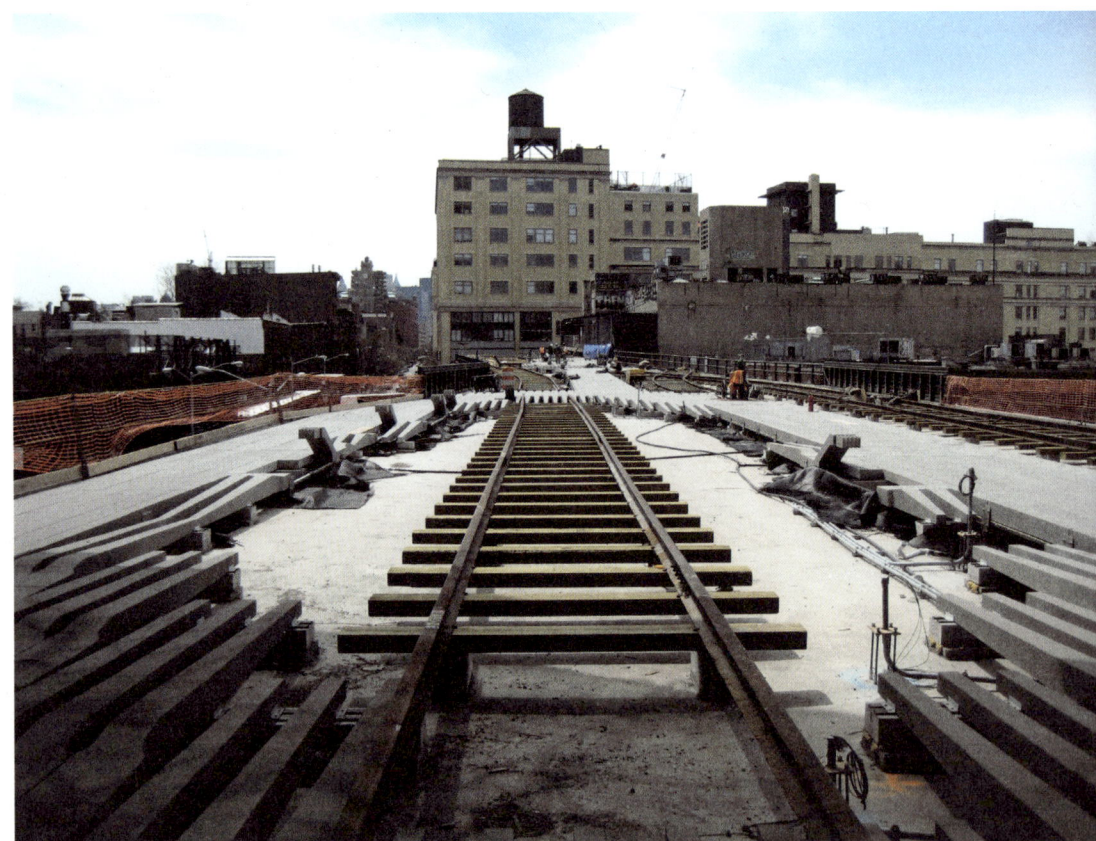

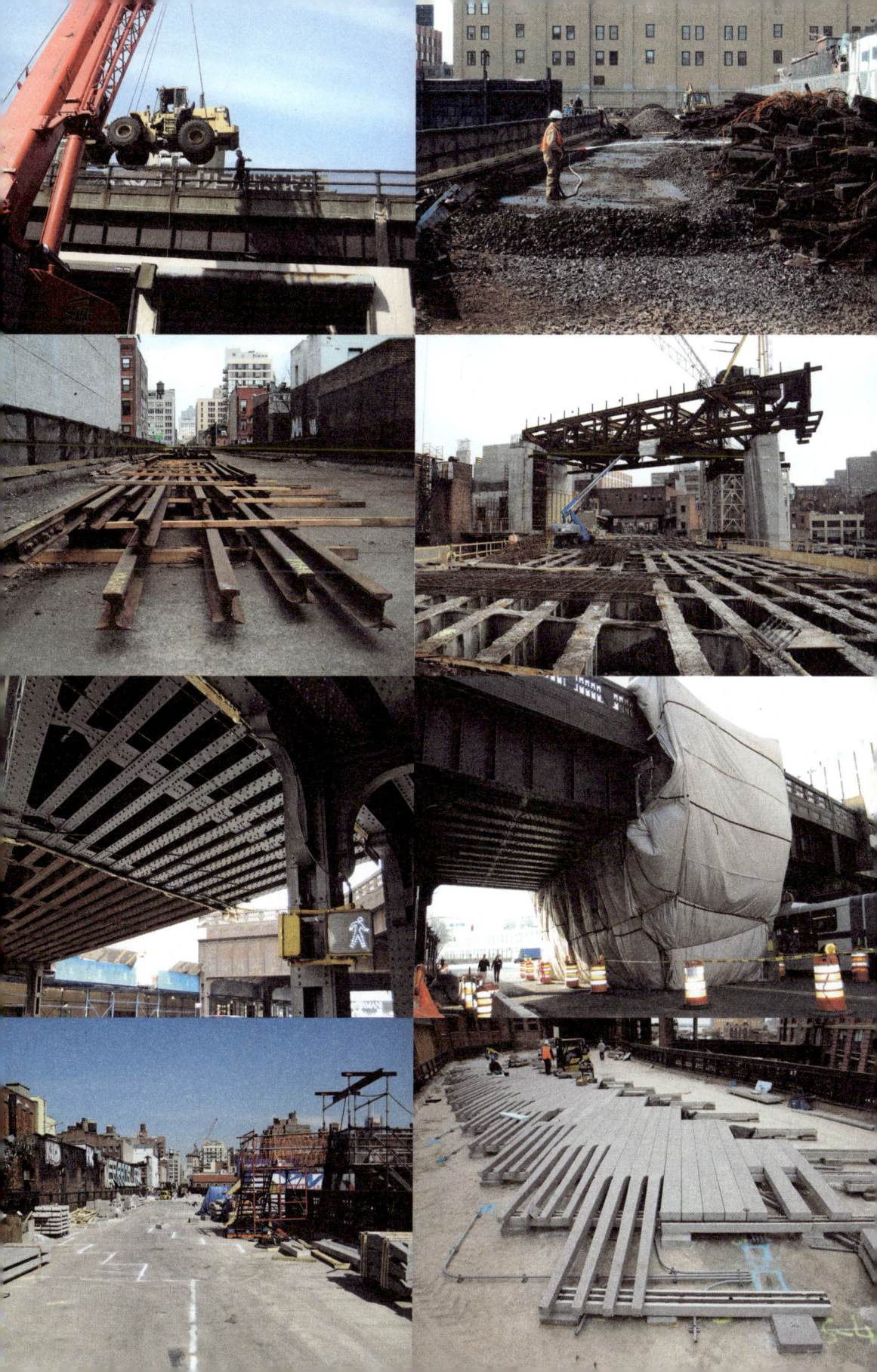

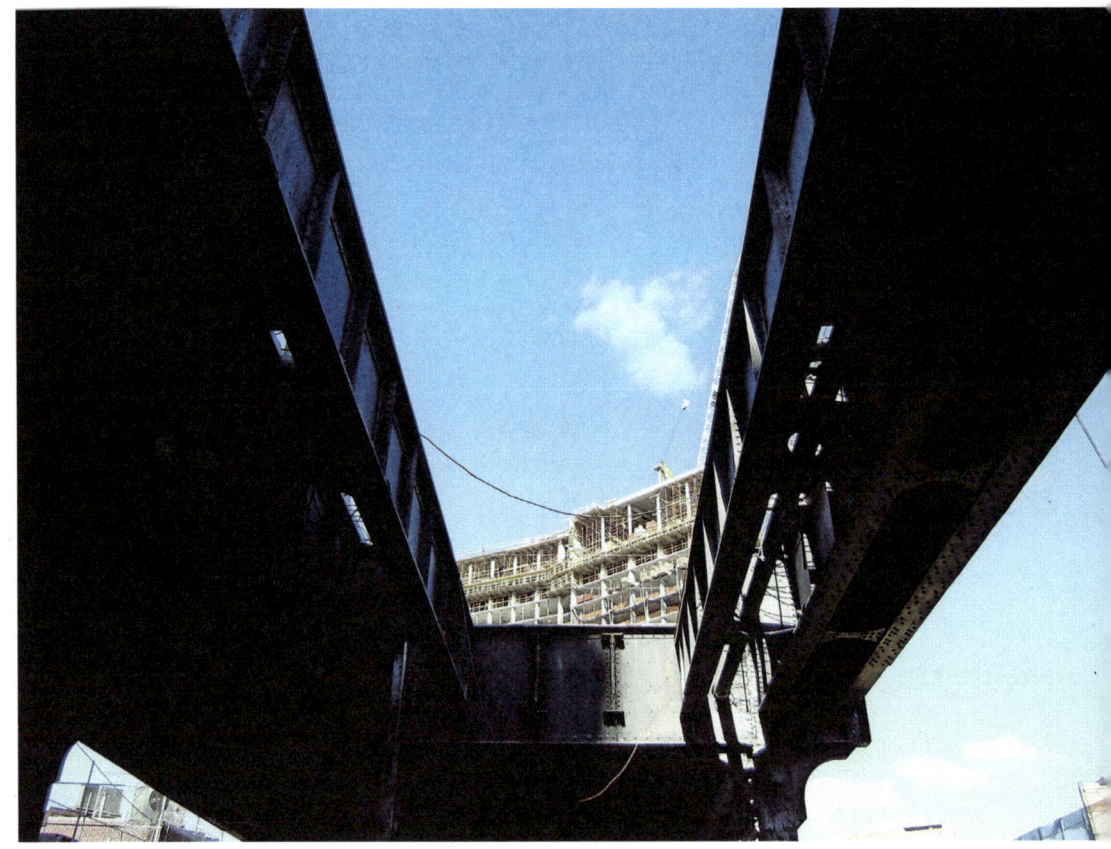

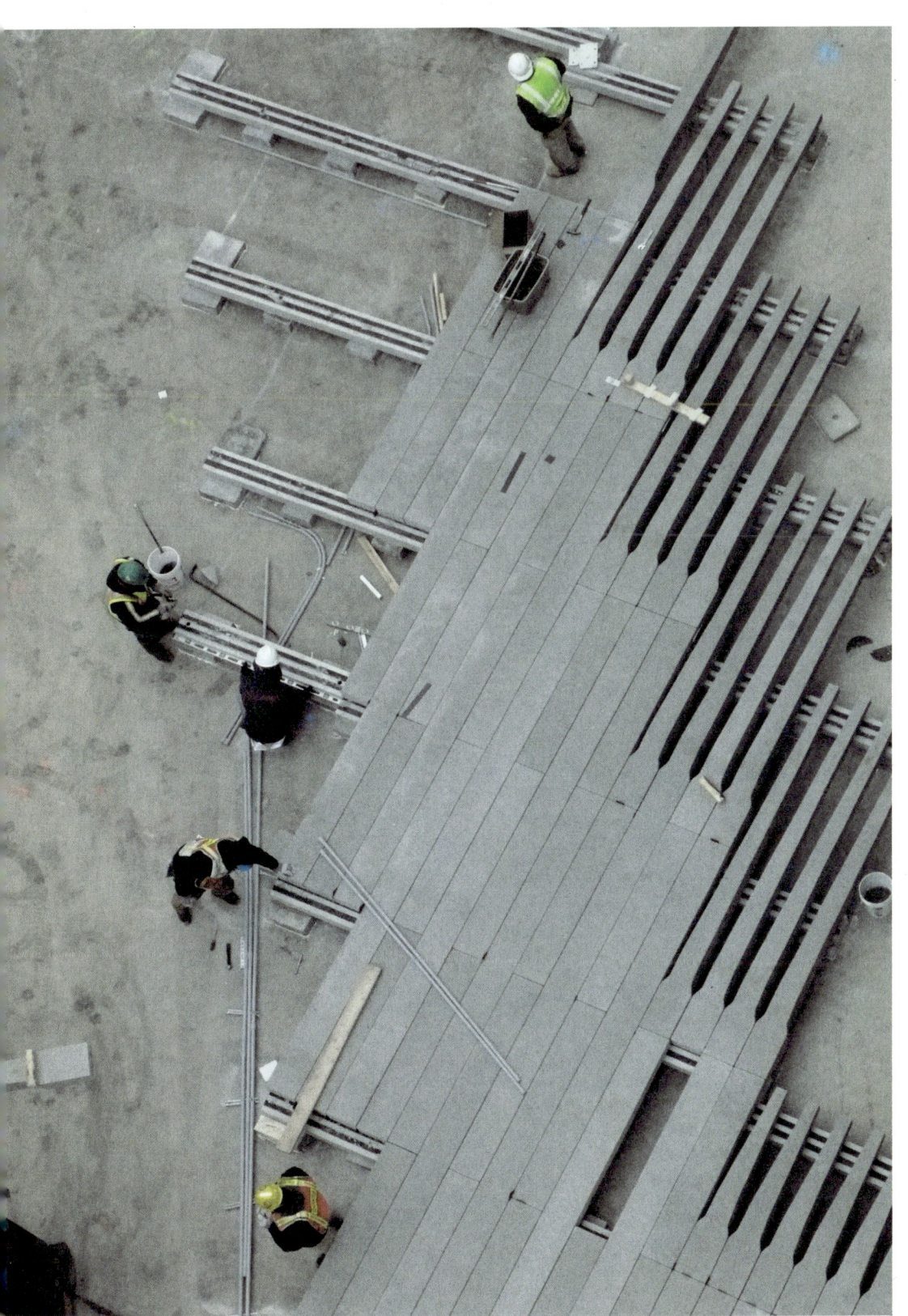

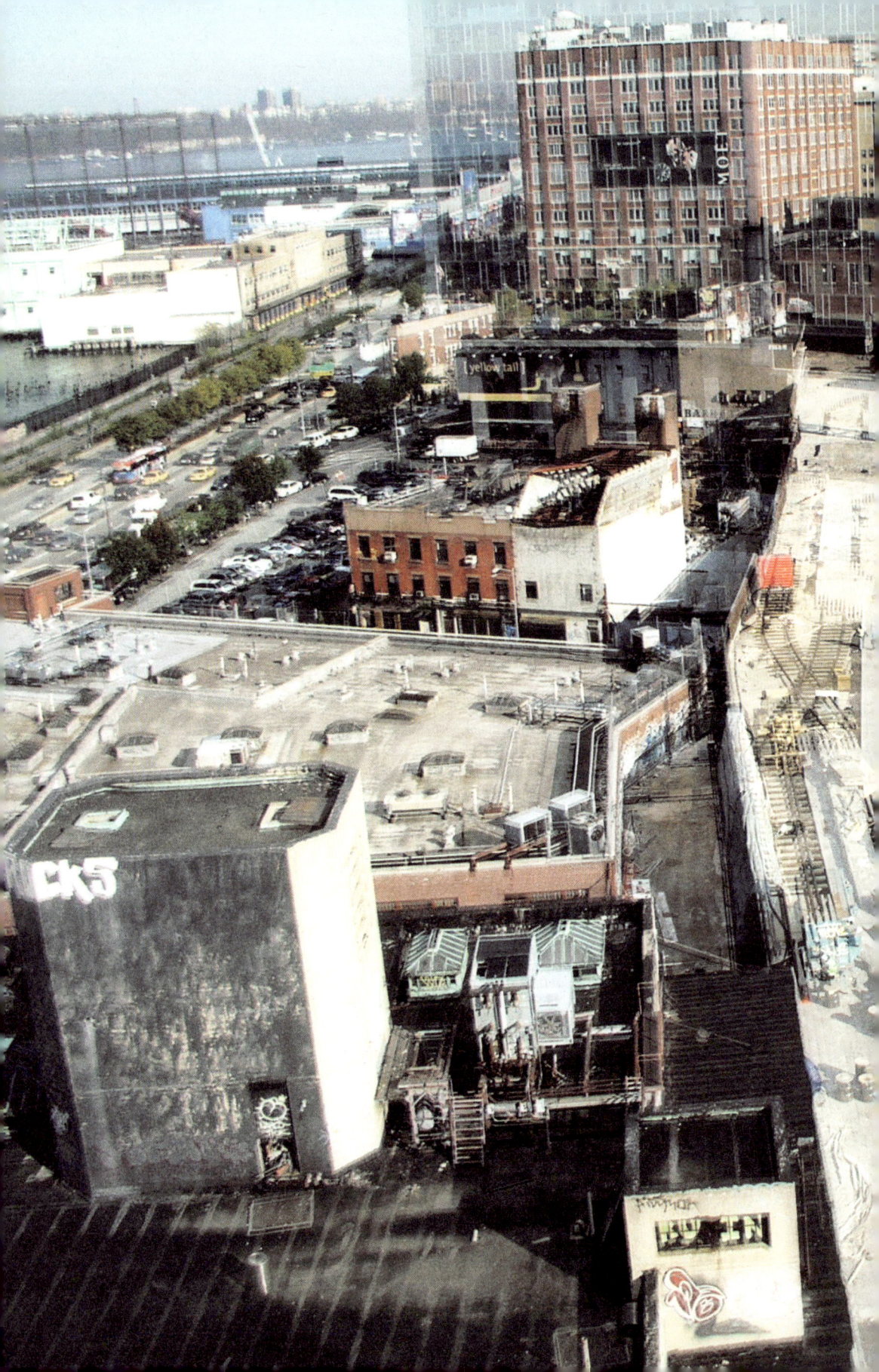

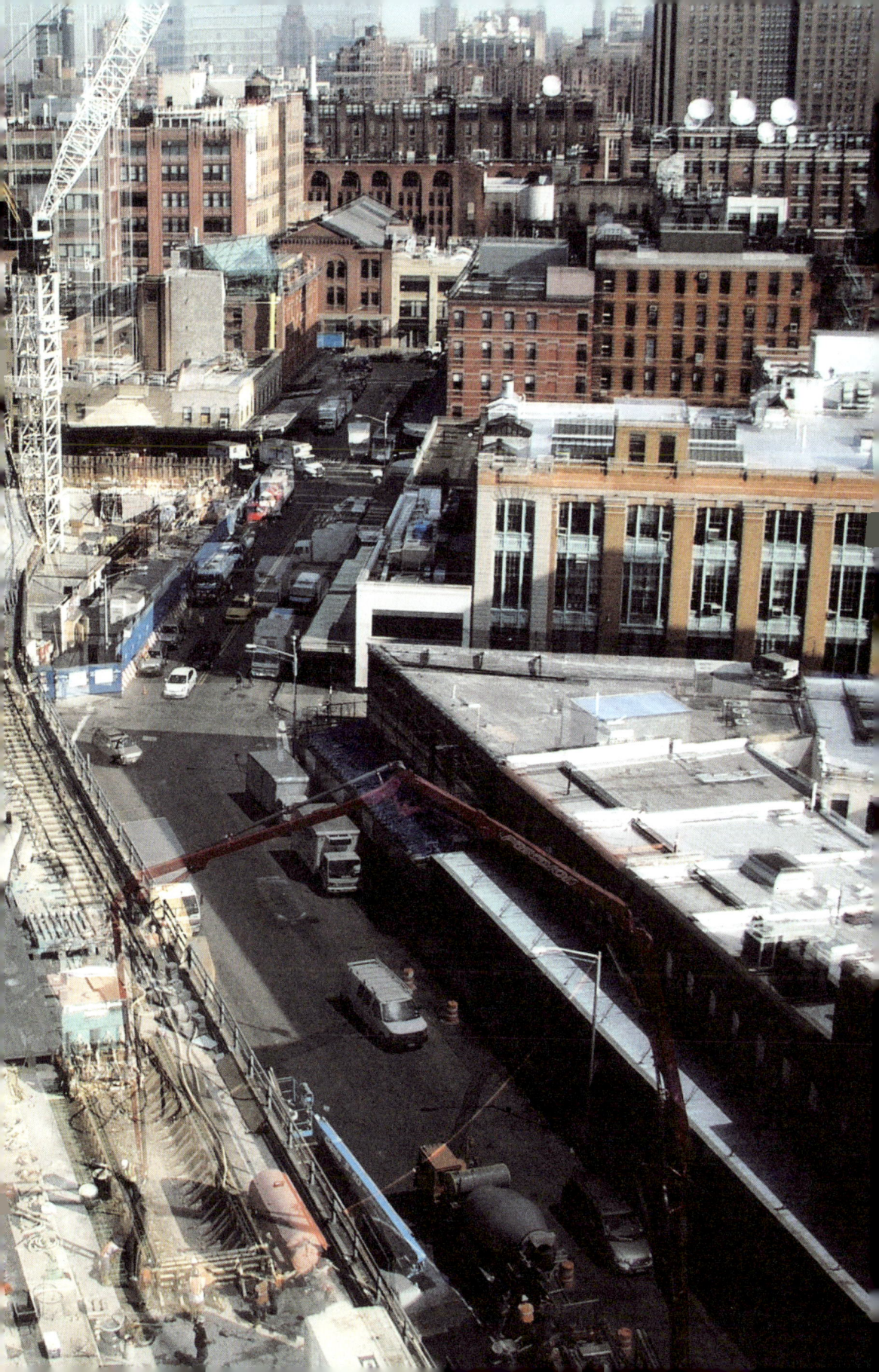

Section 3: Rail Yards

Friends of the High Line is still working to preserve the entire historic rail yards section of the High Line – one third of the entire structure. The City of New York owns the High Line south of 30th Street, where construction is now underway on Sections 1 and 2. But the future of High Line at the rail yards, from 30th to 34th Streets, depends on the final plan for the redevelopment of the site. Friends of the High Line is grateful to our elected officials and their staffs and our community partners for their support in this effort. We look forward to working with the developers who plan and build at the rail yards to ensure the preservation of the entire historic structure.

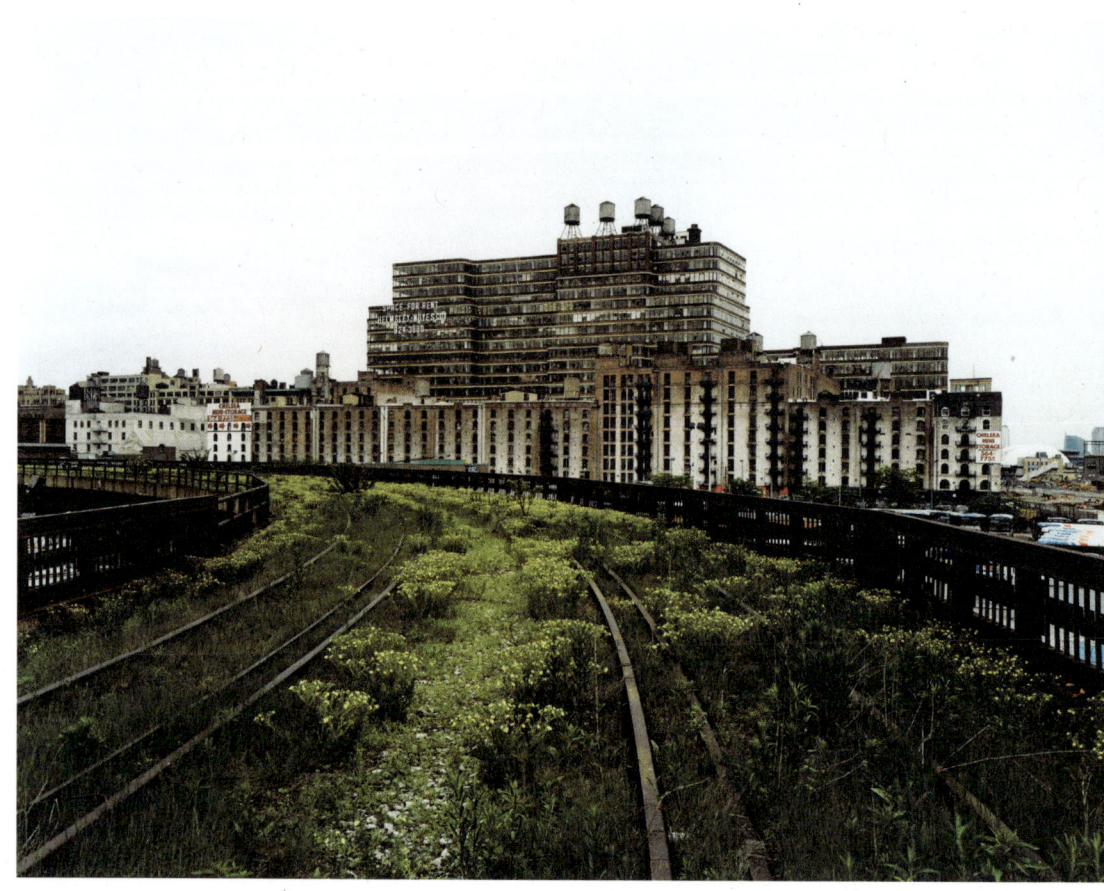

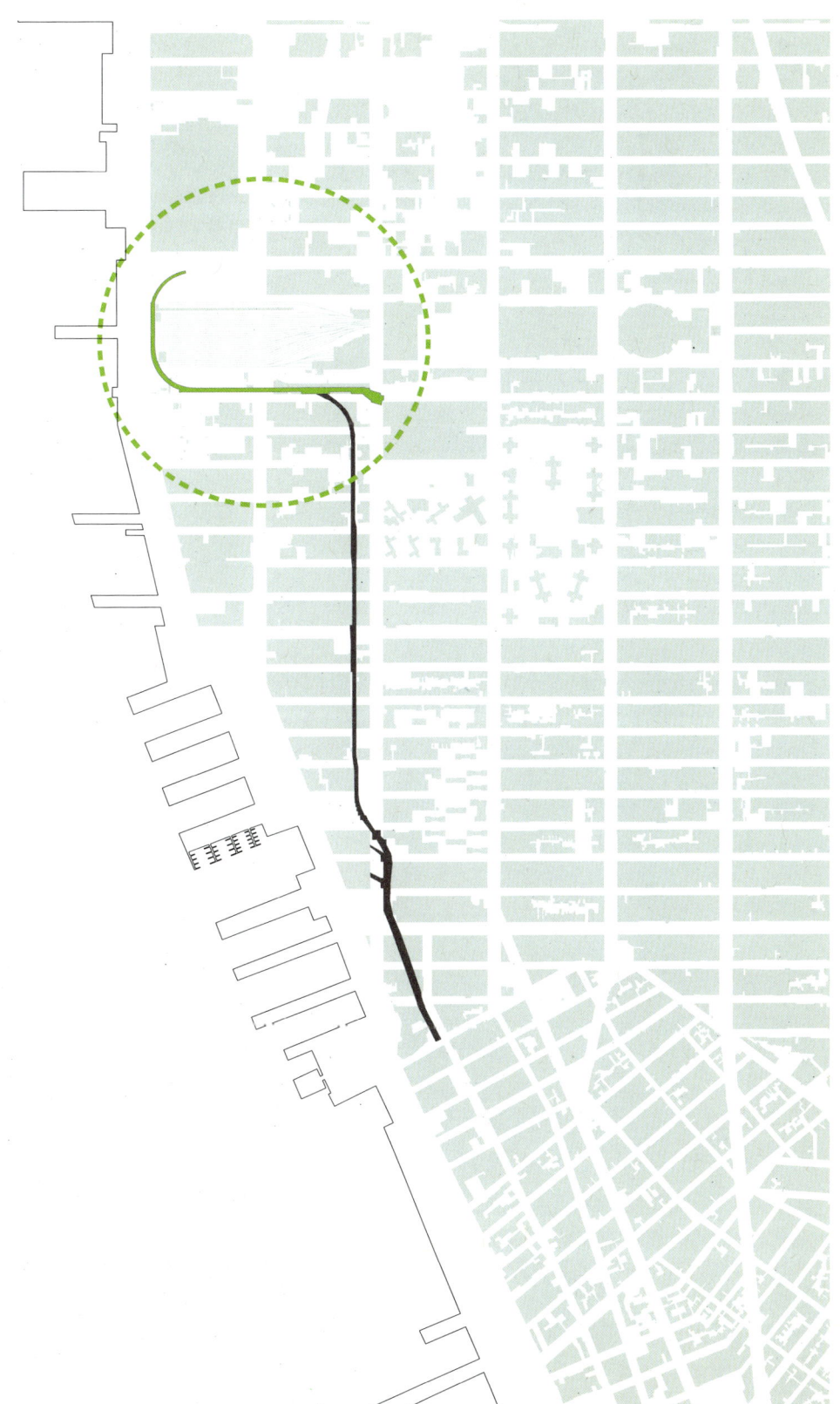

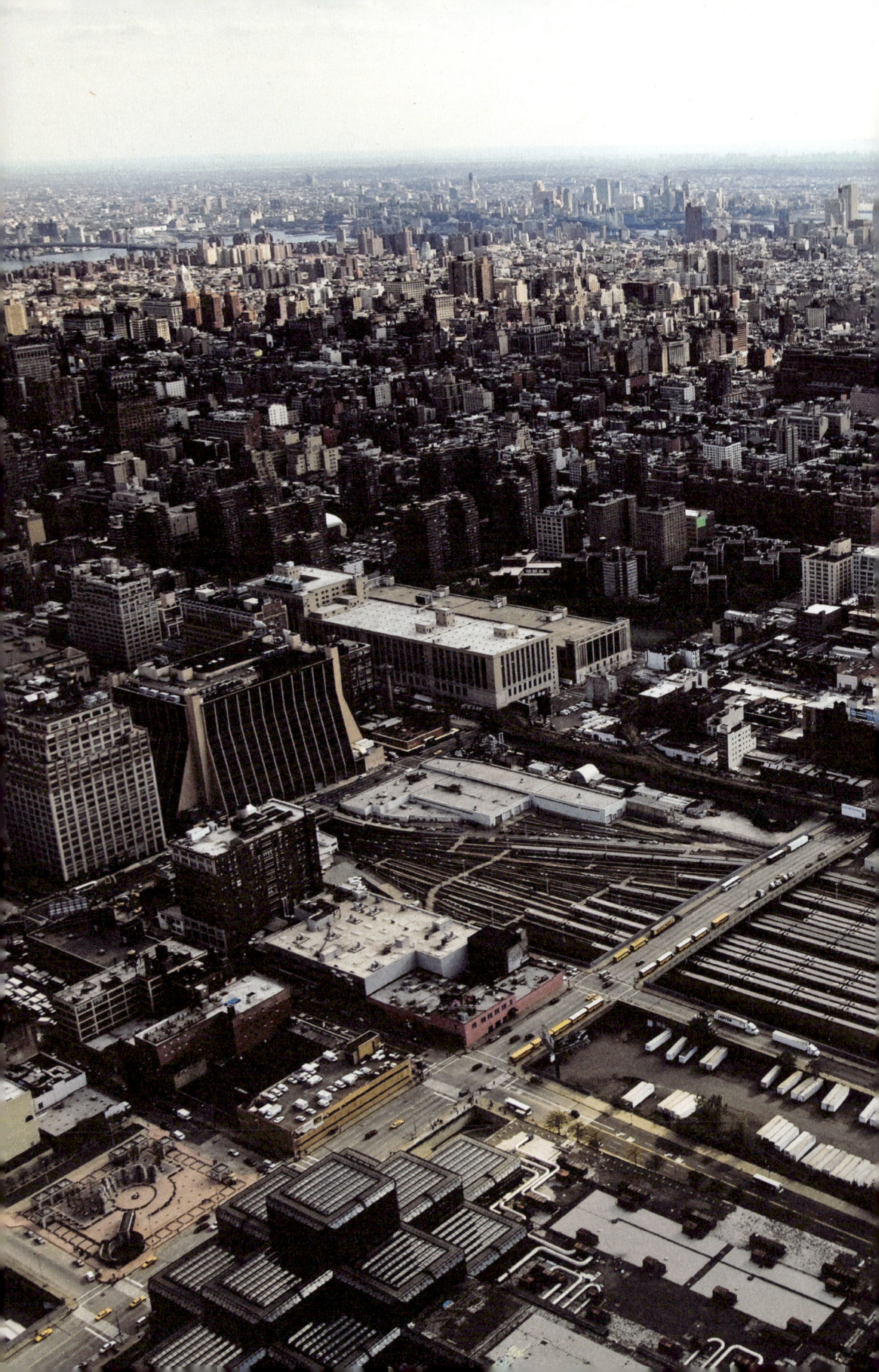

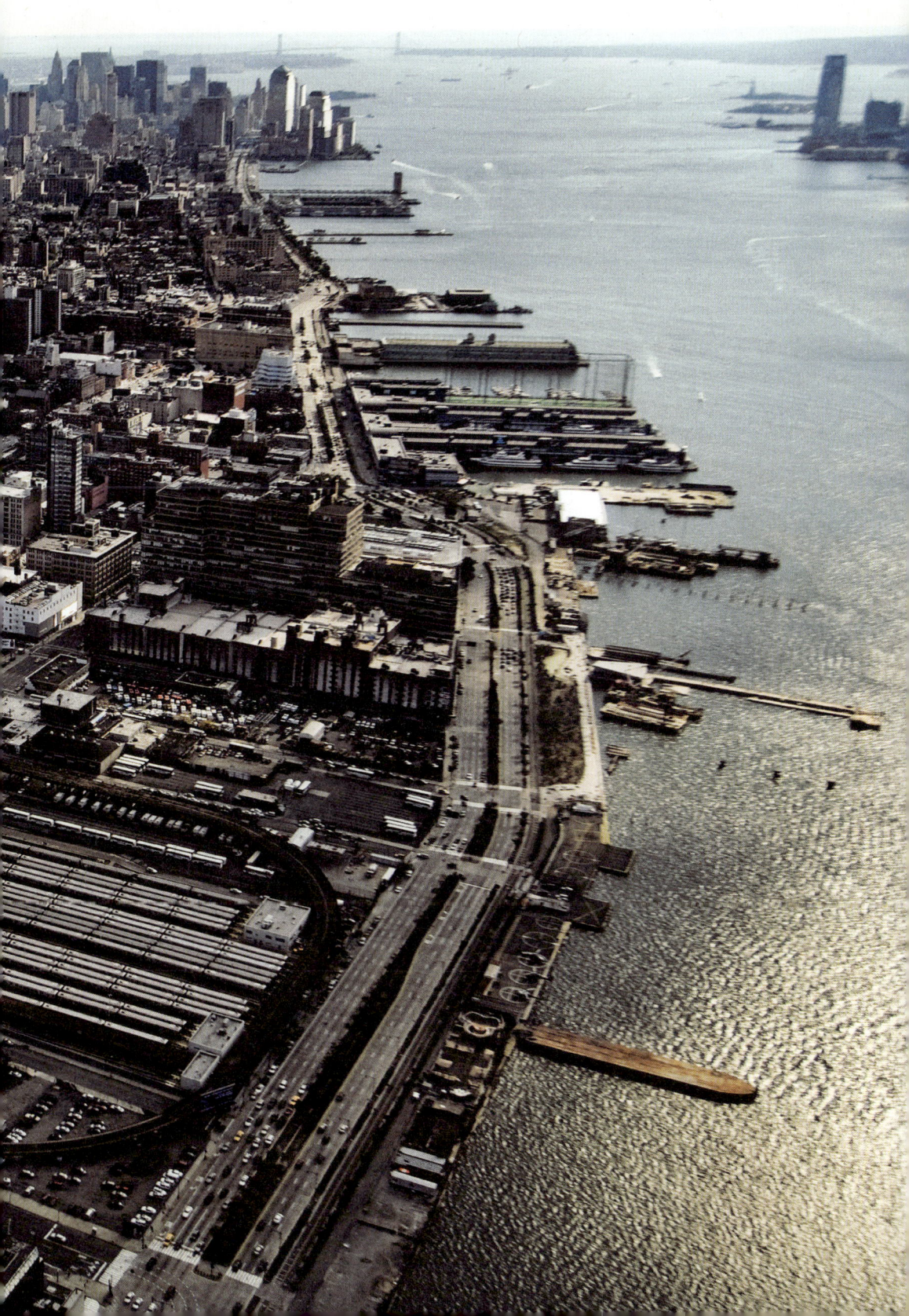

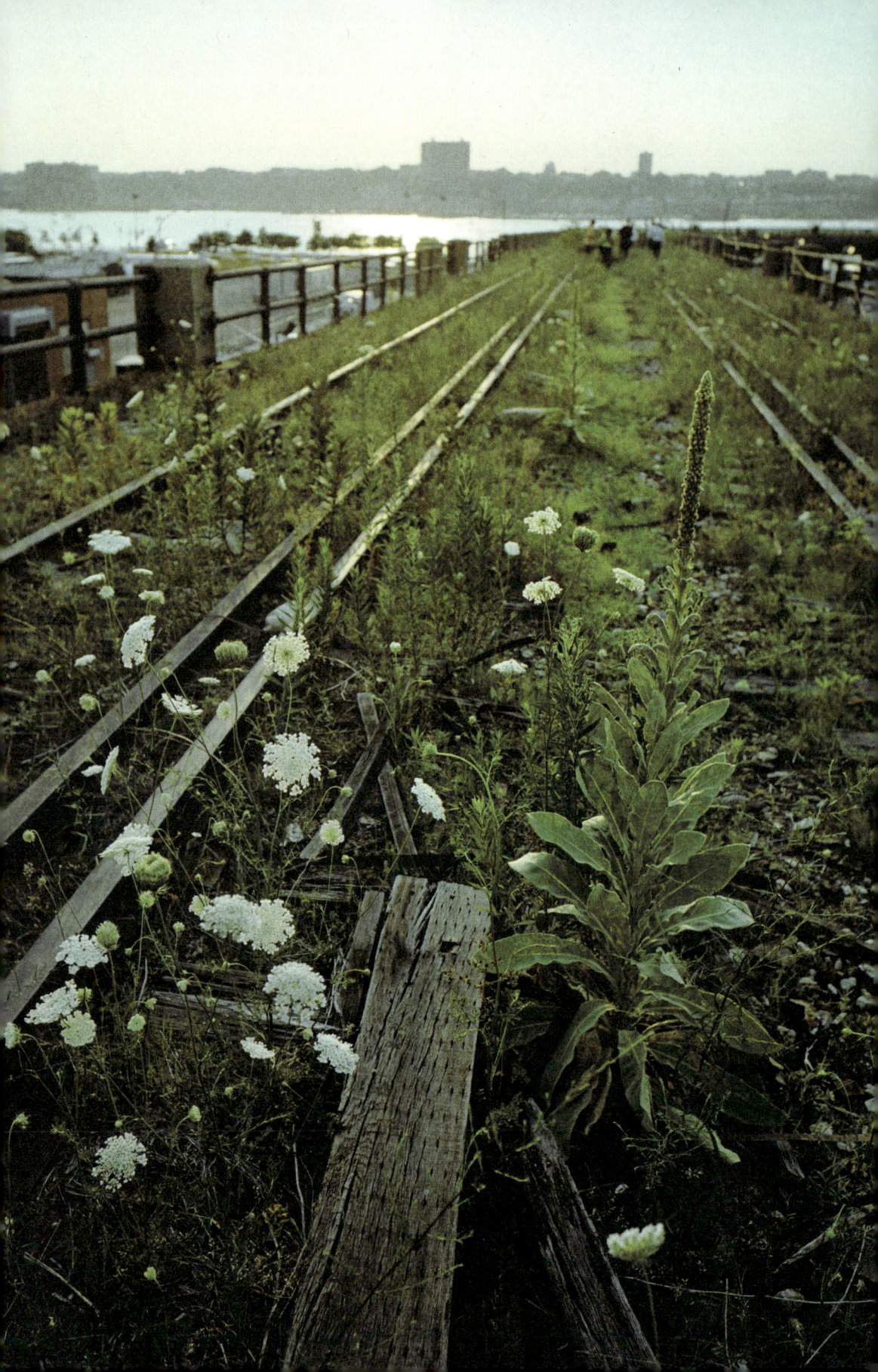

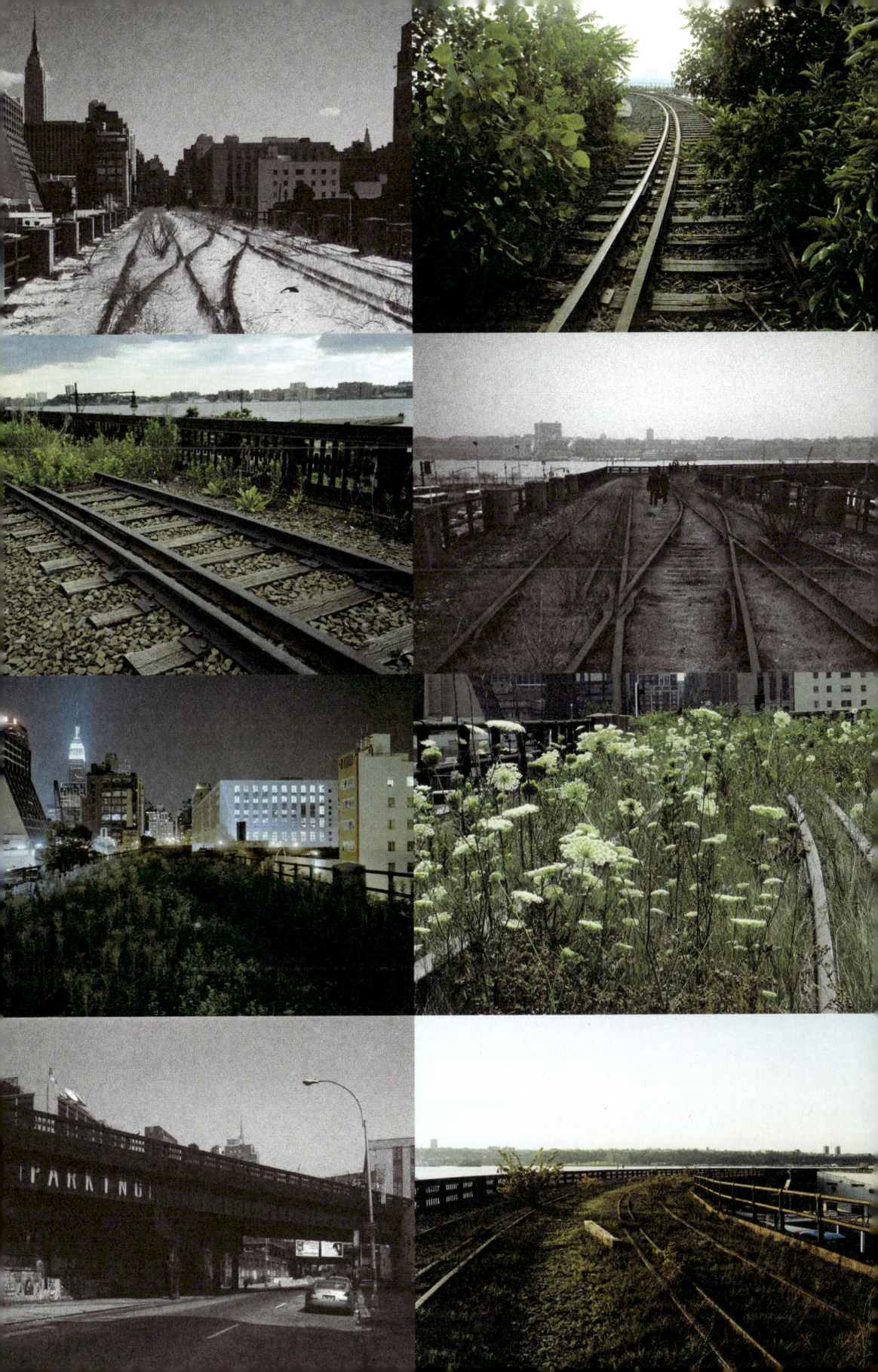

Credits

Project Team

Friends of the High Line thanks the following elected officials and their staffs, who have worked diligently to bring major public funding allocations to the High Line's capital construction:

New York City Mayor Michael R. Bloomberg
New York City Council Speaker Christine C. Quinn
Manhattan Borough President Scott M. Stringer
U.S. Senators Charles E. Schumer and Hillary Rodham Clinton
U.S. Representative Jerrold L. Nadler

Many thanks to all our elected and government partners for their support of the High Line.

City of New York
Michael R. Bloomberg, Mayor
Christine C. Quinn, Speaker, New York City Council
Scott M. Stringer, Manhattan Borough President
William C. Thompson, Jr., Comptroller
Patricia E. Harris, First Deputy Mayor
Robert C. Lieber, Deputy Mayor for Economic Development
Seth W. Pinsky, President, Economic Development Corporation
Adrian Benepe, Commissioner, Department of Parks & Recreation
Amanda M. Burden, Chair, City Planning Commission
Jean-Daniel Noland, Chair, Manhattan Community Board No. 4
Brad Hoylman, Chair, Manhattan Community Board No. 2

New York State
David A. Paterson, Governor
Thomas P. DiNapoli, Comptroller
Andrew M. Cuomo, Attorney General
Thomas K. Duane, Senator
Richard N. Gottfried, Assembly Member
Deborah J. Glick, Assembly Member

United States Congress
Charles E. Schumer, Senator
Hillary Rodham Clinton, Senator
Jerrold L. Nadler, Representative

New York City Team (2004-2008)
Office of the First Deputy Mayor Nanette Smith **Office of the Deputy Mayor for Economic Development** Marc Ricks, Joshua Sirefman, Laurel Blatchford, Jed Howbert, EB Kelly, Zachary Smith, Jennifer Sun-Vigoreaux, Andrew Winters **Department of Parks & Recreation** William T. Castro, Amy L. Freitag, Joshua Laird, Betsy Smith, Michael Bradley, David Carlson, Bruce Eisenberg, Jennifer M. Hoppa, Keith T. Kerman, George Kroenert, Charles McKinney, Alessandro G. Olivieri, Leslie Wolf, Namshik Yoon **Economic Development Corporation** Melvin Glickman, David Kane, Anne Cochran, Len Greco, Jeffrey Manzer **Department of City Planning** Vishaan Chakrabarti, Ray Gastil, David Karnovsky, Erik Botsford, Jeffrey Mulligan, Keith O'Connor, Jaime Ortiz, Erika Sellke **Law Department** Howard Friedman, Joseph Gunn **Mayor's Fund to Advance New York** Megan Sheekey **Art Commission** Jackie Snyder, Joyce Frank Menschel, James P. Stuckey **Department of Buildings** Christopher Santulli **Landmarks Preservation Commission** Robert B. Tierney, Mary Beth Betts, Diane Jackier, Jared Knowles **Mayor's Office for People with Disabilities** Matthew Sapolin, Robert Piccolo **Mayor's Press Office** Jennifer Falk, John Gallagher **Department of Transportation** Margaret Forgione, Kerry Gould, Anne Koenig **Manhattan**

Community Board No. 4 J. Lee Compton, Jean-Daniel Noland **Manhattan Community Board No. 2** Maria Doerr, Brad Hoylman

High Line Development Team (2004-2008)
Office of the Deputy Mayor for Economic Development Marc Ricks, Laurel Blatchford, EB Kelly, Zachary Smith, Jennifer Sun-Vigoreaux **Department of Parks & Recreation** Michael Bradley, Leslie Wolf, Jennifer M. Hoppa **Economic Development Corporation** Len Greco, Anne Cochran **Department of City Planning** Keith O'Connor, Erika Sellke, Erik Botsford **Friends of the High Line** Peter Mullan

Design Team (2004-2008)
Field Operations *Design Lead/Landscape Architecture/ Urban Design* James Corner, Tom Jost, Lisa Switkin, Nahyun Hwang, Sierra Bainbridge, Danilo Martic, Tatiana von Preussen, Maura Rockcastle, Tom Ryan, Heeyeun Yoon, Hong Zhou **Diller Scofidio + Renfro** *Architecture* Elizabeth Diller, Ricardo Scofidio, Charles Renfro, Matthew Johnson, Tobias Hegemann, Gaspar Libedinsky, Jeremy Linzee, Miles Nelligan, Dan Sakai **Piet Oudolf** *Planting Design* **L'Observatoire International** *Lighting Design* Hervé Descottes, Annette Goderbauer, Jeff Beck **Pentagram Design, Inc.** *Signage* Paula Scher, Drew Freeman, Rion Byrd, Jennifer Rittner **Buro Happold** *Structural/MEP Engineering* Craig Schwitter, Herbert Browne, Dennis Burton, Andrew Coats, Anthony Curiale, Mark Dawson, Beth Macri, Sean O'Neill, Stan Wojnowski, Zac Braun, David Bentley, Elizabeth Devendorf, Alan Jackson, Christian Forero, Joseph Vassilatos **Robert Silman Associates** *Structural Engineering/Historic Preservation* Joseph Tortorella, Andre Georges **GRB Services, Inc.** *Environmental Engineering/Site Remediation* Richard Barbour, Steven Panter, Rose Russo **VJ Associates** *Capital & Operating Cost Estimating* Vijay Desai, Sushma Tammareddi, Chongba Sherpa **ETM Associates** *Public Space Management* Tim Marshall **Code Consultants Professional Engineers** *Code Consulting* John McCormick, Laurence J. Dallaire, Kevin Morin **Philip Habib & Associates** *Civil & Traffic Engineering/Zoning & Land Use* Philip Habib, Sandy Pae, Colleen Sheridan **Northern Designs** *Irrigation Consultanting and Design* Michael J. Astram **Control Point Associates, Inc.** *Site Surveying* Paul Jurkowski, Eneser Enerio **CMS Collaborative** *Water Feature Engineering* Edison Becker Bonjardim, Roy Kaplan, Tanya Larson **Pine & Swallow Associates, Inc.** *Soil Science* John Swallow, Robert Pine, Mike Agonis

Construction Team (2006-2008)
LiRO/Daniel Frankfurt *Resident Engineer* Jim Eckhoff **SiteWorks** *Landscape Construction Management* Annette Wilkus **Helen Neuhaus & Associates** *Community Liaison* Howie Harrington **KiSKA Construction** *General Contractor* Naushad Hassan, Robert Marriott **Bovis Lend Lease** *Construction Management* John Skiadis

Friends of the High Line Staff
Joshua David, Co-Founder, Robert Hammond, Co-Founder, Melissa Fisher, Jeff Hafner, Patrick Hazari, Sanaya Kaufman, Rick Little, Katie Lorah, Tara Morris, Peter Mullan, Matthew Shakespeare, Michelle Sharkey, Danya Sherman, Meredith Taylor **Former Friends of the High Line Staff** Alana Buckley, Scott Dubois, Dahlia Elsayed, Deana Hare, Diane Nixa, Juliet Page, Justin Rood, Olivia Stinson

Acknowledgements

It is with deep appreciation that Friends of the High Line recognizes these individuals and other funding partners for their visionary support of the Campaign for the High Line, which supports construction of the new park and an endowment for its future maintenance and operations.

Capital Campaign Donors
The Diller-von Furstenberg
   Family Foundation
Hermine and David Heller Foundation
Sukey and Mike Novogratz
Donald Pels and Wendy Keys

Philip and Lisamaria Falcone
Brittany and Adam Levinson
Mack Family Foundation
Pershing Square Foundation
Tiffany & Co. Foundation

Philip Aarons and Shelley Fox
   Aarons, MD
John deC. Blondel, Jr.
The Bobolink Foundation,
   Wendy Paulson
James Capalino, Capalino + Company
Kristen Dickey
Olivia Douglas and David DiDomenico
The Estée Lauder Companies Inc.
Michael and Deborah McCarthy
Edward Norton
Elizabeth and Michael O'Brien
Mario J. Palumbo, Jr.
Jonathan and Joelle Resnick
Ten Twenty-Six Investors L.P.
   c/o Douglas Oliver
Anonymous (3)

Joshua David and Stephen Hirsh
Mark Diker and Deborah Colson
Robert C. Greenhood
Robert Hammond
Gary Handel, Handel Architects
Jack Resnick & Sons
Katie Michel and Adam Schlesinger
Pamela and Gifford Miller
Donna and Alan N. Stillman
The A. Woodner Fund
Bronson van Wyck
Anonymous (1)

This publication was created to coincide with Friends of the High Line's 8th Annual Summer Benefit.

Benefit Honorees
Hermine Riegerl Heller and
   David Heller
Sukey and Mike Novogratz

Benefit Chair
Lisamaria Falcone

Major Benefit Donors
(as of June 1, 2008)
Philip and Lisamaria Falcone
Cardinal Investments, 511 West 25th
Sonia & Paul T. Jones

Alf Naman, HL 23
Charles Blaichman, Alexandre von
   Furstenberg, and Mal Serure,
   CB Construction
Christopher and Sharon Davis
Fiona and Stanley Druckenmiller
Janet and Howard Kagan
Terry Polistina, Applica, Inc.
Annie Hubbard and Harvey Schwartz
Caroline and Tiger Williams

This publication was made possible with generous support from:
Trust for Architectural Easements
The New York Community Trust

Very special thanks to CSX Transportation, Inc., for helping make the High Line's transformation possible.

We gratefully remember the late Peter Obletz, railroad aficionado, community leader, Chelsea resident, and champion of the earliest movement to save the High Line.

For more information about Friends of the High Line, visit www.thehighline.org.